Rising Above It

Rising Above It

An Autobiography

Edna Gardner Whyte

with Ann L. Cooper

Orion Books ▪ New York

Published by Orion Books, a division of Crown Publishers, Inc.,
201 East 50th Street, New York, New York 10022.
Member of the Crown Publishing Group.

ORION and colophon are trademarks of Crown Publishers, Inc.

Manufactured in the United States of America

Library of Congress Cataloging-in-Publication Data

Design by Deborah Kerner

Whyte, Edna Gardner.
    Rising above it : an autobiography / Edna
Gardner Whyte ; with Ann L. Cooper. — 1st ed.
        p. cm.
    1. Whyte, Edna Gardner. 2. Air pilots—United States—Biography.
3. Women air pilots—United States—Biography. I. Cooper, Ann L.
(Ann Lewis) II. Title.
TL540.W485A3   1991
629.13′092—dc20
[B]   91-12534
                                                                      CIP

ISBN 0-517-57685-6

10 9 8 7 6 5 4 3 2 1

First Edition

This book is dedicated to those who helped to make it possible: to Edna Gardner Whyte, who contributed to the history of aviation with courage and determination; to my editors, Peter Ginna and Candace Hodges, who helped to shape a manuscript into a book; to my loving family and friends with whom there has been sharing and mutual inspiration; and especially to Charlie Cooper, whose loving support and encouragement have been invaluable.

ANN L. COOPER

Contents

Contents

Rising Above It

Aftermath— the Nineteenth Amendment

I had lived for eighteen years before women were "given" the vote through ratification of the nineteenth amendment and I share the indignation with which feminists bristle at such a patriarchal inference. I became imbued with the fervor of the early feminists. My mother told me, "Women are demonstrating and are speaking out. They are begging men for the right to vote." I wondered, "Why should women have to beg the men?" The injustice inflamed my spirit.

In a deliberate decision in 1931, I specifically chose to enter aviation, a man's field in a man's world, spurred by a fierce desire to *be* someone. Betty Friedan, spokeswoman for the feminist movement in the United States and author of *The Feminine Mystique,* described the surge of independence and goal-oriented sense of self that pervaded the thoughts of outspoken women in the early years of this century, the time of *my* birth and coming of age. She described the strong-willed suffragettes, the avid women who fought vigorously and intelligently for the societal acceptance of blacks and women.

Friedan pinpoints World War II as a pivotal time, a time in which war-torn scenes of deprivation and family disruption sent women *back* into the home, *back* to the Victorian concept of being demure, accepting women—those primarily concerned with "diapers and dishes."

Appalled by the backsliding of the post-World War II years, I delight in the maturity and the prevailing attitudes of the nineties. I applaud the selection of young women to fly jets in our nation's military forces. Can I be blamed for wishing I had been offered that chance? I cheer my female flight students when they aim for the captaincy of commercial airliners. Can I help but feel jealous that I was never allowed to be selected? I cannot help but resent the damnable men who were at aviation's helm and who stood in the way when I sought commercial flying jobs. My male students—those *I'd* taught, those who learned everything they knew from *me*—were often hired while I was rejected. When I am accused of being a man-hater and a woman ahead of my time, I wonder, am I? Was that true of a younger me, a thirty-year-old in the 1930s?

I remember the spring of 1932, a year after I'd arrived at the Newport Naval Hospital, my second nursing assignment with the U.S. Navy. In Newport, Rhode Island, fall's tweed blanket of colorful foliage is famous, but spring was my favorite season. May's trees, in every imaginable shade of green, hung lavender blossoms over the gray rock walls that outlined every field. Lilacs sweetened the pungent odors of the shore. I can still picture Aquidneck Island from above—a brilliant emerald nestling comfortably in the palm of the swelling, whitecapped Atlantic Ocean. As a pilot, I treasured the bird's-eye view.

I shared the sky with the birds. Hundreds of them flitted between leafy branches and soared on the brisk sea-sprayed wind. Some migrated but most responded to their instinctive urge to mate, darting from limb to post to claim nesting territories. In one season, birds accomplish what most people seek throughout a lifetime—to define their place.

That spring—1932—a man left his parked touring car to approach me, his face shadowed by the brim of his hat, his mouth set in a grim, determined line. He glanced furtively over his shoulder and hesitated as I turned. Perhaps my clothes put him off? Unlike most women, I wore a pair of spattered white coveralls that reeked of gasoline and castor oil.

He stared at the wrench in my hand. Shadowed by my wooden hangar on Colonel Green's Round Hill Airfield north of Newport and in further defiance of feminine tradition, I tinkered with my prize and joy, my first airplane—a Travel Air.

"Lady," he said in a hurried, husky voice, still eyeing the wrench, "I was told you're a crackerjack pilot. Will you make a flight over Martha's Vineyard? I need to know the color of the flag on the mast of a ship in the third inlet."

He glanced at my face and stepped closer to hiss, "There's twenty dollars in it for you."

Twenty dollars! In 1932 most people reeled with the deepening devastation of the Depression. Twenty dollars was a fortune! I remembered watching millionaire Howard Hughes pass twenty-dollar bills to several men at our Newport airport as if dealing so many cards of a poker hand. The Hayward starter of his S-39 Sikorsky amphibian had needed air and several men scurried to rig electricity and an air compressor. Hughes flew to Newport to visit heiress Doris Duke. A few times I saw her drive her long, black car to our grass field to meet his plane, closely followed by her bodyguards in a matching black limo.

The Depression seemed to have no effect on people like that, but I was not one of the rich and famous of Newport's grand mansions. I was a registered nurse in the Naval Nurse Corps. In 1929 a commission in the Navy had offered me the security of employment, board, room, and a small paycheck—my flying money. For three years I'd eked out a living. As I added payments on a six-hundred-dollar biplane, monthly hangar rent, repair bills, and gas, the struggle had become acute. Now, just imagine! Twenty dollars for what I loved the most—a solo flight over the blue waters of Buzzards and Narragansett bays and the whitecapped waves of the Atlantic Ocean.

"Sure," I said with a shrug. I matched his wary style with a false nonchalance. Could I do it? I hadn't spent a great deal of time out over the water. What if the motor quit?

Twenty dollars was too much to refuse. I swallowed my doubts and tightened the cowl on the engine after stashing my tools in the corner of the hangar. What the heck? It would be fun. With suppressed delight, I tucked my short, curly brown hair into my helmet and grabbed my goggles, glancing at the movement of nearby tree branches to check the speed and direction of the wind, eager to fly—and to be paid for it!

Once propped, the motor blustered into action. As I swung a foot onto the lower wing and climbed into the cockpit, I murmured, "The flag on the ship in the third inlet." I could have shouted. Sounds disappeared in the propeller slipstream, drowned by the motor's roar. The birds were stilled, over-powered by my Curtiss OXX-6.

The man shrank into the shadow of my hangar and lit a cigarette, his hand cupped around the match as he drew a puff. I tightened a safety belt around my waist and gunned the throttle. I taxied the growling, lumbering Travel Air, weaving to be sure that the way ahead was clear. Taking full benefit of the length of the grassy field, I swung the craft into the wind at the edge of the woods and gunned the motor. The trees ahead grew taller as the craft hurtled toward them, then dropped away beneath us as the plane and I leaped into the air.

Would I ever tire of flying? Each takeoff made me catch my breath. I was lifted, literally and emotionally, on outstretched wings. As the wheels left the rough sod, still spinning, and the airplane banked to fly over the ocean's swells, my craft and I became one. Bright sunlight cast our dark shadow on frothing whitecaps below: our miniature, black spectre skimmed each wave crest and dipped into each trough. The fuzzy replica flew with us in distant formation.

"Let's fly, Travel Air," I yelled. The slipstream pulled the words from my mouth. "We're earning money, you and I."

When we cruised above the loading docks of the famed resort island of Martha's Vineyard, I banked to the left and right for a full view of the ships in the inlets. "The flag is red," I called out to the wind. The Travel Air and I wheeled over the docks a second and third time, to be certain—and for the fun of it.

Nosing toward Newport, we chased the gulls toward the coast. Within minutes, my first gainful employment as a pilot was over. The craft and I touched down and I heard the familiar *whoosh* as the wheels met the sod and parted the grasses. I couldn't hide my smile. Little could compare with the joy of a smooth landing. The prop whirred to a stop in front of the wooden hangar and the waiting stranger.

"Red," I reported, gaily. I climbed easily out of the cockpit, yanked off my helmet, and jumped off the wing.

He slipped twenty dollars to me with a limp handshake, said, "Good, lady. I'll see you another day," and left. I wanted to wave the money around and shout for joy.

As promised, he returned and I flew to Martha's Vineyard often, pocketing twenty dollars each time. Sometimes a green flag waved on the mast of the moored ship, sometimes white or red. I was happy to be paid to fly my open cockpit biplane. Solo flight was fun and I was eager to have the money that helped to pay the monthly thirty-five dollars owed toward my Travel Air. I could also pay the hangar rent, my gas bill. I was making *money!*

"Edna Gardner," chastised a friend, a self-appointed keeper of my conscience, "do you know what you're doing?"

"No, and I don't *want* to know," I retorted firmly. "I'm flying my airplane. I'm making money. I don't need to know anything more than that."

"You're under surveillance!" he persisted. "You're telling rum-runners when and where to pick up liquor. You're working with bootleggers!"

Rats. I didn't need to be reminded that I worked for the U.S.

Navy. My own conscience was intact, but my money-making flying came to a screeching halt.

Memories like this one often pop into my head in the earliest hours of morning and I jot highlights on the yellow steno pad on my bedside table. Each memory is a bubble that holds a bit of my life. As bubbles sometimes elongate and warp, some of my memories have distorted and stretched. I guess I can't help that. It has been a long time and there are so many memories, so many stories.

Another story, one that exemplifies a problem I was to have all my life, happened at the 1940 All-American Air Maneuvers in Miami, Florida. I'd flown to Miami from my home in New Orleans. Still buoyant from having won a women's air race in a Lambert-powered Monocoupe the prior year, I was eager to race, to repeat my success. But Monocoupe president Clare Bunch knew full well that the Lambert-powered craft had been given a good handicap in '39 and was too slow for the '40 competition.

Mike Murphy, well-known as an aerobatic pilot, stunted Bunch's Clipped Wing Monocoupe at Miami's air races. "Edna," Bunch told me, "get into my Clipped Wing when Mike is through with his airshow act. It's fast. It will put you at the front in the women's race. We want that Knight Culver prize."

Everyone knew about the Culver-Bunch dispute. Bunch stung with Culver's takeover of the Dart airplane and the capture of talented Al Mooney, the designer, to boot.

"Sure, Mr. Bunch. I'll find Mike and get him to check me out."

After Mike flew his "hoops and zooms" in the stub-winged monoplane and taxied to a stop, I ran over to the Monocoupe and said, "I'm Edna Gardner, Mike. Mr. Bunch wants me to race in this. Will you check me out? I've never flown the Clipped Wing."

"There's no point in a dual flight—there's only one set of controls," Mike said, shrugging his shoulders. "Just remember: this Monocoupe has straight legs. It's no typical production

6

model. On landing, get that tailwheel down—get it *planted*—or the gear will go every which way but straight."

I sat in the bird for a few minutes to get some idea of depth perception. The wings were short! I could really hug close to every pylon with that stubby airfoil. I could hardly wait.

When the loudspeakers blared the call for the women's race, Mike propped the Clipped Wing for me, and the airplane and I leaped off the field, out in front of the pack. We raced, tightly circling the pylons, kicking up sand as we zoomed lap after lap, rising during the turns, dipping close to the ground on the straightaways. We held on to the lead and we won! What a thrill! There's an adrenaline rush to racing and an indescribable high to winning. As the Monocoupe and I passed the checkered flag, we climbed high above the race course, exulting in the euphoria of the win. I was tempted to do a victory roll, but decided that I'd better concentrate on bringing the Clipped Wing in for a successful landing. It would never do to win the race, then crash-land in front of the eighteen thousand air race fans, or worse, in front of the other pilots.

As I brought it in, the straight-legged gear grabbed the ground and held. By the time I got it parked, I was on cloud nine. We women pilots clustered—hugging, laughing, and all talking at once:

"Where were you on the third pylon?"

"I was right on your tail."

"It went so fast. What speeds do you figure we averaged?"

"Christ, Edna. You flew so low! Did you mow sea grass with your left wingtip?"

We dissected each exciting moment of the race while we strode back from the flightline and crossed in front of the grandstand. Keyed up, I couldn't stop grinning—a winner!

Then came the biggest slam of my life. Leonard Peterson, Tex Rankin, Mike Murphy, Johnny Livingston, Vincent "Squeek" Burnett, and other male pilots lounged in front of the announcer's stand—smoking cigarettes, jostling, joking, and talking. Their hands carved aerial descriptions of flying—the only topic that rivaled sex as their favorite. They elbowed one another, nodding toward us, and one of them, Addie Polley, called out, "Hey, Edna, do you know what Tex Rankin said about you?"

"No, what did he say?"

"He said, 'Edna Gardner is one woman who flies like a man!' "

I screamed! Some of the women pilots grabbed my arms. I wanted to slap Tex Rankin across the face. I yelled at the entire lot of men. "That's a slam! I don't fly like a man. That's a slam!"

Tex Rankin added insult to injury. He later wrote in a magazine article, "During the past 20 years I have personally instructed . . . 3,000 students, . . . about 40 women. I found that many women require about 50 percent more dual instruction before solo than does the average man. I believe this is caused principally by the woman's lack of mechanical knowledge. Men are taught mechanics from the time they are old enough to hold a wrench and a pair of pliers. . . . If a woman has a conception of the mechanical side of aviation, has good depth perception and is healthy, I see no reason why she shouldn't become as good a pilot as any man."

Damn him. I fly like a man? A woman has a "lack of mechanical knowledge"? A woman *could* become "as good a pilot as any *man*"?

I can't count the times I've found myself pitted against some of the men who dominated the field of aviation in the late twenties and early thirties. By the 1980s, young men accepted working side-by-side with women, even working for a female if she proved herself, knew her stuff, and inspired them with her management. But their grandfathers weren't so generous. They put us down and held us back. They saw to it that a woman's search for identity and success in aviation was a constant, damnable uphill battle.

Men were my nemesis. I often said, "Men are such fools!" when they frustrated me yet turned to putty with a little manipulation. I couldn't have learned to fly had it not been for the encouragement and support of several men; yet aviators proved to be two-sided. They represented a challenge for my zest, the outlet for my appetite for learning, living, and loving,

8

but simultaneously erected a bastion of male ego, pride, and supposed superiority. They built a wall that was difficult for any woman to scale.

Another story comes to mind as I recall the "Man's World" of flying. In 1934, I taught flying to students at air fields near Washington, D.C. I read a posted flyer that advertised a race: "Curtiss Wright Airport, Baltimore, Maryland. PYLON RACE, $300 in Prize Money and Trophy."

What fun! I telephoned Guerdon W. Brocksom, the flight instructor who had been my mentor, to whom I owed so much for having taught me to fly and soloed me in 1931. Guerd was still living in Newport, Rhode Island, where we'd spent almost two years together.

"May I borrow and race your J6-5 Aristocrat, Guerd?" I asked. "They've advertised a pylon race."

"Sure you can, Edna," Guerd affirmed. "I'll fly it to Washington for you and you can keep it with you for a while. Perhaps you can even sell it for me." Guerd was a pilot of no mean ability and an equally skilled mechanic. I knew his high-wing monoplane would be finely tuned and running well. I knew, too, that the Aristocrat could be the fastest competitor in a racing field that included Travel Airs, Swallows, Wacos, and other biplanes. It could win.

Race day came and I was the only female pilot entered in the race. I was fired with enthusiasm, my adrenaline flowing. I flew as close to the ground and as tight around the pylons as I could swing the wing. The J6-5 engine pulled us out into the lead and we polished the pylons, low and as close as I dared so that no one could creep inside, force me high and wide, and pass me. The throttle was wide open. My heart pounded in rhythm with the engine and, more than once, I wanted to wipe the sweat off my palms along my thighs. But, I knew better than to release the stick for even an instant. There'd be time to wipe sweat after the race.

We won, that Aristocrat and I! But the male pilots huddled after the race, furious to be bested by a woman. They tried to disqualify me and to weasel out of giving me the prize money and the trophy. Incensed to the man, they stalled the award ceremony until those gathered for the trophy presentation were obviously uncomfortable. One of the pilots, a more enlightened man, finally grew exasperated and said, "Listen. You let her enter that race. She entered it, she flew it well, and she won. You've no choice. Give her the prize and the trophy!"

Fury was replaced on most of the men's faces with steely-eyed, tight-jawed resignation. They gave in; but they got even. The following year the same race was posted. "Curtiss Wright Airport, Baltimore, Maryland. PYLON RACE, $300 in Prize Money and Trophy." At the bottom it said, in huge black letters, *"MEN ONLY!"*

It never ended. I have story after story of the prejudice and discrimination that affected my sixty years of flying. One bastard after another crossed paths and swords with me. Have I had some fears and doubts? You bet. Have they gotten the best of me? Not at all. Instead of intimidating me into submission, I formed an unparalleled level of determination and competitiveness. When women are portrayed as being desirably faint-hearted, demure, and subservient, I resist. When femininity is restricted to a woman's body and beauty, the enticement of men, the serving of husband and children, and is considered to be confined to the home, I rebel!

In still another scene and another time, I once telephoned to reserve an airplane at the airport in College Park, Maryland. Flying hours were precious as I had to juggle the demands of my nursing career with the demands of a growing list of flight students. I climbed out of my car at the airfield and found an arrogant pilot at the plane, helmet in place, goggles hugging the top of his forehead. He was rolling "my" airplane out to perform a preflight.

"I reserved that airplane for this hour," I protested to him. "Did you check the schedule book?"

He brushed past me to continue checking the craft, totally deaf to my words.

"Hey!" I insisted. "I've got that airplane. What do you think you're doing?"

"Get outta my way, lady," he snarled. "I'm taking this plane and you're *off* the schedule, even if some fool mistakenly put you onto it. You should be home doing diapers and dishes!"

I stood on the ground and watched the man fire up, taxi out, and turn the craft into the wind for takeoff. Rage welled within me. My hands balled into fists. If I'd been a man, I'd have punched him!

No, if I'd been a man, there would have been no confrontation. I would have had uncomplicated access to the flying schedule. How infuriating, how completely frustrating that a woman could be treated so shabbily. It was one of the many times that I wished I'd been born a man.

All I ever wanted was to secure my place in life and to earn the money to live that life successfully. Flight instructing gave me the chance to be competent and confident. It provided me with a virtually limitless group of friends and acquaintances in relationships in which I was in control. Aviation has been my sanctuary, the sum total of whatever success I can boast. Energy? Determination? Competitive zeal? I have more than my share of each. I've learned to be damned tough. I've *had* to be! I've had to harness and direct my energies and keep anger, hate, and revenge from misdirecting my vigor.

People have said that I am a liberated woman, born too soon. I was born too soon to be accepted as a military pilot, although I was qualified to *teach* male military pilots. I was born too soon to be chosen as an airline pilot, yet I trained *hundreds* of pilots who now fly for various airlines. I wasn't born too soon. I was very much a woman of my time, an independent woman of the 1930s.

When Betty Friedan pinpoints the post-World War II years as a time in which women "returned" to the home, the dramatic return and narrowed sense of freedom was not limited to the United States. The Hitler regime in Nazi Germany also proposed for women *"Kinder, Kuche, Kirche,"* (Children, Cooking, Church). Our vigorous mothers and grandmothers had made significant forward strides for feminism at the turn of the century. What happened to the momentum? Did the cause lose its thrust once the primary goal of the right to vote was satisfied? After 1920, the militant movement began to wane and then reversed its direction. Clearly it faltered too soon with too little accomplished for women.

Ambassador Clare Boothe Luce said, "Because I am a woman, I must make unusual efforts to succeed. If I fail, no one will say, 'She doesn't have what it takes.' They will say, 'Women don't have what it takes.'" Luce spoke for all creative, vital, intelligent, courageous women. In the 1930s, with few options open to me, I persevered. I joined the Navy, I fully supported myself. I learned to fly—an ultimate liberation. I was determined to show that I, and other women, have "what it takes."

$\mathscr{A}$ $\mathscr{L}ark$ and a $\mathscr{R}ogue$

I didn't hate men when I was young. I don't hate men today. But my first and what ought to have been my best relationship was devastating. My father, Walter Gardner, was killed in 1910 when I was only eight years old. I felt cheated. Before I could build trust and lasting love, he was gone.

I remembered his strong hands under my arms, hoisting me aboard a steaming, noisy locomotive. "Up you go, my pretty girl," he told me cheerfully. I was three and we boarded a train in Minnesota to move to an Oregon farm where Father dreamed of forging a good life for his family. He was tall and slim with unruly brown hair drooping over his forehead. Deep laugh lines crinkled around his eyes and he smelled of a mixture of tobacco, aftershave, and new-mown hay. I felt safe in his hands as he swung me through the otherwise terrifying steam that boiled and hissed around the huge train wheels. He settled me on a seat next to my mother and baby brother and kissed us all. "Have a safe trip," he told us. "I'll just be a week behind you in the freight train with our team of horses."

Father tried farming in Oregon, but gave it up to become an engineer on the new railroad that snaked through the wild, rugged Oregon Cascade Mountains. Five short years later he was dead. A locomotive driven by his own brother smashed into the handcar he was driving and tumbled it down a rocky, tree-covered ravine. Not even lucky enough to be killed outright, he was driven four hundred bone-jarring miles to a Portland hospital where he died later of internal injuries. He was only thirty-two.

Family life—security—died with my father. Soon after his death, my mother, Myrtle Gardner, contracted tuberculosis and was sent to Onalaska, a sanitarium in Minnesota. She received no widow's benefits. After suing the railroad company, what meager money she received went to the attorney and hospital costs. Mother abhorred the idea of giving us up for adoption but, sick and incarcerated, she had no choice but to depend upon relatives and friends.

My sister, brother, and I were farmed out. My two-year-old baby sister, Vera, went to live with our Grandmother Gardner. Donovan Dean, my six-year-old brother, and I were separately placed and remained apart until our teens. For eight years I moved from pillar to post. Was it because families couldn't afford another mouth to feed? Did I cause problems? I don't remember, but I know that I moved often. I felt unloved and unwanted—an outsider in other people's homes.

And *poor*. It still hurts to remember receiving a limp, yellowed, hand-me-down petticoat when the girl of the house twirled in new stiff crinolines, three layers thick. Dean told me that Mother once sent new wool mittens to him, but they were given to the son of the family while my brother wore a ragged, used pair.

Most families undoubtedly tried to make me feel welcome, but I felt neglected and ignored. I ached to be loved, to belong. I felt as if there was no one I could trust, nowhere I could turn, no one who cared. My poverty was not only financial, it was emotional.

Yet, deprivation can teach self-reliance. Determined to better my position in life, I became independent and learned to set goals. I chose my own friends, defined my own directions, forged my own life. Few dared tell me what to do, what to think, or how to act. I remembered my mother inspiring me with the her favorite phrase, "Rise above it." Mine became a competitive and rebellious spirit with a fierce determination to succeed.

As Mother's health improved, she was hired by various farmers as a housekeeper. She took Dean with her, adding ten additional dollars a month for his work, although Dean was grown before he realized that any payment was made for his labor. He was expected to attend school and return to farm chores each afternoon. Life was hard and, to complicate it, Mother had to leave several farms when bachelor farmers pressed for her sexual favors. She and Dean moved as often as I did.

After high school, tired of farm work, Dean had hopped freight and wandered about the West with two equally footloose buddies. His intelligence was masked by a lack of self-esteem and a pessimism toward his future. Slender and wiry, Dean never weighed much more than 150 pounds. His light brown hair outlined a thin, angular face with a small, straight nose. I envied his nose. Mine had been broken in a high school basketball game and, although I wanted to, I could never justify the expense of plastic surgery.

By 1926, I had graduated from New Salem High School in Wisconsin, entered and completed nurse's training, and become a registered nurse. On staff at the University Hospital in Madison, Wisconsin, I was eager for some excitement. Newspaper headlines reported, "Trotsky Expelled from Soviet Union" "Richard Byrd and Floyd Bennett Fly to North Pole"; "Goddard Fires First Liquid Fuel Rocket"; and "Gertrude Ederle—First Woman to Swim the English Channel." That swim was fourteen years after Harriet Quimby had become the first woman to cross the Channel in a flimsy, open-cockpit airplane. In 1926 a young Louise Thaden snared a rare opportunity. She accepted a job with Walter Beech at the Travel Air Factory in Wichita, Kansas, and was offered flying lessons. It seemed that the world pulsed with excitement. In mundane contrast, I finished a course in pediatric nursing that chained me to the hospital nursery—feeding formula, burping babies, and changing diapers.

"You're as restless as I am, aren't you?" I asked my brother, Dean one day in late fall of 1926, knowing full well that he was unemployed.

In an impetuous stab at maturity and stability, he had married earlier that year. At my question, he frowned with pensive brown eyes eyes devoid of laugh lines, which darted warily like those of a fox. Our father's death, family separation, and poverty had taken its toll on both of us.

I turned to question his petite, vivacious bride, Velma. "Wouldn't you like some excitement, Velma? It's already dead here and winter hasn't even started. Let's get out before the first snow. What do you say?"

Velma's blue eyes danced. But, with a glance at Dean's unsmiling face, she shook her head. Her dark bobbed hair accentuated her gesture. "How, Edna?" she asked with a shrug. "Dean and I don't have a car. Could we fit three in your little Studebaker coupe? Besides, what about my job? Since Dean's out of work . . ."

"There's no money, Edna," finished Dean. "You ought to know that."

"Oh, come on, you two. I'm stuck in pediatrics and have had enough of babies to last a lifetime. You've nothing holding you here. The last I heard, you weren't crazy about your secretarial job, Velma. I say this is a good time to get out of Wisconsin. My coupe would rather be in the sun—not covered with a foot of snow."

"Money, Edna," Dean repeated, tonelessly.

"I've saved enough from my nursing to get us underway. We could get jobs and earn enough to keep going, couldn't we? You did that when you hopped freight, didn't you, Dean?"

Dean nodded slowly and Velma's eyes sparkled. She and I

were primed for opportunity. Dean finally agreed to the adventure. I mentioned our uncle and aunt, Sam and Margaret Gardner, in Seattle and we decided to drive to visit them—the long way. We had no deadlines, nothing specific in mind.

"We can work our way south where it's warm and eventually wind up with our relatives. Besides, Mother can't complain too strenuously if we're heading for Sam and Margaret's home, can she?"

Dean tilted his head and raised his eyebrows. "Hunnh, well, that's an idea," he said. He grew more cheerful and swung an arm around Velma's slim waist. "We can call it our honeymoon, baby."

Velma giggled, put her arms around his neck, and leaned against him, nibbling at his ear lobe. He turned to look at me when I said, "Let's drive south until we can shed these bulky winter coats."

Dean put his other arm around Velma's waist and pulled her tightly to him. "What d'ya say, baby? Let's get outta here and have a lark. Doesn't that sound..." Velma stopped Dean in mid-sentence with a kiss.

I finished his thought aloud, "...like fun. Hmmm. For you two. Just try not to drive me crazy. God, you can't keep your hands off each other. Remember, two's company and it's *my* Studebaker."

"Spoilsport," Velma taunted with a giggle. She shook her head. "Can I put in a resignation tomorrow? I can't wait to see the look on the face of that dirty-minded old insurance broker when I quit. Heck, I can get a secretarial job any place we go."

"Yeah," agreed Dean. "One where there aren't lecherous men."

"Just you, baby," Velma cooed. "Just you." She snuggled into his arms.

"I'm sure that I can get a nursing job. God willing, it won't be in pediatrics. I won't miss changing crib sheets and messy diapers, that's for sure. I've had my fill of making formula and nursing babies. I'll never have any of my own." The look in

Velma's eyes as she smiled at Dean and tightened her arms around his neck told me that her ideas were the complete opposite of mine.

We told Mother that we had decided to visit Uncle Sam and Aunt Margaret. We didn't think she needed to know much more than that and neglected to mention plans for heading south. When she protested feebly about the cost, I reminded her that Dean had worked his way west before and that both Velma and I had marketable skills. Urging her not to worry, we told her that we'd write. We packed some things and piled happily into the small car.

"Let's go, Studebaker," I directed aloud as I gunned the motor. "Let's get outta here."

What a joy to drive away. We sang songs and laughed, giddy and carefree, relieved and revived to be on the road. We joined the adventurous and, since Velma didn't know how to drive, Dean and I shared the driving.

"Tulsa, Oklahoma," Dean announced, stretching from his turn at the wheel. Velma was sleeping. "Wake up, baby," he said as he shook her shoulder gently, then reached past her to nudge me. "Edna, I'm going to stop for gas. In the sunshine, the breeze feels pretty comfortable. Maybe it'll be warm enough to stay. They might even be hiring in the oil fields."

The wind stung sharply when we stepped out of the Studebaker. We drew our coats tighter instead of chucking them. "Well, so much for Tulsa," I said, shaking my head. "Maybe Texas will be better."

"It's not hot enough here," added Velma. She giggled again and took Dean's hand.

"You drive, Edna," Dean told me after we'd gassed the car. He climbed in first, pulling Velma onto his lap. There was no point in conversation. They weren't interested in talking at all. My Studebaker wasn't big enough for me and for lovebirds. They were pains in the ass.

Velma was the first out of the car when we stopped in Dallas. The day was sunny and inviting.

"It's warm," she crowed.

"It's finally as hot outside the car as it is inside," I said flatly. "I'm about ready for a break. Let's find a room for rent and see Dallas."

Our dispositions had worn thin. With too much time in too close proximity to one another, we chafed. Since childhood, Dean and I had lived under the same roof for only three of our high school years. We were quite different; he more introspective and insecure, and less confident than I. I was the one who instigated this long jaunt, owned the car, had an education and a career. Whatever fears and doubts I had were squelched when I chose to accept the responsibility for the trip. However, it was of little comfort to be in charge with a lovey, newly married couple only inches away day and night. It accentuated my loneliness and made me yearn for my own man and romance. Instead, I had to look for a job and be practical and realistic.

We rented a room on Mapelon Avenue. I was hired to nurse at the Parkland Hospital, which later gained fame as the hospital where they took John F. Kennedy at his assassination. Velma joined an insurance firm, but Dean found himself up to his elbows in dirt and grease with a job that offered a commission on sales of gas stoves. He was quickly disillusioned.

"Sure!" he complained angrily when he came home one sultry evening, slamming the door behind him. "Clean and adjust old stoves and *then* convince homeowners to buy a new one. What a joke. I don't get a red cent unless I make a sale."

"Develop a line, Dean," I encouraged. "Take an advantage and use a little sweet talk. Turn on some charm to make a sale."

"Don't give me that, Edna. What do you know? You priss around in your white dress in an antiseptic hospital all day. Every blasted house I visit has somebody in it who wants their filthy stove cleaned, but not a damn one of them wants to purchase a new one. Hell, I get as dirty as the stoves. By the time I'm through, they don't want to even look at me, much less listen to me or buy from me. I haven't earned a blasted penny.

I've scoured and adjusted dirty stoves for nothing. Not one single fat dime. I tell you, I quit! You two can have Dallas and Fort Worth, too."

"Okay, okay, Dean," I cajoled. "There's no reason we can't move on. Velma, do you have some money to help buy gas?"

"Well, a little, but I've been paying for groceries, too, you know."

"Don't whine, Velma. I'm just trying to figure it out in my head. Oh, who cares? If we run out, we'll stop in Midland or Odessa or even El Paso and earn some more. We're free to do as we please. We've no ties in Dallas." I shrugged and added, "Let's just drive. Maybe there's something special waiting for us in Seattle or California."

"Something or someone, Edna?" mocked Velma. She rolled her eyes at Dean and giggled. Damn her, she always giggled.

"You haven't found a Texan yet, huh, Edna?" Dean taunted. Damn him, too. Sometimes I couldn't stand them.

We baked all the kitchen leftovers into one cake—flour, corn-meal, cereal, raisins, sugar, dried fruit. It staved off hunger and stretched what little travel money we scraped together.

On the road again, the cake stashed along the seat back, we broke off pieces while we drove. Dean made a big deal of taking a chunk, circling his arm around Velma to pop it into his mouth, then snuggling into her neck to eat it. They giggled and tussled until I felt the car shake.

"Cut it out, Dean. Lord, I get sick of her giggling. She'd probably quit if you'd let up. Can't we just drive?"

"Whoa, big sister. Don't get your dander up. You get mean when you're mad. What's your problem? The weather's nice, the car's performing, we've gas money, something to eat—what more could we want?"

"Who provided the gas money?" I snapped angrily.

"It wasn't my fault that I couldn't sell any damned stoves. The weather's too warm," Dean retorted.

"Well, maybe if we keep driving you'll get interested in the Texas and Arizona scenery and stop playing with Velma. There isn't room in the front seat of this car. Especially with *me* in it with you."

"You're a pain, Edna."

"You aren't as much fun anymore, Edna," Velma complained with a pout.

"You need our company," added Dean. "You insisted that we come along. You wouldn't have gotten this far alone. Quit grumbling."

"Let's drop it," I said with a sigh. "We'll kill one another before Seattle at this rate."

We drove in tense silence for several miles. I concentrated on driving, although the roads were nothing to brag about. In the centers of cities and towns, roads were paved, but rural roads slowed us and contributed to our tension.

"As long as it stays dry," Dean said, "these dirt roads won't be any problem. I'll bet we can make forty or forty-five miles an hour."

Velma wrinkled her nose and added, "As long as we can stand the dust. Can you taste the grit?"

"Yeah. It chokes you, doesn't it?" Dean agreed. "Man, we'll never forget Texas: dirty stoves, roads that are remote and rough as hell, heat with dust that'd gag you. Are you as thirsty as I am? I'm dry as a bone."

Velma nodded.

"Now you're grousing," I interrupted. "Dust beats a snow drift or getting caught in a blizzard, doesn't it? Come *on!* Either you can't keep your hands to yourselves or you can't stop complaining. Honestly. It's harder to take your fussing than your lovemaking."

"Who's grousing?" asked Dean. "Sounds like sour grapes to me, Edna. By the way, why didn't you bring a water jug?"

They say that timing is everything in life. Well, Dean's timing stunk. He had no sooner mentioned water when the sky darkened and the skies unleashed a torrential Texas thunderstorm. Rain pounded the dirt road, spattering mud over the car and across the windshield, turning the road into oozing, sucking muck. The skies blackened with dense clouds and heavy, pelting rain, then flashed a brilliant white with unpredictable bolts of lightning. Temporarily blinded, we felt each shock of the shattering claps of thunder that followed closely. Much too closely.

Gullies flooded both sides of the road. Dean got drenched putting on tire chains, but they were ineffective. Mud packed under the fenders and we skidded and slipped. We crept, never getting out of low gear. Driving was exhausting and Dean got out repeatedly to dig at the muck around the tires.

"Can't you dig any faster?" I griped at one point. "We probably would have zipped through Montana. Hard-packed snow couldn't possibly have been this terrible."

"Edna, you've a sense of humor that won't quit, don't you?" He jabbed futilely at mud clinging to the tires and wheel wells and under the fenders. "Next time we get a harebrained idea to drive to Seattle via west Texas, I'll pack the tools. All you brought is this useless tire iron. I can't believe it. You need a man in more ways than one."

"Shut up, Dean, and drop that damned subject. We'll just drive slowly and eventually we'll get to better roads."

"Brilliant. Is there another choice?"

Finally, east of El Paso, we found respite. "Hey," I said, nudging Velma awake. She'd been sleeping, again. What did she care about the miserable roads? I pointed. "There's a tourist home. Let's spend at least one night. It'll give the roads time to dry out and let us get out of this car. We might even get a bath. God, that would be heaven."

"Fantastic!" agreed Velma.

Dean was wet and filthy—delighted to anticipate a bath. We pooled our meager money and reveled in the luxury of a place to stay. The beds were clean and comfortable and the food was good. The owners invited us to join them in the parlor to tell of our travels. We felt sophisticated and worldly—for the first time in our lives.

The stay signaled the start of a dramatic improvement for our trip. The next day, just south of Las Cruces, New Mexico, I pointed at a man on the shoulder of the road and slowed the

Studebaker. "There's a hitchhiker—a good-looking one at that. Let's ask him where he's headed, Dean. He's miles from everywhere. It would be criminal to leave him standing in the desert."

Dean's grin was mocking and I avoided looking directly at him. He couldn't deny that I was right. No driver strands a person in the desert. If it so happens that the hitchhiker is a handsome, smiling man, well? That's even better. The trip suddenly tingled with promise.

The hitchhiker clutched his belongings in a shoe box and held out his right hand, thumb up. He'd no tie on his slightly crumpled white shirt, and his rolled shirtsleeves exposed a pale but muscular arm. The breeze waved his loose beige trousers against his legs and a hat perched jauntily on his slick brown hair. A jacket hung casually across his right arm and his smile was disarming and confident. I wondered how many people, if any, had passed him by.

"He sure travels light," Dean was saying. "But, on the other hand, it's lucky he doesn't have a suitcase. We'd never get them both into this car."

I stopped the car and Dean rolled down the window and called, "Where are you headed?"

The hitchhiker smiled broadly. "I'd really like to get to Los Angeles," he answered. "Any chance you're driving that far? I'd appreciate a ride, eh?" He put his hand on the window sill and bent to smile at each of us in turn.

Dean glanced at me and, at my nod, opened the car door. He took the man's shoe box and stashed it beside the cake tin. He helped a giggling Velma onto his lap to make room for the hitchhiker, then told him, sarcastically, "It just took us an eon to get through West Texas. If there is any rain in New Mexico, we may never make it to Arizona, much less Los Angeles."

I spoke up, "Oh, we will so, Dean." I looked at the man and asked, "Are you in any hurry? The three of us are driving all the way to Seattle. We're just having fun, or trying to. I hope you don't have to be somewhere at any certain time."

"No hurry for me," he said, good-naturedly.

"Well, climb on in," said Dean and reached to shake his

hand. "We'll get to Los Angeles and even Seattle—eventually. No promises as to when, though. This is my wife, Velma, and my sister, Edna, is at the wheel. I'm Dean Gardner and you're...?"

"Gordon, Gordon Hutton." The slim, athletically built fellow grinned and pumped Dean's hand as if he'd found a long-lost buddy. He smiled warmly at me and nodded pleasantly to Velma.

"Where is your home, Gordon?" I asked, sizing him up as covertly as possible. I was glad to be driving.

"I'm Canadian. You'll deliver me fairly close to home by the time you get to Seattle, eh?"

"Well," I said, ignoring the knowing glance Dean was sending to me. He wasn't going to leave us in L.A., hmmm? My cheeks must have reddened. I felt flustered. "After Las Cruces, it's Deming. Let me know, will you, if anyone needs to stop for any reason?"

Gordon was as much fun as his first bright smile had suggested, a joy to have along. He liked to sing and, as we dallied west, we sang every song that we knew. In Arizona, we found a dance hall.

"Come on, Edna," Gordon suggested gaily. "Let's dance." He slid his arm around me and I felt my breath catch in my throat. His touch was masterful. From that evening on, I could scarcely wait to find another town, another dance hall. Gordon was not only a good dancer, he was clever and likeable, intriguing. The chemistry crackled between us. Gordon could have left us in California, but he stayed until we reached Seattle. He was penniless, but that hadn't stopped us yet, so we thought little of it. We shared whatever we had and the trip became a lark.

When we reached Seattle, Gordon said, "Give me your Uncle Sam and Aunt Margaret Gardner's address, eh? I'll catch up with you later in Bremerton."

"Do you know people in Seattle, Gordon?" I asked.

"Oh, a few," he answered easily. "At any rate, you ought to get reacquainted with your relatives before I arrive on the scene."

Dean, Velma, and I found our aunt and uncle and immediately started thinking about jobs and places to live. Velma landed secretarial work and Dean took a job at a print shop. They stayed with Aunt Margaret and Uncle Sam. I found a nursing position at the Virginia Mason Hospital in Seattle with quarters in a dormitory nearby. Gordon? He evidently was a fugitive and a thief. He found notoriety.

After Gordon's crimes were featured in several newspaper articles, Aunt Margaret began to fret. She tried to talk to me, but I wasn't interested in her lectures. I had heard tirades on morals and propriety from my mother and they irked me. I knew the facts of life—I was a nurse, wasn't I? My mother harped on the subject. She told me, "It is wrong to have sex before marriage, Edna," and she repeated herself so often that I resented her interference, rebelled against her authority. I had lived without parental discipline too long. Why did she think she had to tell me anything? And Aunt Margaret? What business was it of hers? I had my own place to live. I earned my own way. I wasn't *her* daughter.

But Aunt Margaret felt responsible for her young relatives. I discovered later that she sent news clippings to Mother in Minnesota. One said, "Gordon Hutton of Canada was caught by Seattle police for stealing a violin at a skating rink. Once apprehended, it was discovered that Hutton is wanted by police in El Paso, Texas, where he is charged with breaking out of jail and for transporting a stolen car from Chicago to El Paso."

Aunt Margaret wrote to Mother, "Edna picked up this Hutton fellow outside of El Paso. The police suspect Edna as an accomplice to his crimes. She went to court and was questioned until the judge decided she was a 'Good Samaritan,' an innocent accomplice; but, Myrtle, I am concerned about her. She is involved with an unsavory character."

What is so fascinating about a rogue? I often thought that Dean's sales of stoves in Dallas might have been more successful if he had some of the persuasive banter of Gordon Hutton. Hutton was a con artist—a charming, attractive con artist.

Aunt Margaret persisted. She sent every news clipping to

Mother in Chatfield, Minnesota. Another said, "Jailed on charges of car thievery, Gordon Hutton of Canada fashioned a key from a piece of brass and escaped from his cell. He repeated his offense, stole another car, and, once nabbed by the Seattle police in the act of a house break-in, was transported toward jail. Again the wily Hutton thwarted officials as he grabbed the steering wheel of the police car and put the car over an embankment into an unoccupied shack below. Hutton managed to wrest the keys from the dazed deputy, remove his handcuffs, and attempt a second escape. This time he was apprehended quickly by alert policemen. He remains incarcerated awaiting extradition to El Paso."

Mother insisted repeatedly that I return to Wisconsin or to Chatfield, Minnesota. Such a move would put me right back where I started, or worse, back with Mother and her second husband, John Hander. I had lived with them in Chatfield during my high school years, from 1918 to my senior year, 1920 to 1921. John Hander was a frugal farmer, but there was no love lost between us. Would I ever learn to choose a man that enhanced my life? I'd no father. Now I had a relationship with a rogue that not only upset my aunt and my mother, but was also abruptly ended when he was carted off to jail.

I remembered living at Hander's farm in Chatfield. By 1918, my mother was out of the sanitarium and working as a housekeeper for Hander. He was no fool. When she applied for the job, he assessed the value of hiring Mother and also getting two teenagers with strong arms and strong backs for farm chores. As opposed to several others for whom Mother had worked, he allowed her to bring Dean and me to live with them. It was the first time that we were under the same roof since our father's death, eight years before. Mother had begun to consider marrying Hander, but Dean and I complicated their lives. I had been elected the captain of the girls' basketball team and wanted to participate. Dean and I worked at farm chores every day, but Hander wanted us to work full time on the farm.

I remembered hearing them argue in the night. "I want an education for my children," Mother complained. "I don't want

Edna and Dean to quit school to work on the farm. I want them prepared to take care of themselves. What if they are dealt a blow like mine?"

"I survived with just a third-grade education," argued Hander. "Dean and Edna are strong and healthy. Why should they play games at school when they could be helping with the dairy cows or working in the fields? You spoil them."

Mother sacrificed for her children. To keep us in school until we received a high school diploma and an opportunity for higher education, she left Hander. She moved to another housekeeping job in New Salem, Wisconsin, as I was ready to enter my senior year of high school. I graduated in 1921.

"I believe that you should be trained, Edna," she insisted. "You should have an education, be prepared to support yourself, competent in a chosen career. If you marry, your education won't be wasted. You can use it as you raise your family. It is important that you are able to support yourself."

Mother's eyes filled with tears as she recalled her hardships, but she was proud she hadn't put us up for adoption, that we'd survived the depths into which Father's death had plunged us. After I held a diploma and entered into nurse's training, Mother sent Dean to ask Hander if she was welcome to return to Chatfield. Invited, she became Mrs. John Hander.

I never related well to Hander. I found it a continued struggle to develop trust in men. Dean and I had worked hard at farm chores for him for a few years and I never regretted learning the value of physical labor. But I missed the warmth of a father's hug, a father's love and encouragment.

I missed dancing and being held by Gordon Hutton, too. When Gordon escaped for a final time from the Seattle jail, it just happened to be a fellow Canadian named Bob Martin who was nearby with a waiting automobile. Bob Martin, after whisking Gordon from jail to freedom in Canada, returned to Seattle and called me. It was Martin who first awakened me to the true love of my life—flying. He owned an airplane, a Canuck, Canada's version of the Curtiss JN-4 "Jenny" biplane, and he shared with me the fabulous realm of flight.

"Have you ever been for a ride in an airplane?" Martin asked.

I'm sure my eyes shone with excitement at the very idea. "An airplane? No, I've never been near one. I've never even touched one."

"I've got my own airplane. I keep it tied down at a field in Renton. If you'll drive there with me Saturday, I'll take you for an airplane ride."

I had no idea that letters flew between Aunt Margaret and my mother. Margaret wrote, "Myrtle, I don't know what to think about Edna. No sooner was that Hutton fellow out of circulation than she took up with a friend of his. He owns a *flying machine.* I'm afraid her adventurous spirit will land her in a heap of trouble. Will you write to her?"

Mother wrote, desperately urging me back to Minnesota. "Think about returning to school to become a doctor, Edna." I ignored her. I wasn't even slightly interested. I'd left Wisconsin in 1926 to find adventure. I liked the Seattle area. I enjoyed nursing at the Virginia Mason Hospital, and, as we started into 1927, there was a chance for some real excitement. Flying! What a thrill. A ride in an airplane! I could scarcely wait.

3

Renton and a Canuck

On Saturday morning, Bob Martin stopped in front of the nurses' quarters and swung open the passenger door to his forest green coupe. I grinned at him, feeling reckless, tossed my coat between us, and slid onto the pale green matte upholstery, smoothing my gray flannel skirt beneath me. We headed toward the field in nearby Renton to his plane.

"Well, Edna. Are you set for a ride in my Canuck?" he asked. "It's a little different than a Jenny, but not much."

"Canook? Jenny?" I asked, curious. Bob was excited. He tensed toward the steering wheel and his eagerness was contagious. His heavy leather jacket hung comfortably from his broad shoulders and his tan jodphurs fitted tightly to his calves, wedged into tall black boots. With curly, ash-blond hair, deep-blue eyes, and a tapered moustache, he personified my image of the swaggering, dashing pilot. He gave me a cocky, lopsided grin, well aware of the interest that he and talk of his airplane generated.

My cheeks must have been flushed like his, my eyes as shining. "I can't even picture what your airplane must look like," I told him. "I've seen a few overhead, but never up close. Are they terribly noisy? While you're flying, do you ever feel as if you might fall right out of the sky?"

Bob's grin widened knowingly. He knew things that I'd never experienced and his superiority was masked by a tantalizing, secretive smile.

The Seattle area, tempered by surrounding water, enjoys a mild climate; but it was still winter, early in 1927, and we were lucky there was no rain. A crisp, sunny Saturday morning greeted us, the skies lightly spattered with high, puffy white clouds. I felt even more giddy and carefree than when I left Wisconsin with Dean and Velma or when dancing in the crook of Gordon Hutton's arm. I rolled the car window halfway down and let the breeze riffle my hair. The air smelled fresh, tinged with the aroma of pine.

I had a million questions. "Did it take you long to learn to fly? Have you ever been scared? When you're flying, do you feel suspended, as if you defy gravity? How fast can your airplane go?"

"Whoa! Hold some of those questions until you can try flying for yourself. And, just wait until you hear that wind whistling through the bracing wires. It will make *that* sound like a whisper," Bob said, pointing toward the open window of the rushing automobile. "I've a helmet and a pair of goggles that you can wear to keep your hair from getting too windblown, although that doesn't seem to bother you. I like a girl who doesn't worry if a few hairs are out of place."

"My hairdo is the least of my concerns. Tell me about your airplane. Where did it get a funny name like Canook?"

He settled back and smiled at me, then casually slid his arm across the back of the seat. "The Canuck, eh? It's the Canadian version of the Jenny, the training plane. There were thousands of Jennies built, so you've probably seen one if you've seen an airplane at all. The Canuck has four ailerons. There are only two on the Jenny. And there isn't quite the same droop to the front of the fuselage at the motor as there is with the Jenny."

More new words—aileron, fuselage. The French influence was obvious, even if the first powered flight was in the United States. Flying has a special language, offers an intimate club for the initiated. Bob Martin didn't know it, but he was fueling a fire within me that would burn throughout my lifetime. How exciting to be a part of aviation, to find a new and challenging world that required talent, courage, and daring, and had a language all its own.

Nursing had its own esoteric jargon, too, but somehow sutures, hypodermics, and stethoscopes paled to insignificance in comparison to bracing wires, fuselages, and ailerons. The idea of soaring with birds, flirting with danger, feeling daring and reckless sent a warm rush through me.

"I'm glad you brought that heavy coat," Bob added, nodding at my folded wool coat. I was wearing a gray wool jacket over my skirt, silk stockings, and a white blouse with a tie at the neck. I found it hard to believe that I'd need an additional coat, but how could I know? I had no idea of what to expect.

"It's an open cockpit and I wouldn't want you to freeze," he finished. He reached over to squeeze my shoulder, giving me another of his crooked, attractive grins.

Was it the man or the machine that left me breathless? My heart began to pound and my hands dampened. As we left the city and drove among grassy fields and stands of evergreens, he talked about his airplane. "... I paid about three hundred dollars for it and the OX-5 was still new, packed in Cosmoline in the crate. I made some repairs to the lower wing, and let me tell you about the wires. It has cabane wires, brace wires, drag wires from the engine, landing wires, flying wires." He took a breath and grinned at me.

"Enough!" I said, laughing with him.

We parked beside a small field, lined with trees and mottled patches of grass. I breathed and took in a heady dose of the pine-laden air. Soon we would rise above those trees. What would it be like? When we got out of the car, Bob took my arm and steered me toward the big biplane tied with its tail tucked into the evergreens.

"Well, here she is," he boasted proudly. "Let me untie her and we'll take a spin."

"Spin? Will we spin around in the air?"

"No, that's not what I meant. There are maneuvers called spins, but we won't do that on your first flight. We'll go for a little ride—follow some roads, turn to the left and turn to the right. I'll show you what flying is all about and we'll see if you like it. Here. Climb onto the wing . . . and don't forget your coat. You're going to need it."

I discovered later he hadn't the least idea how to spin an airplane, but his inflated ego kept him from such an admission. Nevertheless, he settled me into the front seat, pointed to the control stick, and moved it to show me how the ailerons would flip so that, once we were airborne, I could turn and follow a road, turn and follow another. He pointed to the wood rudder bar and instructed me to push with my feet, coordinating with the movement of the ailerons. "Look at the tail of the airplane," he directed. "See? When you pull the stick back, the flipper on the tail rises and makes the airplane tail go down. But, when I let you have it, don't pull back too much, eh?"

"Do you have a stick in the backseat?" I asked, my eyes widening at the thought of controlling the airplane myself.

He snorted importantly. "Of course. Did you think I was going to let *you* take *me* for a ride?"

After he'd handed me the promised goggles and a helmet and had tightened the wide, woven canvas strap around my waist, he grinned and called, "Here we go." He jumped off the wing, trotted to the front of the airplane, checked the radiator, then pulled on the propeller to start the motor. The huge, curved wooden paddles twisted past my view . . . around, then around again.

"Contact!" he yelled.

With a cough and a puff of smoke, the motor belched and

the wooden blades cut through the air. My heart pounded! I smelled the acrid, hot gas and oil and felt enveloped by the deafening clatter of the motor. The wind whipped past, flattening the blades of green grass below us.

Bob jogged to the lower wing, leaped aboard easily, slipped into the other cockpit, and wiggled the stick briskly. "I'm in control," the brisk stick movement told me. It was fascinating to watch the stick's phantom movement fore and aft, side to side between my legs. The wooden bar moved as well.

We started to roll. Down in the cockpit in front of me, the rudder bar danced and the stick jerked back between my legs. Bob snaked the big plane away from the parking place and taxied to the end of the bumpy grass field. The stick bumped teasingly against the inside of first one of my thighs, then the other. I bounced and shifted in the seat—anxious, alert, and very excited.

At the edge of the field, we turned. Bob gunned the motor. We rattled crazily on the sod, then lumbered into the air, first dipping one pair of wings, then the other. The trees dropped away beneath us and we climbed. The stick and rudder bar gyrated at the direction of ghostly hands and feet. Beneath us roads criss-crossed and cars, houses, barns, and churches shrunk to miniature.

Whump. The stick banged sharply against my thighs and I knew that Bob wanted me to take control. "You take it," he told me with the swat of the stick. "It's all yours."

I grasped the stick and glanced over the side of the Canuck. "Follow the roads," he had told me on the ground, so I chose the nearest curving brown line below.

I moved the stick to the right and the biplane shuddered gently in an arcing dance. The left wing rose and we turned to the right. I could feel the stick come back into the center. Bob was helping me from his cockpit. The wings leveled and I chose another road. I pushed the stick to the left. Again the airplane responded. I marveled up at two of the long wings reaching toward the heaped, puffy clouds. To my left, the wingtips pointed toward toy houses and cars, toward the road I followed.

A sparkling blue river riffled over the rocks below and ahead was pristine Puget Sound with the hazy, gray-green Olympic Mountains fringing the horizon. Again a phantom hand guided the stick back into the center and the wings leveled.

The stick made a full circle and I let go. Bob was taking control. He wheeled the big ship and turned for the field that he recognized as home. I was in a reverie, unable to differentiate one field from another. What glorious fun.

But, suddenly, as we descended over the trees, I wondered if anyone was in control at all. The airplane lurched and bucked. The wings frantically dipped, like a wounded bird wobbling crazily through the air. The trees reached out as if to grab us and the plane barely missed them. We careened toward a landing and, at the last possible moment, bounced like an India rubber ball. I grabbed the sides of the cockpit, jarred against the strap. We bounced again and again against the rough ground. The plane surged to one side, then shook and jolted to a halt. I had never seen an airplane land. Perhaps this is the way it had to be. Perhaps they all came banging and staggering to a stop.

Bob dismounted to the wing and offered his hand as I unfastened the strap. He asked, "What did you think? Was that worth eight dollars and seventy-five cents?"

"Eight-seventy-five?" I stammered. This was the first that I'd heard about money. I climbed onto the lower wing and hopped to the ground. I'd returned to the earth, but it would take a while to lose the high.

"It costs me thirty-five dollars per hour to give you a ride," explained Bob, pleasantly. He moved closer to me and stretched an arm over my shoulder to rest against the Canuck. He gazed down at me and teased, "You had fun, didn't you? You don't object to paying for gas and oil, do you?"

"Well, no, of course not. Yes, it was fun. It was great fun. But...thirty-five dollars an hour?"

"You make money nursing, don't you? I can't fly for nothing. But, you're a great sport, Edna. I'd like to take you again. A lot of ladies wouldn't be as fun and daring as you."

He moved closer to me and I slid from between him and the airplane.

"Daring?" I repeated. "It didn't take daring. It was grand. I liked it. I'd really like to fly with you again. But, I only make seventy dollars a *month*. I can't imagine paying thirty-five dollars an *hour*."

"Fifteen minutes at a time isn't so bad, then, eh? That's how long we were up today."

"Could I call them flying lessons? Would you teach me to fly?"

"Sure. We'll plan on next Saturday, same time." He took off his helmet and gave me his most engaging grin.

I could scarcely wait. Seattle rains cancelled one planned flight but soon clear skies blessed another Saturday. This time, once airborne and sailing on the breeze, I took the stick more eagerly, turned the craft to the right, to the left, then around in a circle and felt giddy with the sense of adventure and the challenge.

Martin slapped the stick against my thighs again as the time came for a landing. As he skimmed the trees, the craft rocked violently. As the wheels touched, the airplane bounced even higher than it had the first time. It ricocheted into the air, banged down again onto the wheels, then spun crazily around on the ground, digging one wing into the grass and dirt. I hung onto the sides, my knuckles whitened.

"Damn!" Bob exclaimed, as he climbed out of the cockpit, rubbing his neck absently. He frowned as he looked at the damaged wingtip. "You'd might as well climb out of there, Edna. We won't be able to fly her again for a while."

While Bob checked the damaged wing and landing gear, a stranger approached from across the field. "Lady," he said, "you'd better get yourself another pilot. That's not the first time that two-bit flier has looped her around on the ground. You'd better find someone with more experience. That boy hasn't had but eight hours of flying time in his whole life."

I didn't have much choice. The airplane was damaged and neither of us would fly. My decisions were made for me.

Mother, in the meanwhile, had been listening well to all that Aunt Margaret had to say. When she wrote to insist that I return to Minnesota, I discovered that Aunt Margaret had done a superb job of keeping her informed. Mother knew of the escapades of Gordon Hutton and now she knew all about what she called "flimsy flying contraptions." Thinking that I'd gone mad, she began to write in earnest. Her letters arrived by the drove.

"Come back to Minnesota, Edna," she wrote. "You're getting mixed up with the wrong crowd. What about going on with your schooling and thinking about pre-medics once again? Please give up on your cock-a-hoop idea of flying in airplanes. Consider your career in medicine!"

Mother made a great deal of sense. Both of us were imbued with the spirit of the feminism promoted so militantly by the suffragettes. She insisted that I could make something of myself. I knew that I could accomplish anything that any man could accomplish. After all, I'd graduated from high school and nurse's training; I'd practiced nursing for almost six years; I'd driven an auto for thousands of miles. I'd even flown an airplane, hadn't I?

Mother's letters continued to arrive. "Do you remember the lady doctor that you met when you were studying to be a nurse? She made you think about becoming a doctor, Edna, don't you recall? If you will return and work as a nurse while you pursue pre-medics, I'll help you with a little money; as much as I can."

Of course I remembered that lady doctor. In her long white skirt and mannish, white, tailored coat, she was an unusual sight on the ward at the University of Madison Hospital. Most interns shied from doing rounds with her and many nurses laughed at her behind her back, but I'd always admired her. I respected her for having entered a man's career, a man's world. She became a doctor when it was an uncommon and difficult choice for a woman.

Yet, flying was uncommon for a woman, too. Here I had a chance right at my fingertips. Why should I give that up? And Bob was beginning to be as much fun as Gordon had been.

Leave all this? I liked nursing at the Virginia Mason Hospital. I liked being with adventurous, lively men. I especially liked the taste of aviation to which I'd been introduced. So what if the craft was damaged? Perhaps Dean could help Bob Martin rebuild it and we could have great fun in it. I didn't want to return to the Midwest. Besides, Bob knew Gordon Hutton. I might even see Gordon again if I stayed near Seattle. Bob Martin had his charm, too . . . and his airplane. Mother couldn't tell me what to do.

I dragged my brother out to the field at Renton and introduced him to Martin. Dean had been working in a print shop while Velma continued as a secretary, but it didn't take much urging to convince Dean there was excitement in the sky.

"Would you help me rebuild my airplane?" Martin asked Dean. "You can get out of a stuffy indoor job and, once we're finished, then I'll teach you to fly, too. I'll be happy to pay you."

Dean quit the print shop and worked at the field with Bob for several weeks, although Seattle's rainy weather played havoc with ambitious plans to complete the airplane quickly. Along with woodworking and fabric stretching, Dean learned to rig the maze of wires.

"But, Edna. When's he going to pay me?" Dean complained at last. "I hate being jacked around. This is a repeat of Dallas and those goddam dirty stoves. I'm up to my ears in paint, dope, and woodwork, and I haven't seen a dime. This two-bit flyboy can talk a heck of a lot faster than he can think."

"Be patient, Dean," I urged. "Anyway, aren't you about finished with the Canuck? Bob will probably take you for the next ride. I've been holding my breath for the repairs to be done. For all your efforts, I'm sure Bob will give you a flight. You'll love it, Dean."

Dean was mollified. The three of us were at the airfield when Bob decided that the Canuck would fly. I watched while he handed Dean the helmet and goggles and directed Dean to my coveted place in the cockpit. Bob again pulled the great propeller through, yelling, "Contact!" He scrambled aboard and they both waved to me gaily.

The plane bounced along the field and rose crookedly into the air, the wings waving wildly. But, suddenly, there was silence. The motor quit! The great wooden propeller slowed in mid-swing! Just as they cleared the first bank of trees, the machine dove out of sight.

"Oh, my God!" I cried aloud. I ran for my Studebaker and jumped in. I banged the door shut behind me, twisted the key, and gunned it. Sod spun from the tires and they squealed angrily as the car skidded around the edges of the big field, racing for the road. Oh, God, I hope Dean and Bob are all right. I hope they aren't hurt. What could have happened? Why did the motor quit like that? Do you suppose they crashed into all of those tall trees? My stomach churned and I felt sick. I cried out loud, "What if they're both dead? What'll I do?"

I drove up in front of a nearby nursery, a field covered with row upon row of tiny evergreens. In the midst of several uprooted tiny trees, the Canuck stood on its nose, one propeller blade raised out of the soft dirt, the craft's bent tail high above the scrambled earth and scattered trees. I slammed on the brakes and the car screeched to a halt. I exhaled the breath that I'd been holding, for Dean and Bob stood beside it, alive and well. Bob was scratching the back of his neck with his characteristic gesture. This time he must have said something more powerful than, "Damn!"

When I reached Dean's side he cried, "Wouldn't you know it? The first time I ever get a ride in an airplane and the dad-blamed motor quits! We no sooner got over the tops of those trees than it up and quit. Did you see it? Oh, you must have, you're here, aren't you!"

"I came as fast as I could. Oh, Dean, I'm so glad you're both all right."

Dean kept on talking. "Can you believe it? There goes my paycheck. Big deal. Look at it, Edna. Martin bounced it in here scattering trees to the four winds. That Canuck rolled right up onto its nose. It felt as if it was going to flip over onto its back."

"It's okay, Dean. It's okay. You both made it. Take it easy now."

"Easy! We're damn lucky to be able to walk! He told me that a Canuck doesn't take off faster than sixty-five miles per hour, fly at sixty-five miles per hour, and land at sixty-five miles per hour, but we were doing *ninety* when that nose dropped and we plowed in. We bellied in like thunder, Edna. I've never felt anything like it. The helluvit is, we just finished fixing the damn thing. What a waste! I don't have the heart to start in all over again."

"But, Dean..." I stammered.

"Oh, don't worry. I won't walk away right here and now. I'll help the jerk take off the wings and tow it back to the landing field. But, do you expect me to repeat all the work of these past weeks? For nothing? I've had it, Edna. It's time to go back to Minnesota—to go back home."

We spent the rest of the day disconnecting the wings, locating a flatbed, and transporting the disheveled airplane to Renton Field. Bob was dejected. Dean was disgusted. "All fliers learn about forced landings, Dean," Martin tried to tell him. "Motors quit at the drop of a hat. There isn't a pilot around that hasn't had a motor quit, most of them right after takeoff—lots of them on their first solo flights."

"I know, I know," Dean drawled sarcastically, "and it's very expensive to rebuild any machine like this. You can't possibly pay me for the work that I've already done when you have to turn around and repeat it, right?"

Bob looked at me and scratched the back of his neck again. "Eh? What can I say?" he said, shrugging his shoulders.

"Take me to Aunt Margaret's, will you, Edna? I hurt all over and I'm filthy. I can't think of anything much better than a hot bath right now."

I looked at Bob Martin and shrugged as he had done. "I'm sorry about the Canuck. I really am. I'll see you again, though, won't I? Will you give me a call when you get it up and running? I'm just glad I didn't have to rush you both to the emergency ward at Virginia Mason Hospital."

"Or identify our bodies at the morgue," was Dean's parting shot.

When we arrived at Aunt Margaret and Uncle Sam's home, we were shocked to see our mother. With the failure of her letters to convince us to leave Seattle, Mother took it upon herself to travel to Seattle to retrieve us in person.

"Mother!" I couldn't think of another thing to say.

She covered her mouth in horror when she saw Dean, caked with mud and spattered with dried blood. "What happened? What on earth's going on here?"

"It's all right, Mother," I answered quickly. "He's had a minor accident, but he'll be fine once he's washed and rested."

"Dean?" she inquired.

"I'll be fine, Mother. It was just a rather abrupt fling into the flying world. Actually, it was probably a record: one of the world's shortest flights."

"Flying! I might have known. For heaven's sake, go get into a hot bath. But, before you go, let me tell you both something. I plan to visit with Margaret and Sam for a few days and, Edna, you and Velma give notice and quit your jobs. Be forewarned. We're all heading back to Minnesota as soon as we can get organized to go."

I wanted to protest, but I was outvoted. Everyone wanted to go home except me. With the flying ended as well, Mother, Dean, Velma, and I crammed uncomfortably into my Studebaker and headed east. It had been crowded with three, now Velma had to ride on Dean's lap. In such close quarters, I couldn't help but notice that the thrill of their marriage was gone. They were cold and polite to one another. We made a vain attempt to recapture the pleasure of seeing the country—the carefree fun of the departure from Madison. We managed a pleasant sidetrip to Yellowstone National Park, but the frivolity was gone. We were Minnesota bound. Aunt Margaret probably had her first good night's sleep in six months.

Dean was clearly ready to leave the Pacific Northwest, but that wasn't all. He was ready to leave Velma, too. As soon as they were back in Minnesota, they divorced. "I had no sense of responsibility," Dean later admitted, "and I knew I shouldn't be married. Velma never complained about my not working, but that isn't what I need, Edna. I need someone who understands me and pushes me to improve."

And I needed to plunge back to work. It was 1927 and I was accepted for nursing and pre-medics at Madison's University Hospital, accepting a monthly allowance from my mother. I nursed four hours a day, five days a week and attended classes, too. I was a bit surprised to discover that I loved the coursework and the challenge of pre-medics. I was not fully accepted by the men in the primarily male student body, but perhaps better accepted than most women because of my accrued years of medical experience and status as a registered nurse. Finding medical school intriguing and absorbing, I immersed myself in work and study that filled almost every hour of every day. It was an exciting year.

The year 1927 proved to be a banner year for aviation, too. Two U.S. Army aviators flew to fame crossing from the mainland to the Hawaiian Islands in a Fokker Trimotor. Following the same route, a highly publicized air race—the ill-fated Dole Race — was won by a lucky Art Goebel in his Travel Air, *Woolaroc*. That hazardous race aimed single-motored airplanes and poorly prepared pilots over a watery 2,400 miles of the Pacific Ocean toward tiny dots, the tropical Hawaiian Islands. A navigational error meant death. Any faulty equipment meant death. Several airplanes crashed on takeoff and two racing airplanes were never heard from again. Newspapers thrived on such tales of heroism and horror. The sky captured people's imaginations and the public was bombarded with stories of those daring enough to rise into it.

Excitement was fanned to a fervor by newspaper headlines of 1927 about the first successful solo crossing of the Atlantic by Charles Lindbergh. The tall, handsome flier became a hero, heaped with attention and adoration. Backer and publisher George Palmer (G. P. "Gippy") Putnam raked in a tidy profit with the howling success of *WE*, Charles Lindbergh's book that recounted his unique crossing of the unforgiving Atlantic Ocean. Gippy envisioned a repeat performance, another economic success with a captivating story of the first woman's crossing of the Atlantic. He searched for and found an interested and willing female pilot: a slim, athletic Amelia Earhart. He promoted, pushed, and publicized this "Lady Lindy," chosen to be a passenger in the *Friendship* in 1927, the first woman to fly over the Atlantic. He reportedly had drafted much of the book and took her to his home to complete the account of the flight.

I couldn't escape the lure of aviation. I was caring for the sick and helpless, learning to solve some of the mysteries of disease and distress: a noble career. But I was also changing bedpans, listening to people moan and weep, watching the terminally ill die—a far cry from the glory and the ecstasy of flight. Aviation was a new frontier, a challenge and a joy. Speed, altitude, and endurance records were being surpassed almost as quickly as they were established and publicized. Heroes and heroines were created overnight. I ached to be a part of it. I yearned for some of its fame and notoriety.

4

$\mathcal{P}ennico$
$and\ a$
$\mathcal{R}obin$

A pair of biplanes, the sun glinting invitingly from their wings, lured me from my medical studies one Saturday in 1927. They chased one another among cottony clouds, poking holes in the blue sky. I shelved the books and jumped into my car, homing to them along a maze of roads, craning out of the window to keep them in sight. I parked beside a shack by a sign for Madison's Pennico Field which, with freshly mown grass carpeting the stretch from treeline to treeline, brought nostalgic memories of Renton.

As I watched, one ship sank lightly onto the grass, rolling on the two front wheels then slowly lowering the tail skid to the ground. It didn't skitter and bounce. It landed gracefully with no dreadful twisting and turning. I would have given *anything* to fly like that! That pilot obviously had more flying time than

Bob Martin. I wondered if that pilot would take me as a flight student.

A large red and black metal sign for TEXACO fuel swung in the breeze and creaked on its hinges. Below it Howard Morey was named as the airfield manager and nailed to the door a smaller sign announced OFFICE MIDWEST AIRWAYS INC."

I sat in the car for some time, wrestling with internal doubts. "Well, here goes nothing," I said aloud, when I'd finally built my confidence sufficiently to climb out of the car and enter the office.

I steeled myself as I pushed open the door. A knot of four men, as if in uniform, wore coveralls grayed with wear and generously spattered and stained with grease and oil. They held coffee cups in their hands and cigarettes between their fingers. Their conversation dropped and they turned to watch me enter. One man let out his breath in a low whistle and they jostled one another with their elbows.

"Hello. What have we here?" commented a man at the office desk. He'd been leaning back, his feet propped high on the desk in front of him. "What do you think, fellows?" He swiveled in his desk chair, swung his feet to the floor, and leaned forward. A stocky, broad-shouldered man, he differed from the others in that he wore dark blue trousers and a white shirt unbuttoned at the collar. A cap framed his deeply tanned face and a pencil perched on his right ear. Like the others, a cigarette dangled in his fingers. He took a drag and squinted at me through the exhaled smoke.

One man said, "Welcome to Pennico, miss." I smiled at him. Another said, "Not bad, Jim," as I turned to face the man behind the counter.

"My name is Edna Gardner," I told him. "I want to take flying lessons. Do you teach students?"

"So," he drawled slowly, "this pretty, little lady wants to fly, does she?" He skirted his desk and leaned back casually onto an elbow on the glass countertop. He drew on his cigarette and blew smoke over his shoulder. His mind wasn't on flying or airplanes or aviation. He was assessing a conquest. His thoughts couldn't have been more obvious if he'd reached over to unbutton my blouse.

I stepped backward and tried again, forcing a smile. "Look. I'm serious. I've flown in a Canuck a couple of times."

"Have you now. Are you ready for solo?"

"No. But, I know that I like flying. I came here because I want to learn for myself."

"Hey, Hollywood," called one of the men. "I bet they didn't look any nicer way out west."

"Hollywood?" I asked, turning to the speaker.

"Sure, miss. You're talking to the great Jim Peterson, chief pilot of Midwest Airways, daredevil pilot of the silver screen, the stunt pilot who brings the luster of Hollywood to Madison, Wisconsin, and lets it shine." The men laughed.

Peterson grinned. "I flew in *Wings* and Howard Hughes is planning on another good film—*Hell's Angels*. I'll fly in that, too."

"Of course he thinks it'll be good," interrupted another. "He figures his flying will make them or break them. But he probably won't tell you that they hired thirty-nine pilots to fly in *Hell's Angels*."

"And eighty-seven airplanes," Peterson countered with an easy grin. He turned back to me, "I'll bet you haven't seen that many airplanes on one field at one time."

"Eighty-seven? I thought it was fun to watch two this morning. They lured me out here."

"Lured you? Well, maybe I can do something about that." He was attractive to a fault and undoubtedly knew his way around women as well as around airplanes. But, in aviation, where inflated egos are the norm rather than the exception, Jim Peterson topped all. The limelight had gone to his head. Arrogant and brash, he wore confidence like a badge.

I couldn't back down. Not now. "Do you teach people?"

"Sure I teach," he bragged, relaxing back against the counter. He crossed one leg in front of the other and folded his arms across his chest. "I've been known to teach some things to some people and other things to others." He talked over my head to his male audience, sought approval. He grinned down at me.

"I want to learn to *fly*. I want to learn to *fly*, in an *airplane*."

He sighed and shrugged his shoulders. "Well, Edna is it?" he asked. "You're hard as nails. I suppose we could preflight a Travel Air and get a start on the ten-hour private license that seems to have you drooling. But, I've a better idea. What are you doing later? We could plan an exciting night flight over the lights of Madison, then take in a quiet dinner, some dancing. What do you say?"

"I'm on duty tonight, Mr. Peterson," I lied.

"Call me Jim."

"Okay. Jim. I'm a nurse at the Madison University Hospital and I've duty tonight. But, couldn't we take that flight now?"

"Whoa. You're losing your charm, Jim," called one of the men. The rest laughed.

Peterson ignored the taunt and continued, "A nurse? I can see it now. You want to be "The Flying Nurse" and have us read about you in the papers, 'Do-gooder flies into the hinterlands to minister to the sick and downtrodden.'"

"Well, what's the matter with that? There could be worse combinations of careers."

"Or you could forget about flying and minister to me. I could pretend that I'm sick and downtrodden."

He reached to take my chin in his hand, obviously accustomed to having his way. He wanted me, but he wasn't interested in teaching me to fly. I couldn't understand. Would he lose status if a woman could handle an airplane as well as he? Would it tarnish the image of a brave, daring pilot or diminish his aerial superiority? I wanted to fly. Oh, how I wanted to fly. I wanted to ignore his advances and get a chance to show him that I could learn.

I stiffened and pulled away and he shrugged and became businesslike. "Okay. Okay. I get the point. Lessee, first of all, the C.A.A. is cracking down on licensing. You have to have a medical exam and pick up a student pilot permit."

Now we were getting somewhere. "There is some advantage

to being a nurse. I've done that already. I took my examination and I've student permit Number 4013. Do you want to see it? I'm truly determined to learn to fly."

His jaw tightened and his brown eyes darkened to a cold, hard glint. I apparently touched a raw nerve. He certainly had opinions about women. It was acceptable to invite us to dinner, to seek our favors, but we had no place whatsoever in his sky. We could warm his bed as long as we stayed out of his cockpit. It wasn't hard to imagine where *that* term came from.

We met for several lessons, but Peterson proved to be a reluctant teacher. We flew the Travel Air several different times. In flight after flight, I struggled to learn—to show him that I could take charge, learn to fly. He was tough. He showed me a maneuver, then mocked me when I attempted to repeat it.

"Look at the nose of the aircraft during the turn," he challenged. "Get crisp. You're wallowing all over the sky." His voice was biting and sarcastic. "For God's sake, don't stop flying an airplane ten feet off the ground. You've got to fly it all the way to touch down. What's the matter with you?" The more critical he became, the more tense I grew. He intimidated me and finally sneered, "Give it up, Edna. You're never going to learn to fly. You're gonna kill yourself first!"

I cried myself to sleep that night. But, in the light of the next day I wrestled with the thought of finding another instructor at Pennico. I talked with the field manager, Howard Morey, and begged, "Please, Mr. Morey. Get me another instructor. Surely there is someone who will teach me, someone who will get me soloed. I truly want to be a pilot."

Morey scheduled me with George Hensley, but Hensley wasn't any happier to teach a woman than Peterson had been. Hensley took me flying in a Curtiss Robin and it was a disaster. I couldn't fly that airplane. After we once staggered it into the air, I couldn't get it back on the ground. My approaches were either too fast or too high, too slow or too low.

Hensley finally told me, "You'd better quit, girl. I hear you've already heard that from Peterson and I agree with him. You're going to kill yourself! Quit while you're ahead. Do you want to smash up that pretty face? Settle down and give some nice guy babies."

It was tough enough to eke a few minutes of flying from a few precious moments left over after pre-med study. It was equally tough to scrimp from the meager salary of part-time nursing to pay for flight hours. Adding insult to injury, I was forced to endure sexist remarks, snide criticism, and discrimination. Flying, which could have been exhilarating and joyful, was made unbearable. Give some nice guy babies? Goddam men had to protect the sanctity of their cockpits. Why were they so afraid of allowing women to prove themselves? Couldn't they just teach me to fly and be done with it? They'd sleep with me and crow over the conquest, but no dice at teaching me to fly. Damn them!

By 1929 I'd frittered away precious time and money and I'd obviously gotten nowhere with flying. Somebody warned my mother that I was taking flying lessons again and she stopped sending money immediately. She was interested in helping me get an education but she'd be darned if, as she put it, "her hard-earned money was going to fly out the window on wings." That did it. I had to quit pre-med. (I never knew until much later that Mother had been financially devastated by my father's death, her TB, and the expense of raising three children. I always regretted that she sent money to me rather than the other way around.)

It was a time of decision. As I sought a secure career position, several already-licensed female pilots sought to fly in the first cross-country air race, the Women's Air Derby of 1929. While other females competed for fame and fortune, I applied for a commission in the U.S. Naval Nurse Corps and the promise of room, board, a steady job, and some money. I was sent to my first military nursing assignment at the Great Lakes Naval Hospital in Illinois while Amelia Earhart, Marvel Crosson, Louise Thaden, Florence "Pancho" Barnes, and others gathered in California. Amelia Earhart estimated that there were only thirty female pilots in the United States that were eligible for that air race. How I would have loved to have been among them.

My luck and my timing stank. My student permit expired a matter of days after the lady racers departed Santa Monica on August 18, 1929—the race timed to finish at the opening ceremonies of the first Cleveland National Air Races.

Luck ran out for Marvel Crosson, one of the Derby pilots, too. She died during that race, a victim of too low a bailout over the rough desert country of Arizona. She was found with the silk of her parachute draped over her body. Indicative of the prejudice and discrimination that I'd encountered, Marvel's death provoked a vicious newspaper headline, "Women Have Conclusively Proven They Cannot Fly!"

What rot! Louise Thaden won the race handily. Pretty, vivacious, brown-haired Marvel had been a capable pilot, praised as the first woman pilot of Alaska. She was the sister of famed bush pilot Joe Crosson, the man with whom Wiley Post had flown and the man destined to bring back from Point Barrow the bodies of Will Rogers and Post in 1935 after *their* airplane crash. Ironically, in 1929 it had been Will Rogers and others who dubbed that first women's race "The Powderpuff Derby," or called the ladies "Petticoat Pilots," "Ladybirds," and "Flying Flappers." Rogers made wry and humorous comments at the start of that race. Perhaps he agreed with other men of the times who complained that women pilots were "too emotional, vain, inconstant and frivolous—hazards to themselves and others." To a prejudiced reporter, Marvel Crosson's death apparently confirmed those ridiculous charges. Were there hints of incompetence or inability in the news releases following that fateful plane crash that killed Rogers and Post? I don't recall ever seeing a headline following that crash that read, "*Men* Have Conclusively Proven They Cannot Fly!"

Then came the devastating economic plunge—the stock market collapse of October 28, 1929. U.S. securities lost twenty-six billion dollars in value. The deepening Depression rendered cash, which had always been tight, critical. I was lucky to be in the Navy, but angry anew to have wasted precious money with Bob Martin, Jim Peterson, and George Hensley. I resigned myself to my nursing career, stinging with resentment that men had thwarted me. I concentrated on the Navy, still furious that flight training was denied me, that men had stood in my way.

Adding another irksome angle to the situation was the fact that male pilots were *interesting*. I loved to talk with them, listen to them. I learned more in hangar sessions with men than I learned during any of my flight lessons. With open cockpits, tandem seating, the howling wind and noisy motors, any airplane was a dreadful classroom and I learned almost everything I knew from "hangar flying." But I should have resisted the charms of Jim Peterson and stood up to him. I never should have let my student permit expire. I should have insisted on getting my private certificate.

I couldn't pick up a newspaper in Chicago in 1930 without reading about aviation and air racing activities when the Second National Air Races were planned, not for Cleveland but the Windy City. Chicago airplane builders E. M. "Matty" Laird and Eddie Heath were publicized as two of the many who struggled to finance their homebuilt airplane businesses, ventures that had started into production prior to the Depression and slumped for lack of funds. The popular air races drew hundreds of thousands of spectators, a showcase for newly designed airplanes, and all airplane designers and aviation enthusiasts focused on Chicago.

In a country feverish over setting aviation records—high altitudes, long distances, endurance aloft, fuel economy—the air races focused on speed and paraded airplanes to masses of prospective buyers and flyers, including the government and the military. There was no better stage for a Matty Laird or an Eddie Heath than to have their airplanes growl, spit, and roar, dangerously close to the ground, directly in front of an enormous grandstand of eager, excited fans. Trophy money was precious, but more essential was the fame, recognition, and airplane sales that came from having dazzled the crowd.

In 1930, Matty Laird was commissioned by the B. F. Goodrich Company to build a racing airplane for the Thompson Trophy Race, a closed-course pylon race. The race was a mere month away when Laird accepted the challenge and proposed his famous airplane, which was named *Solution*. The racer, with pilot Speed Holman, *had never been off the ground* until one hour before the start of the race. Holman climbed aboard and flew at an amazing two hundred miles an hour to win.

I envied the Speed Holmans of the Chicago Air Races. I was still infatuated with flying and I envied the female pilots who made it. I raged again at the men who stood in my way. What did I do wrong that made them think I'd kill myself? All I asked was for a chance. I knew I could fly an airplane if one of them would just have the guts to teach me properly. Was it possible that they didn't know *how* to teach me? I began to suspect that they didn't know a great deal about what they were doing themselves. It dawned on me that most men were like Bob Martin, inexperienced and ignorant about what makes an airplane fly, what causes it to turn, or why motors quit. I discovered that hundreds of them had learned to fly with virtually no instruction at all.

Benjamin "Benny" Howard, the famous race pilot, came to Chicago with his sleek racer, *Pete*, in 1930. In 1923, when he eked out ten dollars a month to buy his first airplane for $150, a secondhand Standard, he had simply read a *book* about flying and thought that was all he needed to do. He survived a crash in his biplane that killed a passenger and injured his own hip and leg before he bothered to take a flying lesson.

Vincent "Squeek" Burnett of Lynchburg, Virginia, hung around an airfield, washed and gassed airplanes, listened and watched until the day came that someone offered him a chance to fly. He climbed into an Aeronca and flew. Later he took a lesson—to have someone show him how to make an airplane spin!

I desperately wanted to solo. Many women had followed in the footsteps of female pioneers Harriet Quimby, Matilde Moisant, Katherine and Marjorie Stinson. I read newspaper accounts of Phoebe Omlie, Louise Thaden, Ruth Nichols, Amelia Earhart, and others. As early as 1910 Bessica Raiche had been the first woman in the United States to solo an airplane! I wanted to solo, too.

I could read about the inspiring Stinson sisters, Katherine and Marjorie, by the hour. Katherine and Marjorie's mother, Emma Stinson, was even more liberal and strong-willed than my own. She encouraged both of her daughters and her sons, Eddie and Jack, to fly. When Katherine had one flight in a balloon and read of the money she could earn doing aerial exhibitions, Emma supported her wholeheartedly, despite the strong doubts of male pilots.

"You'll either catch pneumonia or kill yourself," threatened one, refusing to teach Katherine when she asked for lessons. Katherine coaxed Maximilian T. Liljestrand, the famous "Max Lillie," to give her flying lessons. Soloed by Lillie in 1912, twenty-one-year-old Katherine Stinson was the fourth woman to become a licensed pilot in the United States.

The darling of the United States as she toured the country, Katherine performed loops, spins, and the "dippy twist" in her fragile-looking pusher airplane. She was the first woman to fly in the Orient and, in Montana in 1913, the first woman sanctioned to carry U.S. air mail.

Charles Planck, in *Women with Wings*, wrote,

Katherine Stinson watched with shiny dark eyes everything that men did in the air. Then she went and did it herself, just to show that women can fly as well as men. It was inevitable that she would focus attention on the women in aviation, but she did not succeed in getting many women to take up flying. She proved her point, but women looked at the frail, terrifying flying machines that she used, and let her advance her arguments alone.

Katherine and Marjorie Stinson had dared to learn to fly when aviation was in its infancy, dared to succeed in a field that primarily attracted men. They dared to *teach* men: classes of Canadian male pilots for the Royal Navy Flying Service and U.S. pilots for service during World War I. They were remarkable and I wanted to emulate them.

Late in 1930, an article in a Waukegan newspaper caught my
eye: "Waukegan Airfield, opened three years ago on 80 acres
owned by Lindon and Mae Burris, continues to flourish."
Wrapped in my raccoon coat against a chilly October wind, I
climbed into my car and drove to the site to check on it. Three
biplanes, tarps thrown across their motors, frost sparkling on
their wings, stood on the browned, crisp stubble of a hayfield
in front of me. To my left, in a gas station's small cafe and
framed by a partially steamed window, I saw a few men laughing
and gesturing. I parked next to a freshly painted orange hangar
that bore a sign, WAUKEGAN FLYING CLUB, and stated that a
Velie Monocoupe, an Eaglerock, a Swallow T.P., and Standard
airplanes were for hire. A flying club. I'd never heard of such
a thing.

I was torn between excitement and dread and sat in my car
for several moments to allow my mixed emotions to subside.
Suddenly, an airplane motor began to growl. I took a deep
breath before opening the car door and stepping out. Cool air
hit me in the face and I drew my raccoon coat close around
me as much from anxiety as the cold.

A lanky, brown-haired teenage boy loped around the corner
of the hangar. Whistling as he strode in front of my car, he
headed for the cafe. His brown hair fell in a shock across his
eyes and he hunched into the raised collar of his navy blue
jacket. His boots stuck out under high-water blue slacks.

I called to him, "Say, do you have a few minutes?"

The boy grinned widely. "Sure. I'm no dope. I've always got
time for a pretty lady. What can I do for you?"

"Well, my name's Edna Gardner and I'm a nurse over at the
Great Lakes Naval Hospital."

"Hi. I'm Freddy Stripe. Glad to meet you. Do you need directions to the Navy base?"

"No," I told him. I hesitated. "No, I just want to find out if
there's anyone here that would teach me to fly. Is there a flying
instructor?"

"You bet! Come on around the hangar. Guerd is our flight

instructor and he's our mechanic, too. He's working on an OX-5 engine. A whole bank of cylinders went out on our Swallow T.P. when a guy named Lyle Eldridge was flying."

"Did Eldridge crash?"

"Well, he made it back to the field, but, yeah, you could call it a crash. Everybody," Fred added importantly, "expects that these darned motors are going to crap out sooner or later, probably sooner. That's the first thing to learn. You think, right off—where am I gonna put it down if something goes wrong? The T.P. flipped onto its back when Lyle landed."

Fred held up his hand to illustrate the crash. "Up onto her nose and over she went." His grin widened. "The funny thing is that Lyle was okay until he untied his safety belt. He was hanging upside down and got in an all-fired hurry to get out—scared of fire, I guess. When he untied himself, he banged his head and broke two teeth! Honest to God. Guerd's reskinned the Swallow and is repairing the motor now."

Fred added with a laugh, "A dentist will have to repair Lyle."

"Guerd? Do many flying teachers do the mechanic work, too?" I fell into step with the long-legged boy, almost trotting to keep pace with him. He grinned cheerfully and slowed down a bit.

"Sorry," he said simply, then he continued, "Guerd is Guerdon W. Brocksom, the flight instructor who gave me my first flight in an airplane. He took me up in that Velie Monocoupe over there. I do odd jobs to try to earn enough flying lessons to solo one of these days. I wish I was a professional like you and earned what you probably earn."

"I've never been envied for my bank account, Freddy."

"Well, you're a pro. You can tell to look at you. You've got class. I just wish that I could fly an airplane like Guerd Brocksom. I'd be soloed and on my way. He's good."

We'd circled the end of the hangar. Fred grabbed my arm. "Hold it," he said, stopping abruptly. A broad-shouldered man, his heavy brows knit over his deep-set eyes, crouched beside the noisy biplane. He splayed his right hand to signal us, tilting his head to accentuate the warning. "Guerd wants us well clear of that propeller until he shuts off the motor. He always says, 'It'd ruin our whole day if someone walks into a spinning prop.'"

"It'd ruin more than a day for the one who does the walking," I said drily. I knew enough to avoid the propeller, but this Guerdon Brocksom didn't know that. He didn't know me at all. I watched him curiously, dreading that I might find similarities between him and Jim Peterson or Bob Martin. Brocksom, warmly dressed in a dark brown twill coverall collared in thick bearskin, moved with agility as he swung himself up onto the lower wing to reach inside the cockpit. His dark hair curved around his high forehead and accentuated the depth of his dark eyes. His mouth was quite straight, drooping slightly at the edges, his lips slightly pursed as he worked.

"What do you think?" hollered Freddy over the motor's din.

I thought I'd better concentrate on the airplane. "That's a Swallow?" I hollered back. The OX-5 was spitting and coughing.

"That's a Swallow T.P., T.P. for 'Training Plane,'" Freddy shouted. "It's brand-new, or it was before Lyle decided to plow the south forty with it. Matty Laird's Swallow airplanes have been around a long time but this two-placer is a new design. It just came out of Wichita last year. We used to have an old three-place Swallow, but we got rid of it."

I started to yell, "It has a squarish fuselage, doesn't it?" and got out three words when the motor stopped. My voice roared through the sudden silence, ". . . squarish fuselage, doesn't it?" Embarrassed, I looked at Guerd Brocksom.

He grinned and his dark eyes shone. He straightened, wiping his hands on a crimson rag as he jumped off of the wing and came toward Freddy and me. The twill coveralls swished with each step and he absently patted his breast pocket, then unzipped to reach in and bring out a pack of cigarettes.

"Yes, you're absolutely right," he said with a nod of his head. "It has a square fuselage. And squared-off wingtips, too. You sound as if you know something about airplanes." The laughter lines crinkled around his eyes. The crevice in his cheeks deepened as he smiled. Our eyes met and held.

He gestured toward the gear and added, "They call that a

buckboard gear, too, while we're at it." He put a cigarette between his lips and lit it.

I glanced at the wire wheels, the V-shaped gear held apart with heavy bars, then looked back at Brocksom.

Freddy said, excitedly, "This is a nurse from the navy hospital, Guerd. Her name's Edna Gardner and she says she wants you to teach her to fly."

Guerd and I continued to look steadily at one another as I returned his smile. "So," he said. "Does Fred have that right?"

I held out my hand. "Does he ever," I agreed. "He's a quick study. I don't think that there is anything that I have ever wanted more."

Brocksom's eyes never left mine as he took my hand with a welcoming shake. He held it just a little longer than necessary. "Well, Edna," he said, "welcome to the Waukegan Flying Club."

Waukegan—

a

Flying

Club

L et's talk over a cup of coffee," Guerd suggested. Then he hesitated. "Give me a minute, will you? I'd like to shed these coveralls." He swung around and strode toward the large sliding door of the hangar, unbuttoning the brown, bearskin-lined suit and shrugging out of one sleeve as he walked.

"Do you suppose that he'll be willing to teach a woman to fly, Freddy?"

"Judging from the way he looked at you, I'd say he'd be willing to teach you almost anything and enjoy every minute of it."

"Has he ever taught any others?"

"Do you mean ladies? Heck no. As far as I know, he never even flew with a lady before, much less soloed one."

"There are no lady pilots in the Waukegan Flying Club?"

"No. There's a parachute jumper named Evelyn Miller. She

sometimes flies with one of the pilots, Vernon Ramsey, but she's not a pilot. Another of the pilots, Pat Shields, is crazy about her. Let me tell you about her last parachute stunt. She and Vernon . . ."

"Freddy," I interrupted, "tell me about Evelyn Miller later, will you? I'm curious about Guerd Brocksom. I've had some real losers as flight instructors before. When did Guerd learn to fly? Please just don't tell me that he's only got eight hours of flying time or that he flew airplanes in Hollywood for the movies."

"Hollywood? Guerd? That's a good one! I don't think Guerd would last a minute surrounded with fake, glitzy people. He's too down-to-earth. He's straightforward, a real fine man. Wait until you get to know him. He learned to fly right here in Waukegan."

Freddy told me that Guerd had always wanted to learn to fly, had even built a wooden airplane when he was in grammar school. Guerd started flying lessons in a Jenny in 1926, but Les Houk, the guy who owned the ship, would never let go of the controls.

Freddy said, "I mean, how could a person learn to fly if someone else handles the stick and rudders?"

After Houk's Jenny crashed, Guerd pooled funds with another man to come up with the necessary six hundred dollars for a Tommy Morse Scout, an airplane rebuilt by Eddie Heath.

"Heath put an OX-5 on it instead of a Gnome rotary engine," explained Fred. "It carried three passengers instead of just one and, when Guerd soloed that Tommy Morse, everybody said that if he could fly that tricky, squirrelly thing, he could fly anything. He can. He's good. He's been our club instructor here for about a year."

Brocksom came out of the hangar. He'd slicked a comb through his sandy hair, but couldn't tame the stubborn cowlick at the back of his head. Free of his bulky brown coveralls, he looked trim, as if he'd shed twenty pounds. He walked purposefully, his tan slacks outlining his muscular legs with each step. He was rolling one sleeve of his plaid wool shirt, the other already above his elbow. He had a ruggedly handsome face. He looked directly at us as he came nearer. A guarded smile teased the edges of his straight mouth.

"I'd best not get used to wearing that darned flying suit so early in the winter," he said. "I'll freeze my tail by January. It was cold when I got started this morning, but it has warmed up considerably around here, hasn't it?" He directed that at Freddy, who grinned his wide, ready smile in response.

Freddy looked back and forth from Guerd to me. "Yeah. I'd say it has warmed up around here." He seemed ready to make a wisecrack, then thought better of it. He just grinned, shook his head a little and looked down. He scuffed dirt with the toe of his boot until we started for the cafe and service station.

"I told Edna about your start in the Thomas Morse Scout, Guerd. Were you the only man in the U.S. to learn to fly in one of those? I'll bet you were." Fred looked at Guerd, and I would have had to have been blind to miss the hero worship shining in his eyes.

Guerd chuckled and answered, "I'm sure that's not the case, Fred. But I logged some flights in Houk's Jenny. Les Houk was a character. Bill Klingenberger flew with him in that Jenny once and Bill said that the moment after they took off, the motor started missing. Bill said that Les climbed out of the front cockpit onto the wing and started fiddling with spark plug wires to see if he couldn't get the motor to run more smoothly while Bill kept the wings level. The motor was missing like a sonuvagun, but here's Houk—no parachute—out on the wing messing with the plugs. What a wild operation! I'd traded a motorcycle to him for five hours of dual in that Jenny. But, I never could get him to give it to me. When he finally begrudged me fifteen minutes or so, he'd never let go of the controls. The last time we flew, we couldn't get the danged underpowered machine to climb. It wouldn't even clear a hedge at the end of the field and we parked it straight into the bushes. Les got a bloody nose but the Jenny was finished right there and then. The hedge was a little worse for wear, too. Some hedge clippers, those prop blades."

59

"Were you working on this Swallow T.P. all morning?" I asked.

"No. I laid tile with my father. We stirred every rooster into crowing when we left the house this morning. Dad runs a ditcher and he seems to think that it has to be earning its keep before sunup. The closer we get to winter, the harder he works because his customers howl to get ditches dug before the ground freezes. Anyway, when I got here, I should have hung the coveralls on a peg. As much as I need that heavy suit for winter flying, I probably shouldn't mess around drippy, greasy motors in it."

Fred snorted. "How're you going to get away from them?"

"Good point," Guerd admitted. "It doesn't much matter whether I'm flying or repairing, I always end up tinkering with the motor, don't I." It was more of a statement than a question. "An OX-5 is like that."

Freddy punched Guerd playfully on the shoulder. "Yeah. D'you remember Klingenberger's tailspin? He couldn't avoid getting covered with oil and he was still in the cockpit. He was one black mess when he finally landed." He turned to me and continued. "Klingenberger was flying a Jenny and he got sloppy at the top of a loop."

Freddy's hands were carving an arc in the air as he talked. "The motor quit and the ship fell off into an upside-down tailspin. Bill said, 'The oil went out of the crankcase and through the breather pipe. It poured over me like maple syrup on hot-cakes.'"

Guerd laughed with a hearty chuckle. "He was damned lucky he started so high in the air. He tumbled a good two thousand feet before he could get that ship righted. He was lucky, too, when he got the motor started again. You can't always depend on an OX-5 to do that. Then, he was lucky still a third time when he managed to wipe the oil off his goggles so he could see to bring her in. He was so caked with all the dirt that had accumulated on the floor of that old Jenny that he looked as if he'd been tarred and feathered."

We reached the door to the coffee shop and Guerd pulled

it open for me. I stiffened as I stepped in and faced a cafe filled with men. Scratchy music rasped from a radio and a male singer sang, "We'd start in to pet and that's when I'd get her powder all over my vest...." Someone whistled the melody along with the singer and another said, "Sshh," as all eyes turned toward me.

Cigarette smoke hung in wispy clouds throughout the small square room and the smoky odor mingled with that of brewed coffee, grease, and sizzling onions. A few men sat at tables, two sat on high stools at the counter and a dark-haired fellow manned the grill with his wife, a small, blond woman, beside him at the counter. The man stopped frying, his spatula in midair. The woman stared. All gazed at me inquisitively. "Don't let this be another Pennico," I prayed silently, "please, God."

Guerd smiled easily and said, "At ease, you clods. You look as if you've never seen a lady before. Put your eyes back into your heads and meet Edna... it's Gardner, isn't it?" he asked, turning to me.

I nodded and smiled at everyone in turn. Guerd touched my elbow gently and suggested, "Let's sit over here." As we stepped toward a square table he swept his other arm toward the men and introduced me. "Edna, these are the intrepid birdmen with whom you'll have to share the sky—Dick Dillinger, Henry Ekstrand, Pat Shields, Harold VanAlstyne, Ed Casey, Stuart Guest, Charlie Landis. That's Lyle Eldridge leaning on the counter. He looks just as mean in the cockpit behind his goggles but don't let him fool you. He's really at his best when he gets upside down. Let him tell you how to climb out of an airplane that's belly up and no longer going anywhere. Tell her how to do it without bashing any teeth, Lyle."

Lyle laughed, self-consciously covering his mouth with his hand. He said, "Nice to meet you, Edna. Guerd seems to think we should profit from one another's mistakes. My first mistake was flipping the airplane. My second was untying my belt..."

"Aw, tell her about it when you get your store-bought teeth, Lyle," said Ed Casey.

"He can sip through a straw without opening his mouth these days," someone taunted. Everyone laughed.

"What brings you to Waukegan?" asked Henry Ekstrand, running a hand through his straight but somewhat disheveled hair.

"She's wanting Guerd to teach her to fly," piped Freddy. "She's a nurse at the Great Lakes Naval Hospital."

"Really?" said a small, wiry blond-haired man. Gray streaks highlighted his wavy hair. He looked at me appreciatively and asked, "How come I never get a pretty nurse like you when I'm in the hospital? I always get the..."

"You don't get much of anything, Harold. That's why you haven't gotten your transport license yet," teased Charlie Landis, dapper in a brown sport coat and silk tie. Landis cleared his throat and straightened his tie, turning to salute me with a jaunty swing of the tweed cap that he held in his hand. Sparkles of light reflected from the gold ring on his finger and the gold watch chain on his vest. His silk shirt contrasted dramatically with the wool and cotton shirts on all of the others. "A pleasure, Edna," he said. "Perhaps you'll let me show you some places in Waukegan that you might otherwise miss?"

"She'd be well advised to miss some of the places you have in mind, Landis," warned Guerd, good-naturedly. "Watch out, Edna. Charlie's our charmer. Don't let him sway you. But, then, don't consider any of these guys harmless. They're all pilots and now that they soar with hawks and eagles, they've forgotten a bit about humility."

The banter continued behind us as Guerd signaled to the man behind the counter. "Two coffees, Walter. Do you take milk and sugar?" he asked me. When I shook my head he turned back and said, "Both black, Walter, and meet Edna Gardner. Edna, meet Mr. and Mrs. Walter Jack." We exchanged smiles and nods and Guerd stood up to retrieve the cups, suddenly remembering Fred.

"Did you want something, Freddy?"

"Naw. Thanks anyway. I'd better get back out there to sweep

the hangar. I'd headed over here for a broom when Edna stopped me."

"Excuse me, Fred. I didn't mean to interrupt progress."

"No problem, Edna. It's good to have you here. I'll see you later."

As Fred grabbed the broom and went out the door, I turned to Guerd. "I hope I didn't interfere with work he was supposed to be doing."

Guerd slid onto the chair opposite me, gripped his coffee cup with both hands, and gazed steadily at me through the steam that rose from it. "Don't worry about it. He's not on anyone's payroll. You'll find a million Freds across this country—the young kids who'd give their right arms to fly, but who haven't any money to pay their way. They hang around fields every day just hoping to get an airplane ride in exchange for doing odd jobs. He washes airplanes, totes gasoline, runs errands, helps with the mechanic work, virtually anything. He has hopes of being an airline pilot someday and he's a hard and willing worker."

"Freddy mentioned Evelyn Miller. He said something about her parachute stunt?"

"That was really something," Guerd admitted, with a shake of his head. "She's lucky to be alive. She'd jumped before, but this time she was jumping out of Vernon Ramsey's Stinson. They figured that the cast aluminum ring hit the metal step by the cabin and broke."

"Cast aluminum ring?"

"It was an an exhibition chute, a bag, about three feet long and twelve inches in diameter, which was tied on the wing. The shroud lines were all packed into the bag separated with newspapers to keep them from tangling. The shroud ring was of cast aluminum and all the lines, knotted on the bottom of the ring, came from the edges of the chute into the aluminum ring with holes in it."

"Was she killed?"

"Oh man, we thought she was gonna be. As she came out of

the Stinson, the ring broke in three pieces. Two of the lines were attached to her in her harness. The third just floated loose, drifting away from the parachute and spilling the air. The air came out in a streak and Evelyn plummeted toward the ground. Suddenly, the chute filled again, billowed into shape, and slowed her. Then, the whole horrible scene would be repeated. The air would suddenly spill out and Evelyn would sail toward the ground. We watched with horror until, just at the last possible moment, the chute filled and stopped her fall. It collapsed again, but it was close enough to the ground that she just sprained both of her ankles."

Guerd's cigarette tilted into the ashtray in front of him and smoke circled and rose. He reached over to pick it up between his long fingers. His hand was callused, but clean and strong. He drew on the cigarette, one eye closed as he studied my face. With a slow exhale, the smoke framed his head. "So, tell me about yourself. Why do you want to learn to fly?"

I said that I'd read about lady pilots, that girls like the Stinson sisters inspired me, and that I had always loved speed. "When I was a kid in Medford, Oregon, I used to carry my roller skates to my school on the top of a hill. After school, I'd strap on those skates and let fly down that hill. Why, I never stopped until I rolled into the walkway that led to our house. Sometimes I'd get to going so fast, I'd feel like I was flying. Later, in Minnesota, we had skating races, toboggan races. I loved the biting wind in my face, the competition. I especially loved beating the boys."

I told Guerd about nursing. "I enjoy it. I like pre-medics, too; but, I couldn't stand working in the nursery with all the new babies all the time. I thought that if I had to change one more dirty diaper, wash up one more blob of vomit, pat up one more burp, I'd go stark raving mad."

I told Guerd about flying at Renton, Washington, with Bob Martin. "It was in a Canuck. He showed me how to hold the stick, how to work the rudders and to turn this way and that. But, he wasn't much of a pilot. Now that I look back on it, it was a wacky introduction, probably. I found out after we'd flown together that he didn't have but eight hours of flying time."

Reluctantly and finally, I told Guerd about flying in Madison with George Hensley and Jim Peterson and my expired student permit. That episode still hurt the most. "It was three years ago, now. I still get angry when I think about it. They both told me to give up, said that I was going to kill myself. I get so frustrated when I think back. I feel as if I could have soloed that Travel Air if Jim Peterson had given me half a chance. Maybe I want to solo to show Peterson that he was wrong, that I can fly. But, mainly, I want it for my own sake. I want to fly more than I've ever wanted anything in my life."

"Well," Guerd said with a shrug of his shoulders. He took a sip of his coffee, tasting it on his tongue, pressing his lips together as he slowly swallowed. His cigarette had burned down and he took a last drag, then pressed the butt deliberately in the ashtray.

"What do you think?" I asked, impatient for his opinions. "Would you give me a chance? Don't you think that I can learn to fly?"

"I think a person can do anything," he said, slowly and thoughtfully. "I'm sure you can learn to fly if you set your mind to it and if you work hard enough at it. I can tell you better after we've flown together; but, I think it's just a case of desire and practice. As long as you're reasonably well-coordinated and can think, I'm sure you can fly. You just have to want to badly enough."

He stood up. "And, that Swallow T.P. is about as ready to fly today as she's going to be. We can let you try your hand with her. Before I take you aboard, though, I should take her up solo for a test hop. This will be the first flight since Lyle tried to turn her into a ditcher. If you've time and you want to wait, I can fly with you after that. Are you game?"

Was I game? I was ecstatic! He talked about flying—my flying. He hadn't tried to flirt with me. His mind hadn't been in the gutter. He hadn't laughed at me or put me down. Now if I could only do better than I had in that fool Curtiss Robin. I was going to try damn hard to listen to what he told me and to do what he said.

"I can learn to fly. I just know I can," I told him. "You bet I'm game. And you won't be sorry, either. I'll learn to fly if it's the last thing I ever do."

"Well, hopefully, if it's the last thing you ever do, you're still doing it when you're an old lady." Guerd stood up. He smiled down at me. "Hmmm. I don't know if I should leave you in this den of iniquity while I go fly that Swallow or not."

"I can take care of myself."

"Yes. I'll bet you can. I'll bet that you know how to handle yourself even while surrounded with lecherous beasts like these." Guerd smiled at his friends.

"Where are you going, Guerd? Surely you're not leaving a pretty lady all on her own, are you?"

"She wants to learn to fly and I have to check out that Swallow T.P. before the two of us take to the air in it. Walter, will you take care of Edna here? She's obviously capable, but we all know what a ladies' man Landis is. Why don't you fix her a bite of lunch while I take the T.P. upstairs?" He turned to me. "I'll see you in about thirty minutes," he said and walked out the door.

I jumped to my feet and hurried after him. "Don't bother fixing me anything," I called over my shoulder to Walter. "I'd like to watch him." As I caught up with Guerd I said, "You don't mind if I come out and watch your takeoff, do you? I'd rather be out here watching the airplane than eating."

"Be my guest. Stay away from the propeller, though, and don't get out onto the grass. You can never tell when somebody will come over those power lines from the north and be right on top of you. Less than a month ago, a pilot, Fred Hobbs, spun an American Eagle right into the ground across the road. He was doing stalls and wingovers when he lost it—it killed him, although his two passengers walked away from the wreck."

Was Guerd trying to scare me? He went on, "Another guy, a mechanic but not a pilot, Harry Gartley, oiled and greased a Standard one day. He cranked it up and must have decided to take a fling. Harry had a drinking problem and the minute I saw that Standard take off with Harry's wife sitting nearby in their car, I knew who was in the cockpit. He'd never soloed, but here he was climbing to one thousand feet. I never felt so helpless in my life. Harry dipped the nose, dove for the ground, and charged past. All I could do was watch. He was waving like a fool out of the right side of the cockpit while he sheared off the wings on a tree on his left. It killed him outright."

"So, I have to watch out for the men as well as for the machines," I said drily.

"In more ways than one," said Guerd with a quick smile. Then he turned his attention to the biplane. The sun warmed the entire field, drying each shoot of grass and casting short shadows around the various airplanes from almost directly above. I watched Guerd walk slowly around the tall plane, lovingly run his hand along the wooden propeller, caress the leading edge of the lower wing and the fabric of the fuselage where the painted numerals identified it as C8128. Lost in concentration, he carefully checked the big eight-cylinder motor, looking at the radiator, the exhaust stacks, the valves. He didn't seem to remember that I was there at all. He was all business. He took the art of flying very seriously.

Guerd stepped onto the lower wing to bend into the cockpit. I enjoyed watching his every athletic move. He brought out a helmet and goggles and put them on, the goggles crossing the top of his head. He pulled on a pair of gloves as he walked forward to face the big engine and the long, wooden propeller blades. As he swung the big prop through, he lifted one leg to add thrust to the downward pull of his arms. His movement was unhurried and graceful, confident. The OX-5 caught with the same throaty roar as Martin's Canuck—coughing and then settling into a rhythmic chortle. Oily smoke belched around the front end of the craft, then whisked into the prop stream to spiral back over the craft. Guerd strode around the wing, ducked his head to unchock the wheel, stepped onto the lower surface, swung a leg into the cockpit, and turned, at last, to smile at me. He lowered his goggles and gave me a thumbs-up salute.

"Have a good flight," I yelled, but of course he couldn't hear a word I said. I could hardly wait for his takeoff. The sooner he flew, the sooner it would be my turn. I felt alive, excited. He smiled more broadly, recognizing my enthusiasm, then turned his attention to his ship and leaned elaborately to the left and right to make sure that no one was in front of him.

The slipstream riffled my brown hair, fluttered my coat away from my body, and blew my light gray slacks against my thighs as Guerd turned the bird out onto the grass. I pulled the fur close around me as he gunned the motor, reduced it, gunned the motor again, then reduced it a second time. He gunned the motor the third time and swung the stick around in a circle, which caused a flutter in each aileron, the rudder, and the elevators. He was going to fly and then he was going to teach me to fly. I held my breath while the big T.P. was barreling away from me, lurching into the air, and skimming the trees at the end of the field. My breath came out in a rush.

It was October 24, 1930, and I was totally absorbed by the Swallow T.P. biplane circling and climbing over Waukegan, Illinois. Events of interest and importance were gripping the world: Nazis gained seats in the government of Germany; Doheny was acquitted of bribery in the Teapot Dome scandal; President Hoover led the United States; a German, Max Schmeling, claimed the world heavyweight boxing championship; and Bobby Jones won all four world golf titles, the "Grand Slam."

People popularized contract bridge as a leisure activity and the depressed economy continued to decline—the opposite of my now upward-spiraling hopes riding on the climbing, circling winged machine piloted by my birdman, Guerdon Brocksom. My time had come at last.

A
Swallow
J. P.

Fred Stripe yelled to me from the hangar doorway. "Hey, Edna. Come on over. You can watch Guerd from here. He never strays far from the field when he's test-hopping a bird. He may swing over his home at Holdridge Crossing to dip a wing to his folks; but, most of the time, he'll be in view."

"And I'll be out of his way, is that what you're thinking? He already warned me not to wander out onto the grass. I know enough . . ."

"No, no. That's not what I was thinking. I'm sure you're smart enough to keep from being mowed down by a machine with a fan for a nose. I just like your company. There aren't any chairs, but you could lean on the seat of my bicycle, if you want. I can sweep the hangar while you tell me about your flying, your travels with the Navy."

I started for the hangar and had to laugh at Fred's innocence.

I felt years away from having been seventeen. "There isn't much to tell, Freddy. It's like that bank account you envied a little while ago—more wishful thinking than reality. This is my very first assignment with the Navy Nurse Corps so you'll have to wait for tales of terrific travel. Unless I get my flying license. *Then* I could start to travel."

"Will you stay in the Navy once you're a pilot?"

"Do you think there's a future in aviation for me?"

"Well, sure..."

I laughed. "I love this. I drove here today with my heart in my throat, hoping against hope that there'd be someone who would teach me to fly. I haven't so much as touched an airplane and you've got me licensed and a pilot and you want to know what I'm going to do for a career in aviation. That's really rich."

Fred shrugged, a schoolboy with the optimism of youth. But, he had never been a woman. What did he know? He had never been told to aspire to doing diapers and dishes. No, he hoped to become an airline pilot. What man can appreciate how it feels to be denied such a goal? Young Fred was a male in a male-centered world. He didn't have the money he'd have liked, but neither did most people in 1930. Admirably, he rode his bike to the field every day and worked toward his goals. I envied his positive attitude. Perhaps some of his optimism would rub off on me.

The clatter of the OX-5 caused us both to glance up from the hangar door. Guerd was bringing the Swallow T.P. into the wind and down onto the grass. The airplane gracefully bucked a few times as it was buffeted by updrafts near the trees, then settled itself nicely onto the main wheels. It rolled for a few plane lengths before the tail dipped to the grass and the craft slid to a stop. Guerd wheeled around and taxied back away from the wind, snaking his way to the front of the hangar, clearing the way ahead of the propeller. He shut down and leaped out to check the job he had done with the motor overhaul.

As he slipped the goggles over his head and unfastened the strap of his helmet under his chin, he called to me, "Edna. Why don't you put on those bearskin coveralls of mine? Do you see them on the peg? It's pretty breezy up at two thousand feet. I'll check the motor while you do that and then we'll be ready to fly."

"Okay. Thanks!" I called back. I hung my raccoon coat on the peg that had held his coveralls and scrambled into the heavy brown suit. As I buttoned it, I grinned at Fred. He grinned back.

"Oh Freddy. Wish me luck. I hope this airplane doesn't make a fool of me like that Curtiss Robin."

I marched resolutely toward the Swallow. Guerd was satisfied with the quality of his repairs and stood, arms akimbo, beside the left side of the ship. "I know you've had a few other lessons and rides, Edna; but, I find with new students that it's best if I assume that they don't know anything at all. I'll walk you around the airplane and tell you about it here on the ground. Then we'll climb aboard. Are you comfortably warm?"

"Yes, thanks. As you well know, this suit is more than warm enough."

"It gets colder as you climb higher, so it ought to feel good when we're airborne and the wind whips. Let's start with the motor, a Curtiss OX-5."

We walked around the craft while Guerd named the parts of the airplane and explained their functions. He moved the control surfaces and said, "You try it—move them up and down, side to side as I do." He described the fuselage, the tail, the V-shaped, eight-cylinder motor. He moved quickly to hold my attention.

He didn't need to worry. I hung on every word. He was thorough, the first to show me a pre-flying check. Perhaps there were things that he'd yet to learn, but he was good about sharing what he knew. I liked knowing that he was a mechanic and that he knew this particular airplane well. I wanted to be his best student, to make him proud. I didn't want him to be sorry that he'd decided to teach me.

"These are the flying wires," he explained and showed me how to tighten the flying and landing wires. When he moved the elevator he said, "Be certain that it moves freely—no hitches or binds. Go look inside the cockpit—you'll see the stick move as I move the control surfaces. See?"

"Now," he continued, "let's get you settled in that cockpit and see that the belt is tight about your waist."

"That might be hard to do with this bulky suit on. I feel like the bear who once wore it. I'm not sure I can find my waist at all."

"You look pretty good to me," Guerd said offhandedly. "Now, I'll get the Gosport helmet. Have you goggles of your own?"

"No, I've never . . ."

"Wait for a moment. I'll be right back." He jumped from the wing and disappeared into the hangar. Freddy swept the same dirt in the hangar door that he'd been attacking for the better part of our preflight. His eyes were on the T.P. and his grin was contagious. Any anxiety melted as I contrasted this moment with the tensions of Pennico. I could hardly wait to have Guerd reappear, hand me goggles, give me a thumbs-up, and trot around to the front of the airplane to swing the big prop blade into action.

Guerd handed me a helmet fitted with a flexible tube. He explained, "This will let me talk to you from the front cockpit."

"How will I talk to you?"

"You won't be able to," he answered. A grin spread across his face. "That's the distinct advantage of being the teacher. If I've something to say, I'll call into the funnel. If you've something to say it will have to wait until we're back on the ground."

"Okay. I'm ready, Guerd."

"Belt fastened?"

I nodded and he hopped off the wing, saying, "Let's go."

He shouted, "Contact," and propped the big blade. The OX-5 bellowed, blowing a slipstream back into my face. Guerd climbed into the front cockpit. He belted himself in and the control stick moved back toward me. I moved my legs to keep them out of the way.

"I've got it," he hollered into the Gosport tube. The stick

rattled against my thighs, well blanketed in Guerd's coveralls. I waved at Fred. I laughed aloud.

Our thirty-minute flight was one of the best times of my life. The wind brushed icy fingers across my face, my nose tingled, pinched with the cold, as Guerd Brocksom showed me how to guide the Swallow training plane. Flying like the bird for which it was named, we climbed and dove, wheeled and turned. The blue of Lake Michigan met the sky's blue and we used that cobalt horizon line to guide the big airplane.

"Bank and turn, bank and turn," he had said on the ground before we took off, demonstrating to me with his hand. "And be sure you push the nose forward before you turn," he yelled to me as we flew. He showed me—stick forward, then to the side. He righted the ship and banked to turn to the other side. He let me try it.

He called into the tube, "Glance at the horizon. See how the wings and nose look in relation to it?" He pulled the nose above the distant horizon to climb, shoved it over below it to dive. The wind whistled, the motor roared. I was flying. I was free of the earth, free of the babies in pediatrics, free at last.

"I want it to become second nature, want you to fly by the seat of your pants," Guerd yelled to me and the stick came back and sharply to the left. The airplane shuddered as the nose climbed way above the horizon, the right wing arced high above our heads and we wheeled around and around, down, down.

"You've got it," he shouted and I gripped the stick tightly, righted the wings, leveled out the big motor. "Wheee!" I shouted, although I heard no sound but the motor and the wind.

"Look at that field below," Guerd shouted into the tube. "If your motor quits, you can land right there. Let's swoop down and take a look."

The biplane dipped over the trees, then climbed at the other end of the field. "Follow through with me. Feel the controls," he shouted, and the nose covered the horizon, the trees dropped below our sight. "Try this flipper turn."

Guerd tipped the airplane onto one wing, circled around a lone tree in the midst of a nearby field. Then, with a shake of the control stick, he called, "Try it." It was my turn—my turn to copy his maneuver, my turn to *fly*.

All too soon he tapped my left leg and then my right with the stick and called, "We'll land now. Follow through with me again." I put my hand on the stick and felt the stick gyrate, the rudders pump as he brought the ship over the trees and slipped it dramatically to a few feet from the grass. He righted the ship smartly just before the two wheels touched and, with the stick yanked back against my stomach, the tail dipped down and the craft flared and landed. We snaked back to the hangar and the motor stopped. Guerd climbed out onto the lower wing.

I was laughing by the time I had released the helmet and pulled it off. "That was such *fun!*" I breathed. "I can't tell you how much fun that was! Will you be able to take me again soon? Do you think I will be able to make it? Do you think that I'll become a pilot?"

"You did very nicely, Edna, and I'm glad you liked it so well. Let's talk for a few minutes about the air work that we did, outside of the airplane, shall we?" Guerd's calm and patient voice was in direct contrast to my excitement and enthusiasm. "I told you before. I think you can do anything that you set your mind to do. Here, let me give you a hand with that belt and climbing out."

"I can do it. I'm fine, thanks. But, if I'm ever inverted, I promise that I'll remember about Lyle Eldridge. I'd rather not lose my front teeth."

Guerd laughed and stepped to the ground. "Good idea. Your smile is pretty, just the way it is." He offered to help me down, but I jumped off the wing without touching him. Would he offer a hand to a male student? I bet not. Why should it be any different with me?

We talked for an hour over another cup of coffee. Guerd was businesslike. I wanted to talk about flying, but his smile was disarming and attractive. My mind strayed from some of the things he was saying as I watched the light in his brown eyes, the way his lips moved when he talked, his gestures, and the strength in his hands. I wondered how old he was. He wasn't as young as Fred, but I felt sure that he was younger than I.

"Can you make it again on November first?" he asked.

I thought about money. Between the cost of the airplane and payment for Guerd, I would still have to come up with the thirty-five dollars that Bob Martin had expected. At least with Guerd I had a real instructor, but I hadn't been kidding Fred when I told him that my bank account was nothing to brag about. I told Guerd, "I'd like to make it again tomorrow! On the other hand, it's going to take a little doing to set aside some money . . ."

Who was I kidding? I knew I'd find the money one way or another. "Oh, never mind. I'll make arrangements for the money. What time do you want me here on November first?"

Before I left, Guerd put his hand over mine. "Don't be a stranger, now," he said. "You can come by anytime, whether we're scheduled to fly or not. Part of the fun of flying is being around the airfield. I'll put you to work like I do Fred. Well, not *exactly* as I do Fred." I could have kissed him. Maybe I would someday.

I fairly danced through the rest of the month at the hospital, anticipating November first like a kid waiting for Christmas. But, before returning to Waukegan, I wanted to have the warmest togs I could find. I didn't feel that it was right that Guerd Brocksom had to provide my clothes as well as my instruction. When the new month began, I was ready and eager.

As I drove up and parked, I saw Guerd waiting for me by the Swallow. The day was cold and a brisk wind was blowing. Guerd began tugging a cover off the motor as he saw me. I ran gaily toward him. I wanted to give him a hug, but held myself back.

"It's good to see you, Edna. I like your white coveralls. Are they good and warm? Do you want to wear mine?"

"I made certain that I'd my own, Guerd. As cold as it is today—and is apt to be for the rest of the winter—I figured you'd need your own coveralls.

"I was born and raised in this country. I've plenty of warm clothes. Don't ever hesitate to borrow my bear-lined suit. I want to keep you warm or you might decide that you don't like flying at all."

"That will never happen. Never."

"Okay. Then, let's get on with flying. Do you remember when we swooped low over another field during our last flight?" Guerd asked.

"Yes. Of course I do. Why?"

"Because there may be times that the airplane won't want to fly. You should have a spot in mind to put down should the motor quit. *Never* try to get back to the field you just left, if the motor quits on takeoff. Will you promise me that you'll remember that?"

"Never? Even when the next field is rough or there are trees? I should think..."

"I don't mean after you've climbed high enough to have time to maneuver. I mean right after takeoff. If the motor quits, don't turn back, okay?"

"I'll remember."

"Do you want to wear the flying suit?"

"I'm fine. I knew that I was going to fly, *this* time." I grinned broadly. "Last time I was just hoping!"

"Good girl. That's the spirit. Let's do a walk around, then you can climb aboard."

After I was cinched into my seat, Guerd stood on the ground and looked up at me quizzically. His look asked, "Are you ready?" I nodded and he swung the big propeller through. The motor refused to catch. Guerd yelled, "Contact!" and pulled it through again. It took several tries before the chilled OX-5 finally choked, coughed, and rasped. The propeller started to spin.

Guerd pointed to the stick and yelled, "She's all yours. Let's see you keep that stick back and use your feet to steer her out for takeoff." I took the stick with my gloved hands and pulled it to me as far as it would go and he settled himself in his cockpit. I liked seeing his broad shoulders in front of me, liked watching his signals and gestures as he talked to me through the Gosport tube.

As we snaked out onto the grass, he pointed at the windsock to remind me where the wind was coming from. I felt his hand and feet override mine to guide me every once in a while, but he was good about letting me get the feel of the controls.

We gave her the gun for takeoff, started to arc above the trees at the end of the field when—silence! The big propeller stopped. There was no blur of movement. All I heard was the whoosh of the wind and saw the big wooden paddle—stone still.

"Guerd!" I screamed—though of course he couldn't hear me. At first I thought he'd shut off the motor. The trees seemed to reach up to grab at our wheels. Was Guerd testing me or had he had some strange premonition? Did he know that today the motor would quit?

I remembered what Fred had said. He said that Guerd taught him the same thing. "You learn right away," Fred had said, "Everybody expects that these darned motors are going to crap out sooner or later. You have to be quick. You have to decide, 'Where am I gonna put it if something goes wrong?' and you don't turn back. You land dead ahead."

Dead ahead. That was hardly comforting.

The stick swung violently in my hands as Guerd grabbed control. He thought fast and he knew what to do. Down we rushed. I felt as Dean must have felt, diving fast through the trees in the Canuck with Bob Martin. I braced myself as the ground seemed to race at us. Guerd was skillful as he guided the diving craft to a field slightly offset and just to the west of our flying field. The frozen ground was devoid of crops so there was nothing to grab at our wheels, no mud to clutch us to a sudden and disastrous stop, toss us up onto the nose and over onto our backs. We bounced hard, then gradually came to a stop.

"What happened?" I asked as soon as I could undo my belt and climb out onto the wing. "Why did it quit like that?" Guerd had unbuckled and leaped out ahead of me. He jumped off the wing and dashed up front to check the OX-5.

"I'm never sure," he answered honestly. "There's a lot for us all to learn about these darned motors. Look at the carburetor, for gosh sakes. It's encrusted with ice! I'll be damned."

"I'm so glad you took the stick, Guerd. You're the one that found a good place for us to land. What if you hadn't been with me? What if I'd already soloed?"

"Did you learn not to turn? I want that engraved in your mind! If the motor quits on takeoff, land straight ahead or not much more than a slight angle away. I don't want you to fly scared—I just want you to never stop thinking. These damned motors can quit anytime, anywhere. I'll tell you—I wish I knew what makes them tick!"

We waited on the ground until Guerd could see that the ice had dripped from the carburetor. "Let's try to fire up, Edna. I'll pull it through and see if she'll catch. Then, I'll do the takeoff and get us back over the trees to the Burrises' field."

"If the motor doesn't quit."

"Yes, if the motor doesn't quit!"

Guerd managed a safe takeoff and landing that retraced our short flight that day and we parked the Swallow. But we flew again on the second of November, the fifth, sixth, seventh, and eighth. I invested my entire paycheck in the Waukegan Flying Club and became a regular—a familiar sight in Walter Jack's cafe and at the hangar where Guerd often worked when he wasn't taking me flying or flying with another.

Guerd taught me to handle the T.P. in strong winds—the winter winds of northern Illinois that whistled straight off Lake Michigan as relentlessly as mountain streams driving to the ocean, sometimes as straight as an arrow and sometimes whirling and eddying as streams diverted by fallen logs or boulders. He taught me how the big craft feels when it stalls and we made circuit after circuit to practice landings and takeoffs.

On November ninth Guerd suggested ground school. Snow whirled in a veritable blizzard, which precluded flying anyway. "You're getting the hang of flying, Edna, and you're doing a good job of making the decisions a pilot faces," Guerd said. "I think it is time to sit and drum some facts into your head. You will have to pass a written test with an inspector from the C.A.A. and you will have an air test. Let's work on some of the information that isn't easily shouted from one cockpit to another. We'll talk over coffee, all right?"

"Whatever you say, Guerd. I almost didn't even drive over here today. I couldn't believe that we'd fly anyway."

We both drew our coats close around us and lowered our heads into the blowing snow as we walked from the hangar toward Jack's cafe. It surprised me to feel a sudden clutch of desire as Guerd took my arm and it seemed as if we both drew closer together, matching strides as we walked. I should have been thinking of aircraft performance when he directed me to an empty table in the corner, but all I noticed was the attractive smell of his aftershave lotion. I tried to wrestle mentally with aircraft weight, length, and fuel supply, yet I found myself disconcerted by the warmth of his deep-set, dark eyes. I took a long sip of coffee and tried to concentrate on what he was saying.

"By now," he began, "you've had at least thirty takeoffs and landings..."

"With you," I interrupted. "I had some time..."

"Yes, I know you had some flying before me, but I have watched you become more confident every day in the takeoffs and landings that you've done in this Swallow T.P. and I think you should know something more about the airplane that you're flying."

I watched his lips compress as he gathered his thoughts. I wondered what it would be like to kiss him. I smiled as I realized that he was talking about the history of an airplane while I was watching his lips, his eyes. I forced myself to think about the Swallow T.P. and the story of Matty Laird who designed the first Swallow in 1919. I heard Guerd say, "Laird moved from Chicago to Wichita, Kansas, to produce his Swallow. We used to own a three-place Swallow in our Waukegan Flying Club. We sold it just before you came here. There was a place for two passengers up front and it was a real boon for barnstormers. They could earn twice the money when they could carry two passengers instead of one.

"Anyway, by the early 1920s, Laird left the Swallow factory and came back up here to Chicago. Lloyd Stearman replaced him as chief engineer in Wichita and Lloyd designed the 'New Swallow' six years ago in 1924. There have been a series of refinements and, this past year, 1929, this trainer was born. It's different from the all-wood model like the New Swallow."

"How does it differ?"

"It has fabric-covered spruce wings, but it was among the first in our country to have a welded steel tube fuselage. You know there are ailerons on all four wings. Can you tell me the length of the wings and the fuselage?"

"The wings are thirty feet long and the fuselage is twenty-three feet seven inches long."

"Good. I didn't want to be talking just to hear myself talk. You've been studying."

I smiled at him and he continued. "The landing gear is cross axial in a V shape—we call it a 'spreader bar' gear—and the T.P. has, as I've shown you, a 90 hp Curtiss OX-5 water-cooled engine with a frontal radiator."

"Are there Swallow T.P.s with different engines?"

"A T.P. can be fitted with a 90 hp LaBlond, a 95 hp Wright Gypsy, a 100 hp Kinner, or a 110 hp Warner. You can expect to fly at about ninety miles an hour with the OX that's in our T.P. but, unlike the Jenny, she slows down real nicely for landing—about half as fast as the Jenny. That makes her ideal for students and flying training. Now, if you fly a T.P. elsewhere, remember to check the type of engine. Landing speeds may differ."

"I'm just happy to be flying this one. I won't be going looking for another for a while. Of course, I'm in the Navy," I admitted. "I can't know exactly how long I'll be here at Great Lakes. I certainly hope I can get my pilot's license before the Navy dictates a move."

I saw something in Guerd's eyes—a flicker of disappointment

perhaps—when I mentioned moving away. He had known all along that I was a Navy nurse. Surely he wasn't thinking of changing that, was he? He'd never so much as held my hand.

"Well, let's apply ourselves and see if we can't get you that elusive piece of paper," he said quietly.

"What do you want for yourself, Guerd?" I asked. "Are you happy to be here in Waukegan for the rest of your life?"

"This is my home," he told me. "When you grow up some-place and your entire family is there, it is difficult to think of uprooting. Yet...," his voice deepened, "I've been longing for the chance to make a living with an airplane and in aviation. I don't see much of a future as a ditcher and I feel like young Fred Stripe. There must be an airline piloting job for me some-where. In the meantime, I guess I'm happy here in Waukegan. I'm certainly happy that you've come my way. You've brought excitement to the Waukegan Flying Club that had never been here before. Sometime I'll tell you what Fred Stripe calls you. Say, I've got an idea. Could we finish our book work and think about spending the rest of the day together? Perhaps, when the snow lets up, we could take a drive, find a place to have supper, and..." He shrugged. "Would you like that?"

"Wait just a minute. What did Freddy call me?"

Guerd's mouth widened into a broad smile. He leaned toward me, put an arm around my shoulders and gave me a hug. "Fred's no dummy. He says that you are a regular spark plug."

I smiled as I promised Guerd that we could spend the rest of the day together and, on top of that, that I'd learn all about the Swallow T.P. and that I'd have memorized all the numbers by our next meeting. The terms were all so new: *chord* of the wing, an imaginary line from the leading edge to the trailing edge, five feet; *gap*, the distance between the upper and lower wings, five feet two inches; an *empty weight* of 1,240 pounds, the weight of the airplane without baggage, fuel, passengers, and pilot; a *gross* of 1,825 with the useful load included; *instruments* attached to the center section struts for both of us to view. He showed me diagrams to illustrate the gliding angles that gave safe landings over trees, over power lines, in wide-open paths or over water. He talked with me about banking, flipper turns, and how to handle the airplane in different wind situations.

I already knew that much of the fun of flying was the freedom of feeling light, suspended on the wind, defiant of most natural laws, and exhilarated by the sense of being different from those who never left the earth, never tasted the thrill of flight. Undeniably, the other half was smelling Guerd's aftershave, having our eyes meet and hold, watching his deft hand draw diagrams on the paper, listening to the amount of knowledge that he had and was willing to share, seeing his mouth move, and occasionally feeling our shoulders touch. We had drawn our chairs close together and both of us were acutely tuned to one another. I could tell. I could feel it. Did I want to go for a drive? For supper? That sounded glorious. Almost as good as flying!

7

By the Seat of My Pants

B y late November 1930, Guerd and I were involved. Increasingly attracted to each other, affection was probably inevitable. I also dated an interesting doctor named Boe with whom I worked at the hospital, but flying was exciting and Guerd personified that excitement. I spent as much time with him as I could wrest from my nursing schedule and it was no surprise that most of those hours centered around the Swallow T.P. and the Waukegan Flying Club. Training flights progressed and, delightfully, so did my flying skills.

It was inevitable, too, that once I'd become more confident in the T.P., the OX-5 would suddenly desert me. We took off together on another pre-solo training flight.

"Omigod! Guerd, the motor's quit!" I yelled, feeling my stomach knot, my pulse quicken. Over the normal din of the motor, Guerd couldn't hear a word I shouted. Could he hear me in this sudden horrifying silence? I wasn't thinking clearly. I simply reacted, yelling out loud. I'd never realized how comforting the roar of the motor could be. As the wind quietly whistled in the wires, I shoved the nose of the Swallow forward to glide toward the nearest hayfield. I kicked the rudders hard.

Wrestling with the controls and my own panic, I coaxed aloud, "Come on, baby, settle down. There's a field below and Guerd's here. He'll take over. He'll see that we land all right. He'll..."

Whump. The wheels touched the frosty stubble and we bounced. I slammed my foot against first one rudder, then the other, and pulled the stick all the way into my gut. "Come on, Swallow...come *on!*" The big plane bounced again. I tapped the rudder hard. The plane bounced a few more times until it skewered sideways and shuddered to a stop.

"Thank God!" I breathed.

After we'd climbed out of the downed bird, Guerd put his arm over my shoulder and squeezed me. "Great, Edna, you did a fine job! You're ready to solo."

I was shaking. He put his other arm around me and drew me close. In a softer voice, he soothed, "And we're both fine and that's all that matters."

"The airplane is all right, too, thank, heavens," I told him. Belatedly I realized what he had said and I pushed against his chest, frowning at him. He took a step backward as I asked, "What do you mean I'm ready to solo? Do you want me to go through the next motor failure alone?"

Guerd laughed. "No, nothing like that. But, if it happens, and well it might, you'll be ready to handle it. You were the one that brought her down this time. Didn't you know?"

"I did the landing alone? You didn't help me at all?"

"I never touched a thing. You did a fine job."

I hugged Guerd around the neck and smiled at him. "That's great news. I *felt* as if I was doing the flying, but I can't always tell if you're helping with the controls or not. Be honest, Guerd, did I really do it all?"

He nodded and I whooped, "How exciting!" I gave him a big kiss and he kissed me back.

We stood, arms around one another for a few moments. Then, Guerd held me away at arm's length and looked at me steadily. His dark eyes shone. "It must be the cold that affected the OX-5 today. I'm just glad to see how well you responded. I'm becoming very fond of you."

I smiled up at him, "Thanks. I like hearing that. I like you, too. But, doesn't it bother you that I'm older than you?"

Guerd tilted his head warily. "How do you know my age?"

"I sneaked a look at your pilot's license when you happened to have it out."

His eyes sparkled. He put his hands on my shoulders and I could feel his fingers tighten through the heavy fabric of his winter flying suit, which I had begun to wear more often than he. "My lady of the world. My woman of experience. Why would I worry about a few years? What is it, six? Perhaps I could consider that as a few years in which you learned some things to teach me."

"Or, to change the subject, you could consider doing something to get us out of here. I don't know about you, but I'm getting colder by the minute."

"Miss Practical. Okay. You're right, of course. It's just that holding you is more fun than messing with a balky OX-5." He pulled me to him.

"Honestly, Guerd." I shook my head and laughed, pushing him away. "This somehow doesn't seem like the time or the place...."

"You'd rather I mess with the OX-5, I can tell."

"Why don't we get the darned airplane fixed so we can at least take it back to the hangar?"

"Then?" Guerd asked.

"No promises," I told him. "I've got to get back to the hospital for duty this afternoon."

Guerd shrugged good-naturedly. "Oh well. We can enjoy being together at the moment, however odd the place or time.

I'm thankful that you like airplanes so much. Not every girl is as intrigued with flying as you are."

Not every nurse either. As we worked together, our feet chilled by the frosty hay stubble, our hands, though gloved, blackened with dirt and grime, it made me laugh to think of my nursing friends. Most of them would be horrified to have their hands drip with oil and grease. Most wouldn't know the first thing about checking spark plugs, wiping valves, or helping Guerd troubleshoot the OX-5. Some of them liked to come with me to the field, anxious to see what flying was all about and even more anxious to meet the men, the fliers. That was a different story. Intrepid, cocky men with leather helmets, goggles, and silk scarves represented sex appeal, adventure, and daring. I could scarcely fault my friends. But, the dirty work? That appealed to virtually no woman I knew, especially in the harsh winter weather.

"Guerd. It's beginning to snow."

"Well, that will cool me off if nothing else does," Guerd said with a laugh. "Maybe we'd better hustle if we want to hop over the trees while we've still got enough visibility."

We had felt cold before, but with every new gust of blowing snow, the chill seeped to the bone and we began to shiver. The wind was frigid and we stamped our feet and removed our gloves to rub and blow on our hands. Conversation stopped and we worked feverishly. Our cheeks flamed red with windburn and it seemed an interminable length of time before Guerd finally signaled me into the cockpit. He was ready to try it.

"Contact!" he yelled over the blast of the wind. He pulled the propeller through and the OX-5 grumbled and died. Guerd continued to kick and pull, kick and pull. He worked up a sweat pulling the blades through and the motor finally fired. He clambered aboard quickly, yelling, "Just hop over the trees. You've got it." As he slid into his cockpit, I turned the T.P. into the wind and gunned the motor. As we gained speed, snow swirled into our faces. By the time we became airborne, it whistled straight past our heads and the cold was numbing. We rose just high enough to clear the trees and point the nose of the T.P. toward the Burris farm. I chopped the power, aiming into the howling wind to bring the craft down. It was no time to be in the sky flying around.

"Good job!" Guerd yelled after we'd rolled to a stop and he'd leaped out of his cockpit. "Let's get the bloody thing tied down and get inside out of this wretched cold."

Thoroughly chilled, I was also strangely ecstatic. Nobody could take from me the thrill of having made a successful forced landing nor could anyone steal my growing confidence. Nobody could stem the tide of warm feelings that were growing between Guerd and me. We decided to spend the rest of the day together until it was time for me to report for nursing duty and we climbed into my Studebaker to leave the airfield behind.

Several days later, on a crisp, clear, sparkling winter morning, I said to Guerd, "Don't you think that I'm ready to solo? I feel sure that I could take the airplane around by myself." Then my voice took on an added tone of urgency. I felt as if I was begging. "Please, Guerd? Don't be like Jim Peterson. Please let me take her up and around the field alone. I just know I can fly her safely."

"Okay, Edna. That sounds fine," he promised. "But, you need to understand stalls and spins before I'll let you go alone."

"Stalls and falls? I'll bet that's what they'll be like," I said with a grin.

"We'll do stalls, spins, and spirals to the right and to the left. You haven't done those yet and I can't solo you until I feel that you can do those well. I'm not much of an acrobatic pilot, but, knowing you, I suspect you'll like twisting through the sky in an airplane."

On December 8, 1930, Guerd, the Swallow T.P., and I climbed high toward puffed, white clouds while Waukegan, Illinois, shrunk to miniature below. Like a hawk soaring on rising air currents, we circled upward into cold, clear air to get plenty of altitude for acrobatics. Our breath streamed each time we exhaled, our hands and feet grew numb with cold, and, as we neared the bases of some puffy white clouds, I could see miniature ships on the distant blue of Lake Michigan. Snow dusted the landscape all the way to the base of Chicago's tall buildings to the south, along the lake shore, and sprinkled a white sugar coating over the small town of Racine, Wisconsin, to our north. Still we climbed higher.

Guerd yelled into the Gosport tube. "I'm going to show you what it looks like to be in a spin. Tighten your belt."

I yanked at the end of the belt and felt it press against me as he pulled the nose of the Swallow up, up into the air. The motor labored, the acrid smell of the exhaust spilled over me, the wires wobbled and sang, the big biplane shook and shuddered and then dramatically slewed off to the right, turning around and around—or was it the earth that was spinning so rapidly around instead? The blue of the lake blurred into the snowy white landscape and smeared into a blue and white arc. It was fascinating.

The stick slammed forward, the rudders moved briskly beneath my feet and the spinning stopped. The wires changed from a vibrating hum to a high-pitched whine. We were diving straight for the ground! The cold air rushed back into my face, stung my cheeks, tore at my helmet. I couldn't see Guerd's encouraging smile, but I knew that he could bring us out of anything. He was so cool, so competent. I felt the stick creep back toward my abdomen, the big craft groaned as she righted herself and soon we were level, the clouds once more above us, the earth below, all in order as if never stirred into a swirling confusion at all.

I laughed aloud. "That was wonderful," I screamed to the wind. "That was absolutely wonderful!" Guerd twisted around in his seat and grinned at me from beneath his tight goggles. I yelled, "Let's do it again!" I spun my hand around in the air to signal another and still another.

I saw him reach for the Gosport funnel. "I guess you liked that as much as I thought you would," he yelled. "We'll do it again, but this time to the left. Follow through with me."

"I'd love to, Guerd," I said into the wind. "I'm with you."

Once more the nose of the big plane started up. The stick came back to my abdomen, all the way back. The rudders danced, the nose of the craft shook, and the pungent gas assailed my nostrils again. I could feel a buffeting that I'd never felt before today, could see the stick shake as it had never shaken, and the wires vibrate like guitar strings plucked by a giant hand. The left rudder slammed against the stop and it happened again. Around and around we went. The blue and white earth spun rapidly to the right; indistinct, a blur. We turned faster than a spinning leaf whirled by the wind.

"Wheeeee!" I yelled and then I saw the stick move briskly, the right rudder pedal kick forward beneath my foot, and the rotation started to slow. I felt my body jerk to a stop. The nose of the airplane had been pointed down, now it dipped even lower, as straight and unswerving as an eagle diving toward its prey. The wind screamed in my ears. When the spinning ceased, the wings righted and gradually the phantom hand guided the stick back, back, back toward center again. The airplane's nose took a rightful place just below the distant horizon and the world calmed.

So this was spinning. I felt a surge of love and gratitude to Guerd. How grand that he was showing me the joys of flying, sharing with me his segment of the sky. (And what a relief that I wasn't aloft with Bob Martin, the man with so few hours, so little experience. It was a blessing that Martin's airplane was harmlessly wrecked in ground loops or he might have attempted to teach me what he probably didn't know anything about!) I was learning to fly. Better than that, I was learning to fly well. I was being taught by a patient, careful, caring instructor. I would soon be a pilot—I knew it. I would be, however, a much better pilot for having learned from Guerd.

Three stalls and two spirals followed the spins, but they paled in comparison. After I heard, "This is a stall," through the Gosport tube, I gently toed the rudders, took the stick lightly into my hands. I wanted to feel what Guerd was doing, but I didn't want to interfere. I'd heard stories about students "freezing" on the controls in panic. I didn't want to be that kind of student. Besides, I wasn't scared. I loved twisting through the sky just as Guerd had supposed I would.

"This isn't like a stall in a car," Guerd yelled to me. "The motor should have no reason to stop. The wing will stop lifting, that's all. Watch now." Again, the stick crept back, it tapped the insides of my thighs through the thick coveralls, and the rudders danced lightly under my feet. The nose of the airplane bucked a few times as the buffeting began and then drooped forward. When Guerd put the stick forward, the buffeting stopped. He brought the nose back toward us again. There wasn't much to that, I decided.

"You try it, Edna," I heard Guerd call to me. I felt the stick rap my thighs and I grasped it firmly. I pulled it back toward me and, instead of the nose of the airplane coming up, it slewed to the right. "Don't forget those lazy feet," Guerd yelled through the tube directly into my ears. "Get your rudders moving, Edna. Dance!"

The view of the horizon was obscured straight ahead, but I watched the ground and the lake over the sides of the craft. I struggled to keep the wings even, to pull the stick and push the rudders. Wham! The nose dropped and so did one pair of wings, cockeyed, twisting.

"I've got it," yelled Guerd. He righted the ship and yelled again, "Feel it through with me, Edna. Feel what I'm doing."

He made it look so easy. Just as the airplane began to buffet, he did everything smoothly and correctly.

"One more time, Edna. Try it one more time. You can do it. Keep those feet moving."

I was tiring. My numb fingers slipped on the stick and my toes felt like ice cubes chattering on the rudder pedals. My leg muscles twitched with the effort and I yanked back angrily on the stick, pushed my right foot against the pedal. I felt the ship shudder and shake, then the nose pitched down.

"Great!" yelled Guerd. "Now, ease the stick back to recover and let's get to the airfield. I could use some hot chocolate."

He was a good teacher and he didn't like to quit when a student was tired, discouraged, or feeling inept. He liked to stop at a moment of success. The minute he said, "Great!" I knew we would be returning to the airfield for a landing. That was all right with me. Few places are colder than an open cockpit airplane at high altitude over one of the Great Lakes in the middle of winter. The spinning and stalls had been fun until the reality of frostbite seemed imminent.

"Let's spiral down," Guerd hollered into the tube. "Follow through with me. This is a good maneuver for a rapid descent from altitude. You can spiral to the landing. Can you see the field from here?"

The wind had drifted us, the landscape was frosted white up to the shoreline of the brilliantly blue lake. I strained to look for familiar landmarks as Guerd turned the craft around and around, losing altitude, yet staying over one point. Down we circled to the left, then he righted the craft. "Your turn," he hollered.

I swung the wings into an arc and down we descended, not quite as smoothly, but under control—under my control. When I located the Burris barn, Lindon and Mae's big house, and the hangar next to the cafe, I leveled the wings, then banked to descend toward the field.

"Good job!" Guerd yelled. "Very good! I'm proud of you."

After getting the T.P. tied down, we thawed out over a cup of hot chocolate and a piece of Jack's apple pie, warmed in the oven, luscious with freshly cooked fruit. As we sipped, warming both hands around the ceramic mugs, Guerd brought up ground school training again. "You really must study, Edna. You have a test ahead of you and need to apply yourself toward that."

Guerd and I spent countless hours studying what he termed "dead reckoning" and we planned and flew several cross-country flights. They served the dual purpose of teaching me to navigate over long distances and of taking us away from familiar sights, known terrain, and, sometimes, prying eyes. We

grew closer and more fond of one another day by day. My
piloting improved and my confidence grew—about flying and
about being a woman, a capable and a desirable one.

One day we flew in an Eaglerock for a change and then Guerd
helped me conquer a Curtiss Robin, my nemesis when first
flown with George Hensley—flights that, along with those with
Peterson and Martin, had begun to fade into oblivion. It seemed
as if the person who flew with those men was another woman
in another place at another time.

When the weather was less than perfect, we'd shoot takeoffs
and landings—always practicing. When the weather was favor-
able, we flew to various airports in the area, pushed my limited
navigational skills and our relationship. We felt carefree and
giddy, taking time for ourselves away from the circle of friends
that seemed to envelop us whenever we were at the Burris field.
We cherished the flights and grew more familiar with northern
Illinois, southern Wisconsin . . . and each other.

Christmas came and went and, on New Year's Day 1931, the
weather dawned clear and crisp with a slight southwesterly
breeze. Guerd met me at the Swallow T.P. and smiled warmly
at me. "The day couldn't have been better if we'd ordered it,"
he said, an arm draped loosely over my shoulders. "I want you
to take her up alone today."

"Are you serious? Solo? Oh, Guerd, at last. I've been praying
for this day—thinking about it, wishing for it. I won't disappoint
you. I'll do so well that you won't regret having taken me as a
student . . . not ever."

"Not ever," he parroted. He kissed me lightly on the cheek
and turned to walk to the front of the airplane. "Let me know
when you feel as if you've completed your pre-flying check and
are comfortably situated in the cockpit. Don't be surprised when
the ship seems much lighter and more willing to fly. I'm taking
all 165 of my hefty pounds out of there."

"All 165 hefty pounds," I scoffed. "You can't mean that the
airplane will notice that you're gone."

"You'll be surprised. She'll be peppier than you've ever

known her. Have a good time. Let me see two fine landings, will you?"

"You bet! And, thanks Guerd. I'll sing all the way around the entire landing pattern."

"I'll be listening. I'll be watching, too. Happy landings."

He yelled, "Contact!" when I was situated and had given him a thumbs-up. It was good to have a simple helmet on, no tubes dangling into my lap and snaking into the seat. Indeed, I'd spent all my flying time in the backseat, and I'd grown accustomed to seeing his strong back and broad shoulders in the front cockpit. Now I was alone! What a thrill. Nothing would compare to this for a long time to come.

Guerd was right, as usual. The airplane fairly leaped off the ground. I felt as if I'd suddenly taken off in an unfamiliar bird or that Guerd had done something with the engine to give it more pep. "Whoa," I called. Did I think that the airplane would hear me and slow down? It was up and flying before I had caught up with it and I squirmed in my seat, danced the rudders and lightly dipped the wings to ensure that I was mastering the airplane and not the reverse. I could almost hear Guerd's voice in the imaginary Gosport tube. "Take charge, Edna. Fly the airplane."

The sugar-coated pine trees dropped from beneath me and I banked to the left. I could see cars rolling down the nearby streets, tractors parked for the winter, smoke curling from the chimneys of houses and crisscrossed cow tracks across nearby fields. I started to sing. Puffs of breath streamed from my mouth and I knew that I'd never been happier in my entire life. I was alone. I was solo. I was totally in charge of a Swallow T.P. airplane and loving every second of it. I sang even louder, but still couldn't hear a sound above the airplane's din.

I glanced down at the hangar, strained to see Guerd on the ground. There he was flanked by Freddy and at least four of the others who had piled out of Walter Jack's cafe, coffee cups steaming in their hands, all looking up at the Swallow and me. I was solo! What a wonderful, memorable day.

When it came time for the landing, I wanted to be perfect. I didn't want the airplane to bounce. I didn't want to slew around on the ground, out of control, dipping a wing. I wanted to touch down as sweetly as possible, let the tires kiss the frozen ground, crunch on the thin frosty layer of snow that barely covered the brown, dead grass. "Just watch me, Guerd and Freddy," I sang. "Just watch, all of you men. I'll show you what a woman can do. There, that's where the American Eagle spun in. Not me. I'm flying. I'm solo and I'm going to have the best time of my life. Here I come."

The airplane shuddered gently as I pulled back on the stick, my feet dancing on the rudders, swinging the big rudder on the tail behind me to the left and to the right. The Swallow seemed to sigh onto the ground with a soft whoosh. I did it once, then I gave her the gun and repeated the circuit to erase all doubt that my first sweet touchdown was a fluke. "Just watch me, fellas," I sang aloud. "I'm having a heyday. I'm free. I'm soloed. I can do it without you." I would probably never be the same again. This moment would change my life forever and I could hardly wait to see what lay ahead. "I'll go across the country, I'll race to the moon. I'll fly high and wide and I'll never look back."

After the T.P. and I touched the earth and slid to a stop, I could hardly wait to stop the motor and untie my belt. I jumped out onto the wing, tore my goggles from my eyes, unsnapped my helmet and ran into Guerd's arms. He was laughing, Freddy was patting my back excitedly, and the men were all praising and cheering. What a wonderful day. They ushered me, noisy, jostling, laughing, and pushing like so many chattering magpies into the cafe for a cup of coffee.

They gathered around me and raised their cups in salute, "To Edna! Our spark plug! You did it, pretty lady. You soloed and now you're a pilot!"

"Were you glad to get rid of me?" Guerd teased.

"You bet. I was glad to be rid of any man who has tried to teach me to fly. Some of them have been nothing but anchors around my feet." Then I softened, when I saw the quizzical look that passed over Guerd's face. "Hey, I appreciate all that you've taught me. I really do. But, you know that I'm glad to be soloed. I've wanted this day for so long. Do you know what I'd really like to do? I'd like to fly to Madison and climb out of the airplane right in front of Jim Peterson and George Hensley. I'd like to show them!"

Everyone was still talking and laughing between themselves when Guerd moved closer to me and, in a lowered voice, said, "I'm proud of you, Edna. I told you that you could solo an airplane if you set your mind to it and worked at it. You've done just that. You've worked harder than any student I've ever taught. Now let's finish the job and get that ten-hour private license you've wanted. I'll wager the C.A.A. has one with your name on it. You've still got to fly some distance flights and have me teach spot landings, spirals, steep flipper turns, and figure eights."

"I guess I still need you quite a bit."

Guerd's eyes were soft and dark. His smile was sincere and affectionate. "I, for one, am delighted to hear that. I would say that 1931 has started off with promises of being the best year of our lives. Happy New Year, Edna." We kissed, then grinned at the catcalls and jeers that came from the men who surrounded us.

The joy of the moment was spoiled with feelings of guilt. I didn't know how to tell Guerd that I was expecting an assignment from the Navy. I also didn't want to admit that Dr. Boe planned to precede me to the east and was urging me to visit him in Boston. I wondered how much time it would take to get the ten-hour private license. I wondered what would Guerd think if I left Waukegan in a few short months.

8

Round Hill and a Travel Air

Guerd told me in mid-May of 1931, "Tomorrow's the big day, Edna. Your check ride for a private pilot's license will be in Palwaukee. Mr. Hughes of the Department of Commerce will be there."

"Am I ready, Guerd? Am I really ready?" I watched his features, anxious for him to be honest and expecting to see the answer in his eyes as well as in the words. His dark eyes softened as he slightly tilted his head and curved his mouth into a loving smile. He put his hands on my shoulders and nodded. "You're ready, Edna. You'll do fine," he assured me. He bent forward and kissed my lips.

Well, I was *somewhat* prepared. Guerd had taught me flipper turns, stalls, and spins. He had drilled me in the coordination required to swoop around ground pylons in tight figure eights, climbing and diving to pivot around the chosen point despite the natural wind. He prepared me well, but there was no anticipating the likes of a heavily browed, black-suited, somber Mr. Hughes.

I was nervous yet confident as I soloed the Swallow T.P. to Palwaukee, landed, and left the ship in a safe spot on the field. My reserve drained as I faced the cold, stony-faced government inspector holding court in a big open hangar on the field. Once introductions were completed, two male pilot hopefuls and I were handed a fifteen-question written test. For that, Guerd had helped and I had spent hours in study. I breezed through the written test ahead of the two men and handed my results to Mr. Hughes. He directed me to sit quietly and wait for the others to finish with a curt nod and a flick of his wrist toward the chair. He smoothed his slick hair with a hand that brandished a large gold ring and straightened his dark tie, picking an imaginary piece of lint from his jacket lapel.

When the men had finished, Mr. Hughes stretched to his full six-foot-two frame, signaled one of the men, and commanded roughly, "All right, you are first. You've passed your written portion of the federal exam. Let's see what you can do in the air."

Mr. Hughes stood rigidly a distance from the hangar to watch the prospective pilot take off in a Waco. Although bursting with curiosity, I didn't dare go to the doorway to see the flying test. I dutifully stayed in place, glancing occasionally at the second applicant. He fidgeted in his seat and kept his eyes straight ahead. He repeatedly wiped his hands along his upper thighs.

It had been 1926 before the federal government decided to license pilots. Prior to that, pilots had logged countless hours without the constraints of rules or regulations or written tests or flying tests. By 1931, testing was mandatory and every pilot who wanted to fly legally had to climb into an aircraft under the scrutiny of an inspector to demonstrate being capable and practiced. This particular examiner seemed to be a master of intimidation and I tried desperately to calm my rising fears.

Mr. Hughes ordered the second man to take off into the air as soon as the first was finished and the paperwork had been completed. I watched the nervous man quake under the icy glare of the gruff inspector. His shoulders drooped and his step was halting as he approached his craft, another Waco. I swallowed a rush of acrid bile that rose suddenly into my throat and squeezed my hands together in my lap, fighting for self-control.

I waited for what seemed an eternity. Alone in the barn of a hangar, I leaned stiffly against the back of the wooden chair and concentrated on the wisps of dirt that swirled upward from the floor, circled in the sunlight that streamed through the cracks in the wooden building. Crickets chirped and birds twittered in nearby trees. A bee buzzed lazily near a stray clover growing in an inside corner of the hangar and finally his droning song was lost with the zoom of the approaching biplane. The second man was returning to Mr. Hughes.

My heart pounded. My hands sweated and I smoothed my cotton skirt along my thighs for the umpteenth time, wiping my palms and trying to calm my nerves. I checked again the bow at the neck of my white blouse and reprimped my bobbed curly hair.

Mr. Hughes entered the dusty building through the huge hangar doors and scuffed dirt swirled around his polished shoes as he strode to a makeshift table that served as his desk. He pushed papers around and dashed notes on the margins of written documents. He never looked at me. Was he never going to take me? What was the matter? I was the first completed with that test. Had I rushed too much and been careless? Had I made foolish mistakes? I began to doubt and became more frustrated by the moment.

Finally Mr. Hughes sighed and stood up. He barked, "Miss Gardner, will you come outside with me?"

I was startled. I dutifully followed him out and around the side of the weathered wooden building, my heart pounding in cadence with my step. I stopped abruptly as Mr. Hughes spun on his heel and faced me. He was cold and curt.

"Miss Gardner, this isn't easy for me," he said, his tone flat.

"I've never given a pilot's license to a woman. Why do you want one?"

I tried to return the gaze of his steely blue eyes and noticed the working ripple of his jaw.

"What do you mean?" I asked.

"Answer my question," he insisted. "Why do you want to fly? I've never given any woman a license and I'm not at all sure that I want to start now."

Tears pricked and burned in my eyes. God, not now—let's not burst into tears *now*. I'd fought showing my emotions since I was a child. I dreaded any show of weakness, especially at a crucial time when I should be strong and most determined. All I could think was, "Don't tell me this man is going to make me forfeit all of the efforts—the time, the money, the practice, the hard work with Guerd." Tears trickled from my eyes and along my nose. I fumbled in my skirt pocket for a hanky.

"I want a career in aviation," I stammered. "Weren't the results of my written test good enough?" I blew my nose.

"Yes," he admitted. "Yes, your written test was all right. Yours was the highest grade. I can't take that away from you."

"I don't understand," I told him, my voice breaking. "Why would you want to take anything away from me? I've worked very hard. I even borrowed money to get the flying time that I needed. Won't you let me show you what I can do in an airplane? I want to fly. I want a license so that I can be a pilot for the rest of my life—a good pilot. I'd like a career in aviation. Am I being denied the chance to take the check ride just because I'm a *woman*?"

Now the tears flowed. I couldn't help it. I couldn't stop them. I cried into my hanky and wiped my eyes and my nose at the same time. I felt my shoulders shake with the thought of all of the money, the months of effort, wasted.

"Oh, all right," he relented. He flipped his hand toward the parked airplanes and added, "Go climb into your airplane. I'll watch. You'd better do a creditable job, though."

Anger welled within me and damned the flow of tears. The

pressure of waiting so long began to lighten. I thought of Guerd's encouraging smile and held my chin a little higher. With my shoulders squared, I faced my familiar Swallow T.P. and decided to show this man. I'd show him that I not only could fly, but that I could handle the controls of an airplane with the same success I'd shown on my written test—*better* than the two men he'd tested.

And I did. I flew for Mr. Hughes for twenty minutes, did a smooth takeoff, two well-executed spins, and a three-point landing that made my insides soar. I couldn't hide a smile. I climbed slowly out of my parked craft and approached him.

He grudgingly handed me my license, number 20000. Once freed, my new ticket tightly clutched in my hand, I went back into the air and did two loops and a spin directly over Palwaukee Airport. "I'm a pilot," I yelled at the top of my lungs. "I'm a good pilot, Mr. High-Hat Hughes, and I'm going to do nothing but get better and better. You just watch." I climbed the T.P. high overhead and spun down, down, down toward the green field one more time before righting the craft, waggling the great wings, and pointing the nose toward Waukegan. It was May 14, 1931, and I could hardly wait to show my pilot's license to Guerd.

Dr. Boe was complimentary when I waved my new license in front of all my colleagues at the hospital. He'd made no bones about the fact that he found me attractive. Now he suggested that I take him flying and share with him tales with which I'd regaled all my medical friends. "I'll pay for the airplane, Edna," he said.

"You'd be my first real passenger," I told him, delighted with the idea and with his generous offer. I'd taken Fred Stripe up for a few fifteen-minute local flights, but if Dr. Boe was willing to pay, I could fly the airplane on a more lengthy cross-country flight.

"Would you like to fly to Chatfield, Minnesota, with me?" I asked him. "I would love to surprise my mother and her husband. Mother always thought that I was foolish to want to fly. Perhaps a visit will make her feel differently."

"I'm game," replied Dr. Boe. "I've never flown in an airplane before. How long would it take us to fly to Chatfield? I'll have to make arrangements to have someone cover for me at the hospital."

Chatfield is located in the southern tip of Minnesota. I measured the course and estimated a two-hour flight, although we both made arrangements at the hospital so that we could be away overnight. I told him how to get to the Burris farm and agreed to meet him early in the morning, May 16. I was apprehensive of facing Guerd when I went to the field, but luckily he was working with his father and was nowhere to be seen.

I was lucky, too, that the weather was cooperative. Dr. Boe drove up not long after I'd arrived and we readied the Swallow. "You're going to like this," I assured him, as I outfitted him with a borrowed helmet and goggles, preflighted the ship, and settled him into a seat. "Except for my flight to Palwaukee to be tested for my license, this will be my first cross-country." My excitement level must have been contagious. Dr. Boe was an eager passenger.

We covered 163 miles over a corner of Wisconsin to the little landing strip at Chatfield. Mother warmed a bit to the idea of my flying and she was pleased to meet Dr. Boe. Even John Hander was impressed that I could fly. A knot of Minnesotans clustered at the airfield to see the Swallow that had landed. We had a pleasant visit and flew back to Waukegan, appreciating the brilliant sparkle of Minnesota's sapphire-colored lakes. They reflected the blue of the sky and mirrored the clouds that chased us. River oxbows snaked between the lakes, and streams emptied into the rivers, swelling them with spring runoff.

Guerd had missed our departure, but I dreaded that he would be at Waukegan upon our return. It was not only that I had flown off for the weekend with another man. The Navy had given me orders and I was concerned about breaking the news of my reassignment. I wasn't sure about Guerd's reactions.

As the flying instructor for the Waukegan Flying Club, Guerd was well aware of the scheduling of the airplanes. He knew that I'd taken the Swallow T.P. and knew that I'd carried a passenger. He greeted us cordially, if a bit coolly, when we touched down the next afternoon. He nodded to Dr. Boe when I introduced them, then asked questions about the Swallow's performance. The mechanic in him was relieved to see that the airplane had allowed me to accomplish a long-distance flight with no complications.

He helped me to tie down the plane after I'd seen the doctor off in his car.

"He offered to pay for the flight," I said, defensively, to respond to the questioning look on Guerd's face. "We flew to Chatfield and visited Mother. She isn't as set against my flying as she once was. She recognizes that I couldn't have come to visit if it hadn't been for the chance to fly. Even John Hander was impressed."

"I'd have to be insane to pretend that I wasn't bothered by seeing you with another man. I'm falling in love with you, Edna," Guerd said, quietly.

"Ssh," I told him gently. "Before you say any more, let me tell you something. I've some news and I'm not sure what you'll think. The Navy is shipping me out. I'm leaving Great Lakes Naval Hospital for reassignment to Newport Naval Hospital in Rhode Island."

"You're doing what?" Guerd took a step backward and stared at me. "You're *leaving?*"

"Yes. The Navy wants me to report to Newport on the thirtieth of this month."

"You'll be gone in less than two weeks? I can't believe it, Edna." He was quiet for a moment and then, subdued, he added, "I guess I knew that it was coming. I knew that persons in military service have to accept the dictates of the government. I guess I hoped that it would be different for nurses—one special nurse, anyway." After a pause, he added, "Well, chalk up one good thing. You got your pilot's license in time."

I put my arms around his neck and kissed him. "Thanks to you. You know? I've been thinking about my drive east. Do you suppose your sister, Tessie, and your mother would like to drive with me? Dr. Boe is leaving this week to be reassigned to Boston.

We could drive there and also see New York City. Wouldn't they like that?"

"Lord. You certainly know how to surprise a man. First you hit me with the fact that I'm not the only man in your life. Now you talk about my sister and mother accompanying you and I'm still swallowing the fact that you're leaving."

"Oh, don't be jealous of Dr. Boe."

"Not much reason to be, is there? I don't suppose we've any claims to one another. You do know that I care about you. As for Tessie and Mother, all you can do is ask them."

"Want to go up for a flight? Then I'll drive over to your parents' home."

"I'll check you out in the Curtiss Robin. That will be a change in comparison to the Swallow. I guess we'd better take advantage of our last few chances to fly together."

I flew in the front seat of the high-winged cabin monoplane, picturing Guerd's familiar broad shoulders directly behind me. I turned to smile at him occasionally, but he didn't grin back at me. I could only imagine what was going on in his mind after the excitement of our meeting, the closeness we'd shared as he helped me obtain my pilot's license, and the suddenness of the bomb that I had just dropped.

Guerd was more than comfortable in an airplane, but this time he flew with his upper body erect and unyielding. I assumed he was braced for flight and perhaps the coming fortnight when I would be gone. Guerd had had other women in his life. He would find another. On the other hand, what was to prevent him from joining me in Newport?

Our friends at the Waukegan Flying Club gathered around us after we landed. It was the first chance they'd had to see me since I'd become a pilot. It was gratifying to see the respect that I'd earned with my medical friends, but it was much more fun to share my new pilot's license with those that understood what I had accomplished, those who knew what flying was all about. We all laughed as I mimicked the dour face of a federal examiner.

Suddenly, I said, "I have an idea. Let's have a race. Let's take the four airplanes and see who can fly to Racine and back the fastest? Guerd just checked me out in the Robin. I'll fly that one, okay, Guerd?"

Guerd shrugged and smiled, "I'm game. Are you interested, Fred?"

Freddy snorted, "You bet!" Then he turned to me and said with a grin, "You're never gonna live down the title of spark plug, Edna. When you're around, things happen."

"Well, let's get started. On your mark, *go!*"

Four of us zipped through quick preflights and hopped our airplanes into the air. I was the first to circle the water tower at Racine, Wisconsin, and the first to land at Waukegan, grinning broadly as I greeted my fellow racers as they landed one by one. "Ante up, you men," I told them. "Let's pool a few dollars, get a trophy. I'll have it engraved with 'WINNER, ROUND-ROBIN RACE TO RACINE.'"

It was my first racing trophy and, after the adrenaline rush of the chase, the thrill of the win, I knew it was far from my last. Air racing suddenly topped my list of interests.

"I'm going to fly to Eddie Heath's field, Guerd," I said, a week later. "He's near Des Plaines, northwest of Chicago, isn't he?"

Guerd nodded. "You bet. He's the one who modified my Tommy Morse Scout and his school has turned out millions of pilots."

"Millions?"

"Well, perhaps that's an exaggeration, but Heath made quite a name for himself as a designer-racer-flight instructor. It was just a couple of years ago—I think it was in 1928 that he came out with the airplane that he called his Baby Bullet. That raced at 142 miles an hour on only 32 horses of power. It was amazing! It won in 1929, too."

"Now that I've discovered how much fun it is to air race, I want to meet a man like Heath who designs racers. Maybe I can learn something. I bet someone like him might even sponsor me with one of his airplanes someday."

I flew in the Swallow and, after landing on his grassy pasture,

I found Heath fiddling with the rudder of a newly designed airplane. I introduced myself to him and asked, "What are you doing? Are you attaching that rudder for the first time?"

"No. I've flown the bird," Heath told me, "but the flight test isn't going as well as I'd hoped. I can't seem to get the rudder responsiveness that I want."

A small, wiry man, Eddie Heath was intense and I didn't want to be a bother. I made a few more comments, then climbed back into my T.P. to return to Waukegan.

As I parked in the customary spot near Jack's cafe, Freddy ran out to my ship. "Edna," he called to me. "Did you hear? Eddie Heath has been killed. He was in a flying accident."

"No he wasn't, Fred. I just saw him myself. I talked to him."

"He was killed, I'm telling you. He took off to test a new design and he augered in. He crashed. No lie."

I couldn't believe it. I felt sick to my stomach. "Where's Guerd, Freddy? Is he around?"

I knew that Guerd would be philosophical about it. His stoic, steadying influence would assure me that life goes on—that, although even the talented and experienced could be killed, this flying world of ours was worth the risk and the challenge. Besides, my time was getting very short and I wanted to spend time with Guerd whenever it was possible. I found him working on the flying club's Velie Monocoupe.

"Fred's right," Guerd told me, wiping his hands on a red rag. "Heath has been a big name in aviation here in the Chicago area. We'll miss him."

"It is so hard to believe," I told Guerd. "I was just there talking to him. I might have even been the last to talk with him. That's hard to take."

"He is not the first nor the last that you will see killed or hurt in airplanes, Edna. Ask yourself, does it make you want to give it all up?"

"Heavens no. It makes me want to become better. It also makes me uneasy. Let's change the subject. Could we fly over to your home and let me talk with your sister, Tess, and your mother? I hope they'll drive to Boston with me. Perhaps we can even take the ferry to New York City and have some sightseeing fun."

I moved close and put both of my arms around Guerd's neck. He looked at his hands, found them clean enough, and wrapped his arms around my waist. "Do you know what I'd like to do, Guerd?"

"Right this minute? Or later?"

I laughed. "No, silly. I mean once I've gotten to the Newport Naval Hospital."

"That's much too far away."

I laughed again and kissed him lightly. "Just listen to me. I'll check out the flying at Newport and perhaps you can join me there."

Guerd let go and stepped back. He shook his head. "This is my home, Edna. You know that."

"Yes, but you're always saying that you want a career in flying. What are you accomplishing here that you can't do or even improve upon in Newport, Rhode Island? What if I find a demand for flying instructors? Or mechanics? I'll look into it the first thing."

"I don't know about following you east, but I do know that I will miss you terribly."

"I'll miss you, too, Guerd. But, who knows? This may be a big chance for us. Perhaps there are fabulous opportunities for flying in the big cities of the East. You'd consider it, wouldn't you?"

Guerd put a hand on each of my shoulders and kissed me. "I'll consider it. I hate that you're leaving and I'll consider almost anything that means we can be together. Now, let's fly to Holdridge Crossing."

Tessie and Mrs. Brocksom drove the long way from Waukegan to Boston with me. We ferried to New York for our first sight of the big city, some sightseeing, and a stage show. We returned on the ferry to Boston to visit with Dr. Boe. He took the opportunity to whisper sweet nothings in my ear and suggest marriage, but I was much too interested in airplanes to want to settle down. Besides, he wanted babies, a family of his own.

That idea held no appeal for me whatsoever. I often said, "I'll look at the man and I'll look at the airplane. I'll always choose the airplane," but that wasn't entirely true, either.

Ever since learning to fly with Guerd Brocksom, my confidence had been building and it was incredible what that freshly inked pilot's license meant to my self-esteem. It posed no threat to become acquainted with Boston and New York. Well on the way toward sophistication, I marveled at the change. Gone was the person who had snaked across the western United States with Dean, Velma, and Gordon Hutton. I reveled in new poise. My nursing was a pleasure and my flying gave me wings, freedom to explore my new environs and to make my mark upon them.

Immediately after moving into the naval nurse quarters at the Newport Naval Hospital, I searched for an airfield and found a few airplanes operating from the grass on the west side of Aquidneck Island on Narragansett Bay. I met Smitty, a fellow who owned a LaBlond-powered Barling and offered to take me for a ride.

I flew with Smitty a few times and began to meet people involved in aviation and with flying. I hadn't much money, but I searched for an airplane to buy and learned of a Travel Air for sale in Fall River, Massachusetts. I asked Smitty to fly to Fall River with me and to help me check on the Travel Air.

"It's a rare bird," insisted the airplane owner after giving me a short introductory flight. "Like you. I haven't met many lady pilots. You'd do well with this Travel Air. There are a lot of them that are powered by the OX-5. This one has an OXX-6."

"How much are you asking for it?" I questioned and turned on my heel when he mentioned a thousand dollars. "Come on, Smitty. We might as well fly back to Newport. I can't afford any price like that."

"Wait a minute," urged the seller. "I really need cash. Give me an offer. Tell me what you can go."

I just shrugged. "Nowhere even near what you're asking. I've just $160 in the bank."

The Travel Air's owner threw his hands up in disgust.

"But," I continued, "I work for the federal government. I'm a nurse at the Newport Naval Hospital. What would you say to the $160 in cash and $35 a month until I've paid a total of $600?"

When the owner agreed, I let out a whoop and grabbed Smitty around the neck. "Fantastic! I just bought an airplane, Smitty. I just bought the first airplane of my life! We can fly back to Newport in formation."

"Loose formation," Smitty joked. "That big biplane would eat my little Barling up and spit it out if we tried to lock wings."

"Now I'm going to have to rent a hangar. I can't have my brand-new airplane sitting out in the rain and ocean spray of Newport."

"I'll show you Colonel Green's Round Hill Airport north of Newport near New Bedford, Massachusetts," said Smitty.

"Colonel Green?"

"He's a good man. He was crippled with polio and will never walk, never fly an airplane, but he loves airplanes. He has built a pretty nice air field."

It was rumored that Green was permanently handicapped because his extremely wealthy but eccentric mother refused to spend money for a doctor for him when he was young. Green built one of the finest airfields of its time—an airfield replete with lighting, a hard-surfaced runway, and many hangars to house the varied aircraft owned by pilots of Massachusetts and Rhode Island.

"I'll take you there and we'll check on renting a hangar," said Smitty.

It was in a Quonset hut at Colonel Green's Round Hill Airport that the Massachusetts Institute of Technology performed experiments as one of the universities that studied uranium-graphite combinations that were expected to result in a self-sustaining nuclear chain reaction. It was on Colonel Green's air-field that a Kinner-powered Bird airplane was hangared not far from mine, a beautiful biplane with a blue fuselage and silver wings that belonged to Anne Morrow Lindbergh and her husband, Charles. I was thrilled to meet them and thrilled to rent my hangar at Colonel Green's field to house my Travel Air.

I wrote Guerd eagerly. "You would like it here. We are surrounded by water and fly from a runway in a green field that dips down to the shore. I have been flying with a fellow named Smitty in his LaBlond Barling, a low-winged monoplane that is a lot of fun to fly. I've had a chance to fly an Avro Avian and even an autogyro, which was a strange experience. Talk about hovering slowly over a landing site!

"I have tested whatever airplanes I could get my hands on, an Aeronca, a Curtiss Junior, and now, for my big surprise, I bought a Travel Air! I hope you will come east and fly in it with me. It is an OXX-6 with ten more horses than our old OX-5 and with two magnetos for ignition. It's true that only one of them ever works, but we only had one with the OX-5, so what do I care? This Travel Air is a 2000 and has 'elephant ears' on the ailerons. I'll send you some pictures of it."

Newport quickly became home to me. I even adapted to the persistent coastal fog, which rarely kept me from spending every free hour from my naval nursing duty in my new Travel Air. From my hard-earned seventy dollars per month, I spent every dollar — all on flying.

I wrote Guerd again. "I've been flying into every weather condition around here—fog, clouds, rain, and sometimes beautiful, clear, sunny days. There's plenty of money here—it doesn't seem that the Depression has ruined life for the very rich. You should see the fabulous mansions with their grand yards and fancy gardens. I like circling over the island to look down at the fancy yard parties and see how high society lives.

"I've practiced landings, flown around the beaches, hopped passengers, learned to handle the crazy wind—it shifts and changes with different moods of the Atlantic Ocean.

"I wanted to try to set some records at consecutive loops, but all I get is dust and dirt and an occasional dead mouse in my face from the bottom of the airplane. I'll keep practicing loops and spins, though. I think it'd be great to set some sort of endurance record.

"Most exciting, Guerd, is news of the Cleveland Air Races of 1931 scheduled for September. They make me think of that race I won when we flew round-robin to Racine."

The races made me think, too, of 1929 and Louise Thaden's win in the first Women's Air Derby. Jealous that Amelia Earhart, Bobbi Trout, Florence "Pancho" Barnes, Phoebe Omlie, and others could get airplanes and backing for their participation in the long race, I often read about them in the newspapers and was interested that they had started an organization specifically for female pilots. In November 1929 those lady pilots and others gathered on Long Island to form the organization of women pilots called the Ninety-Nines, named for the number of those listed as charter members. Amelia Earhart was elected the first president.

In another letter to Guerd, I wrote, "I joined a flying group, the Betsy Ross Corps. It was newly organized, May 1931, and sounds like the kind of group I'd like. They want to use airplanes to make humanitarian contributions and I think that my airplane and I can contribute. I hope it proves to be as helpful as it sounds—flying blood plasma, carrying patients who live too far from hospitals—just the thing for a flying nurse. I joined the Ninety-Nines this year, too, Guerd. I've been told that I will meet Amelia Earhart at meetings here in Providence and on Long Island."

But, more than anything, I wanted to participate in the Cleveland Air Races. When the Navy gave me a two-week leave for September, I could scarcely wait to call Guerd on the telephone. "Will you meet me at Cleveland for the air races? They're to run from August 29 to September 7."

"I've been trying to figure out how and when I'd get to see you, Edna," Guerd answered in his soft, low voice. It was good to hear him. I smiled into my receiver.

"Just think, Guerd. Last year people like Jimmy Doolittle, Benny Howard, Wiley Post, Frank Hawks, and Roscoe Turner all raced. The men and their races are highly publicized, but I heard of a women's free-for-all. Gladys O'Donnell won last year. She averaged 149 miles an hour, can you imagine? She, Mary

Haizlip, and Pancho Barnes were there to race. The Navy has given me a two-week leave and I'll fly from Newport on the twenty-eighth of August and head west. What do you think?"

"Will you race your Travel Air?"

"No. It isn't fast enough to compete with an airplane that zips along at 149 miles an hour and they'll probably go even faster this year. But, I have written to the Triangle Parachute Company and asked them about the performance of their chutes."

"Triangle Parachutes? Oh, come on, Edna. I know you like acrobatics. I know you're hooked on racing, but please don't tell me that you've taken up parachuting."

I laughed. "No, I'd rather do the piloting. But, their chutes are like triangles with one corner open. I guess a chutist can twirl that corner to the rear and sail forward. They promise accurate performance and boast that the chutist can put it down exactly on target. I wrote to ask if they'd furnish a chute and a jumper for me for the air races. The targets are painted circles on the ground and, if the chutist lands in the middle, he and the pilot win a lot of money. If I could just make expenses, it'd be worth it. What about you? Will you meet me there?"

"You bet. I'd like to see you, to hold you. I'll be there. Perhaps, uh . . . perhaps we could talk about a future together?"

I hedged. "No promises. No commitments, Guerd . . . yet. I have been thinking about you, though. You can't imagine how beautiful Rhode Island is from the air. With all the ponds and marshes, a duck hunter like you would call it heaven. I've seen the sky absolutely blackened with gaggles of geese and ducks. And with all the boats, the mansions, the beaches—I know you'd like it here. I've been looking for a flying job for you, but haven't come up with anything. Maybe I'll hear of something before we get together in Cleveland."

"You could undoubtedly use some help with that Travel Air of yours, too."

"Oh, Guerd. It will be great to see you. I'm so glad you'll be there."

9

Cleveland
and a
Cowboy

Damp, misty fog crept across the shore and fingered through the grass as I preflighted my Travel Air on August 28, 1931. Eager to be above it, I hurried my check and took off, headed west toward Springfield, Massachusetts. Excited by the thought of actually participating in the Cleveland Air Races, I was strangely detached from the scene below. Strings of fog snaked along creeks and rivers, ran together to cover the fields and obscure the ground, but I flew on. Fog, a fluffy white cotton comforter that draped over the landscape, began to billow and rise higher into the air. My OXX-6 throbbed rhythmically, but wispy clouds soon enveloped us and the ground ahead disappeared into a sea of white. I dropped to as low an altitude as I dared, straining to see the ground straight down beneath me. I could see nothing out front. I knew this part of the route and recognized a few landmarks, but my hands were as clammy as the creeping fog and my shoulder and neck muscles began to ache with tension.

Luckily, as I neared Springfield, the fog thinned. I recognized the field and brought my ship down for a landing. Relieved to be on the ground, I was also anxious to meet some of the local pilots to hear about preparations for the nationals. Springfield, home to the Granville Brothers, builders of the famous Gee Bee racing planes, had a large stake in the air races. I listened as pilots buzzed with talk of Lowell Bayles and his plans to speed a Gee Bee around the pylons of the Thompson Trophy Free-for-all Race—a ten-lap, 100-mile course. Bayles would race with seven other pilots, each in an airplane that differed greatly from the stubby, bullet-shaped Gee Bee.

A strong head wind slowed me, but I flew into Cleveland on August 30, thrilled to see the grandstands erected on one side of the huge field, the commercial traffic on the other. Guerd was at the field, apparently checking the pilot of every Travel Air that arrived until he found me. He grabbed me in a big bear hug and I hugged him back, comforted by his familiar smell and strong arms. I tore the helmet and goggles off of my head and we clung to one another with a long kiss.

"You can't know how glad I am to see you, Edna," he whispered, his mouth close to my ear, his nose buried in my hair.

After a few moments, I pulled back and smiled. "And what do you think of the Travel Air? This is the first you've had a chance to see it. I've been so eager to show it to you."

"I'll look that over later. Surely you know that the person flying the airplane is of much greater interest to me. That's no surprise, is it?"

"No. That's no surprise. Feeling's mutual, Mr. Brocksom." We hugged again and I asked, "Have you a car? Can we drive over to the other side and see what's going on at the grandstands?"

We both were entranced by the races. I told Guerd about stopping in Springfield, so we kept our eyes on Bayles and the Gee Bee, which was to become notorious. We saw Jimmy Doolittle touch down in Matty Laird's *Super Solution*. He'd raced from California, won the Bendix Trophy cross-country race as the first to land at Cleveland, then refueled and taken off for Newark, New Jersey, hoping to beat the record set by Frank Hawkes for the fastest time across the United States. Doolittle broke the record by better than an hour, covered 2,450 miles in eleven and a quarter hours, then returned to Cleveland to race the *Super Solution* in the Thompson.

"Look, Guerd," I exclaimed during the closed-course Thompson race, "Doolittle's trailing smoke. He's in trouble!"

When we found out after the race that a piston had broken and Doolittle had to get down out of the sky and out of the race, Guerd said, "He probably flew across the country and back again with the throttle wide open!"

Lowell and the Gee Bee were behind Doolittle until the engine blew in Doolittle's monoplane. Bayles's chunky Gee Bee had just rolled out of the factory two weeks prior to the races and they won at an average speed of 236 miles an hour. We had no way of knowing then that Bayles would be killed in a fiery crash of the Model Z Gee Bee in December. He hadn't long to savor his thrill of victory.

Guerd smiled down at me, hugged me, and said, "I can't believe that you are here to compete in the National Air Races with your license less than four months old, Edna. You really are something."

"Hm," I retorted with a grin, "didn't someone call me a ..."

"Yes, Fred called you a spark plug. He's right!"

"Hell, I wouldn't miss this. Just think of the famous people here—the top civilian and military pilots of our *nation*. We'll rub shoulders with them, Guerd. Let's taxi the Travel Air to park it with the other airplanes in the air show. We'll be right out there in the midst of it all. We might even get our names in the papers."

Guerd wasn't as interested in the limelight as I, but we were eager to become reacquainted, happy to be together. We shared the rest of the day. The next morning, as he kissed me he said, "Well, I guess we're here to work. I'll check your bird. Do you have a jumper assigned to you?"

"Yes, the Parachute Company gave me a "Cowboy" LaPierre. Jumpers are supposed to be on the program each day at one and at six o'clock. Let's go to the Air Race Office. Perhaps Cliff or Phil Henderson will show us where to find him."

Guerd and I walked, our arms around each other. I'd almost forgotten the smell of his aftershave, his throaty, sexy laugh, and the enticing depths of his dark brown eyes. "Guerd, there must be hundreds of thousands of people here. Isn't this great?"

Cowboy LaPierre was at the office looking for his pilot as we were looking for him. A hard-looking man, he might have slept in his crumpled black slacks and dingy white shirt—and his scuffed boots, for that matter. He'd slung a creased leather jacket over his shoulder and even heels on his heavy boots failed to bring him up to my height. Undoubtedly he'd spent a lifetime defending his slight stature. He wore a glowering look that challenged all comers. Several days' growth of beard stubbled his chin and his eyes were narrow, suspicious slits.

"Which airplane is yours, lady?" he asked tersely.

"I've a Travel Air 2000. Have you jumped from one of those before?"

"Sure I have," he bragged. "If there's an airplane made, I've jumped from it. But, how about you, lady? Do you really know how to fly the damn thing? I don't climb on the wing with just anybody, you know."

"I know how to fly it, Mr. LaPierre," I bristled. "I got it here from Newport, Rhode Island, didn't I?"

"I'll vouch for her," Guerd added. "I was the one who taught her to fly."

"I don't have to be vouched for, Guerd. I . . ."

"Lady, let me see your airplane. I want to show you how I do this jump before we go. Have you hauled a jumper before?"

I was irritated at Guerd and defensive toward LaPierre. I frowned at both of them in turn and said, tensely, "Don't worry, Cowboy. I'll get you up to the right height and over the right spot. Your job is to maneuver into the inner one of the painted circles in front of that enormous crowd. Your job is to make some money for us. That will make the trip to the Cleveland Air Races worth it for you as well as for me."

"Good luck," Guerd called to us as we strode toward the Travel Air.

"I'll check the surface wind until we take off," said LaPierre. "Then, as we climb, I'll drop strips of crapper tissue to see the drift of the wind as we climb higher and higher. I'll climb out of the front cockpit onto the wing and I'll direct you. If I yell, 'Left,' then I damn well expect you to get us to the left right away. Got that? And don't dump me off no wing. I'll go when I'm damned good and ready."

It was heady to taxi for takeoff in front of the huge crowd, to know that hundreds of thousands of eyes were watching. The crowd was boisterous. The excitement was contagious. I climbed the Travel Air up above the field in lazy circles and finally Cowboy LaPierre started to climb out onto the lower wing. I'd no idea that the ship would swerve with his weight. Much later I learned that the drag of a human on the wing was equal to that of carrying another airplane around. When he stepped into the slipstream of the prop, the wind slapped his body, the ship veered, and I slammed a rudder—an automatic reaction. I grappled with the controls and banged one rudder after another in an effort to control the ship. My legs shook.

"Right!" Cowboy yelled. Then he turned to stare at me, his mouth grim, his eyes wild behind his goggles. "Damn it! Get *with* it! Get this damned thing to the right, under control!" He yelled again, "More right! There, hold it. Cut!"

I pulled the throttle hastily and pushed the nose forward to keep the Travel Air from shuddering, buffeting, or, worse, stalling and pitching. LaPierre dove from the wing. As he kicked off, the airplane veered away from his push. I caught it and breathed a sigh of relief to have him away. Relaxed at last, I circled lazily to watch his triangular chute billow. He directed his drop, guided his direction and, with enormous skill, landed very close to the inner circle painted upon the ground.

"Yes!" I exulted. I could scarcely wait to get to the ground to congratulate him. I mentally began to calculate the amount of money that he was winning for the two of us. I was excited. I was also challenged to bring the ship down in front of the crowd, to land right along with famous aviators like Jimmy Doolittle and Roscoe Turner.

On September 4, I asked Guerd, "Would you carry LaPierre today? I'd love to watch just once. I'll climb to the top of the grandstand and get some idea of what the parachute jump looks like from the crowd."

As I found a seat in the stands, the free-for-all for female pilots was announced. I watched, my heart pounding. Florence Klingensmith, who once sold an airplane to Guerd, raced in a Lambert Monocoupe against Mary Haizlip in a Davis, Phoebe Omlie in a Warner Monocoupe, and Gladys O'Donnell in a Waco. From Springfield, Massachusetts, and the Tait family who sponsored much of the work of the Granville Brothers, Maude Tait raced in, what else? A Warner Gee Bee. Filled with envy, I didn't have to be a genius to realize that a woman could compete if she had money or if she *knew* someone or if she slept with or married a race pilot. Betty Lund was married to racer Freddie Lund, and Mary Haizlip was taught to fly by her husband—the small, competitive, banty rooster of a man, Jimmy Haizlip.

After the women's race I watched Jimmy Haizlip battle it out to take first place from the six-time winner in '31, Johnny Livingston. Haizlip must have loved that! The crowd roared. It was Johnny Livingston's brother, "Bite" Livingston, who gave me a good tip that I stored away in my head for the races that I would run. He told me that Johnny watched the *arm* of the man with the starting flag while he sat in the cockpit, engine revved to full fury for the horserace start. When the starter's arm sliced down, Johnny watched the arm muscles, not the flag. With the first twitch of a muscle, Johnny gave it the gun. He was always the first around the scatter pylon, the first with a jump on the other racers! How I wished Guerd would catch the racing fever. He could help me get a competitive racer.

Guerd was climbing high with Cowboy LaPierre in the passenger seat of my Travel Air. I watched the smooth takeoff and wondered, enviously, if I kept my wings as level, made the craft perform so smoothly and with such apparent ease.

The Travel Air climbed, circling into the wind, staying directly above the drop zone. I squinted and finally saw a tiny figure leap from the wing and grow larger, his triangle opening over his head. Cowboy LaPierre landed smack dab in the inner circle and I jumped to my feet, cheering. I watched until he waved a fist high above his head to acknowledge the cheering crowd, then I glanced up, expecting to see Guerd bring the Travel Air in for a landing.

But Guerd and the Travel Air were nowhere to be seen. I frowned, cupped a hand to shade my eyes and scanned the sky, searching every direction. Where were they? In my concentration on Cowboy LaPierre, I'd lost sight of the Travel Air. It and Guerd had disappeared completely.

My perch high in the grandstands allowed me a view of the entire area—the racers and their swift ships, the acrobatic aerial performers and airplanes using Cleveland's commercial runway a mile away across the field. An earlier rain had left the ordinarily dusty field a darkened brown, dotted with puddles. Gray, leaden skies formed by an overcast of clouds dulled the sun, but would have presented no danger to Guerd. Private airplanes were pushed nose to tail. Mud-spattered automobiles were parked in seemingly endless rows, but Guerd and the Travel Air were gone.

I turned to the man standing beside me in the stands. "Did you see the airplane that last jumper left?"

The man shook his head, his attention on the next event, the next air race.

What could have happened? My stomach knotted. I stared at knots of people clustered around each of the racing planes. Engines screamed at high power as racers rounded the turns of the race course and others competed from their static test sites on the ground. The field buzzed with action and roared with competition.

"What the hell?" I cried out loud, pushing my way down

through the crowd, stepping from one bleacher to the next. "Excuse me. Please let me out. Please..."

As I climbed down out of the grandstand, famous race pilots Johnny Livingston, Steve Wittman, Art Chester, Benny Howard, and Jimmy Wedell zipped past, low, very close to the ground and dangerously close to one another like so many bats loosed out of hell. The noise and the flurry were magnetic, the excitement contagious. The crowd watched, mouths agape. I interrupted their concentration as I pushed between people one after another. Guerd! Where was *he?* Could he possibly have lost control of the Travel Air and crashed? Oh God! What if Guerd crashed?

I felt helpless and drained by the time the racing was over for the day. Who could I turn to? Who could I ask? Pilots and their crews still worked feverishly over the airplanes in the pits, some engines still growled, but the grandstands quieted and emptied, the crowd had gone home. Twilight washed the field with dusky pink when I finally saw my Travel Air splash through a mud puddle to a landing.

"Guerd!" I yelled aloud, running toward the still taxiing airplane. Any panic over his safety vanished and my feelings vacillated between curiosity and fury. I could scarcely wait to hear the whole story.

"Guerd! What happened to you? Where have you been?"

In his easy way, Guerd slid out of the cockpit and shook his head. "Didn't we check this Travel Air over thoroughly this morning?" Laughter lines edged his eyes as he smiled, but his eyes reflected his weariness and his coveralls were filthy. He reached to hug me.

I pulled back. "Just a damned minute. You've been gone all day. We missed the 6 P.M. parachute drop. That costs money. Tell me where you've been and what's been going on?"

"I'm afraid the money lost on the jump isn't the total expense of the day, Edna," Guerd said, leaning back against the fuselage. His eyes were tired. "I spent the entire afternoon and evening in a field about five miles from here trying to repair a broken fuel line. The engine quit immediately after LaPierre left me for the jump and, luckily, I not only found a grassy patch that would let me in, but it was big enough so that I could get out again."

"A broken fuel line? How did you fix it?"

A slow grin spread across Guerd's face. He drew a cigarette from his chest pocket, lit it, and exhaled the smoke with a steady breath. "You'd never guess," he taunted.

"Well?"

"I got a fellow to give me a chunk of rubber tubing from his whiskey still."

"Oh you did, did you? And you probably told him that you needed to test the quality of his sauce, too."

"You know me better than that, Edna." He squinted as smoke curled out of his lips. "I knew you wanted LaPierre to jump again today. I also knew that I'd better get the ship back here for tomorrow or I'd have hell to pay. I did my best, but I'm afraid it's a makeshift job. You'll have to get a repair shop to use proper clamps. I could only scare up baling wire. I was fortunate to land *period*—not to mention find someone who'd admit to having a whiskey still and the narrow rubber tubing. What if they thought I was a Fed? I think I was pretty lucky." As he dragged on the cigarette, the glow from the tip deepened the shadows of his already deep, dark eyes.

"I'm sorry, Guerd. I didn't mean to doubt you. I have been stuck here all day long, not knowing where you were, not knowing if you were all right, not knowing about the airplane . . ." I put my arms around his neck and pressed close to him.

"That's my girl," he said as he kissed me. "Let's get some rest. We'll have to take the Travel Air across the field to a shop tomorrow morning bright and early." His arms tightened around me. It was good to be near him, to be wanted, to be held.

In the morning, I taxied the Travel Air to Sunny Sundorph's shop on the east side of the field. They agreed to fix the broken fuel line, although a mechanic laughed and said, "Where'd you get the fancy rubber tubing? That's at a premium in these dry days." I was relieved that Sunny would wait for payment until Cowboy LaPierre shared the money that he and I were earning together.

I dropped the Cowboy another several times and grew more excited each time. He was landing within the circle—in the money—every time. He was a good jumper, if not necessarily a good man.

On the last day of the races, Sunny Sundorph asked, "Edna, have you any of the money that you owe me? Your bill is pretty hefty."

"I'll ask my jumper, Sunny."

When confronted, Cowboy LaPierre said, "As soon as we finish the last jump, you come to the office at the north end of the grandstand. When the Hendersons pay up, I'll give half of it to you."

The races wound to a finish. I hauled Cowboy LaPierre up for the final six o'clock jump. The skies were clear, cleaned by the recent rain. Lake Erie sparkled with tiny dewdrops of late afternoon sunlight on choppy little waves. The blue Rocky River wove beneath us and the sun glinted from windows of Cleveland's buildings ten miles to the east. Just below, what appeared to be half of the *world* jammed the grandstands and all had their eyes skyward.

LaPierre was masterful. He dove toward the circles like an eagle dives for his prey. Streaming straight toward the smallest circle, he'd rake in a lot of money for us. I'd be able to pay my bill with Sunny Sundorph. I'd be able to pay for the fuel for my return trip to Newport. I'd even have some money left over. That'd be great!

Cowboy beat me to the ground, as usual, and I circled down, aligning the Travel Air for a landing. I felt like part of the air show as sparks flickered back out of the long exhaust stacks, diverted away from me in the cockpit, but decorating my landing.

I taxied my airplane to the parking area at the far south end of the grandstand, away from the air show airplanes and fancy racers. By the time I'd shut down and chocked the wheels, the crowd was beginning to filter out. I ran under the grandstand, kicking aside the gum wrappers and bottles, and wove through paper trash that still fluttered around my head like so much confetti.

At the office, I looked around. No Cowboy LaPierre. "Where's Cowboy LaPierre?" I asked. "He was my jumper. He told me to meet him here."

Other jumpers and some of the race pilots were crowding in the door, lining up for their pay. Cliff Henderson looked up from his desk, holding his finger on his place in the large ledger in front of him. He shrugged his shoulders and said, "Cowboy LaPierre? He's gone. He was paid off about a half hour ago. There's no telling where you'd find him now."

I balled my hands into fists. "Gone? Damn!" I shouted. I wanted to pound on the desk. "He cheated me! He owed me half of whatever you paid him. What kind of a setup is this? Why do you give all of the money to the jumper and give him a chance to get away without paying the pilot? The pilot pays for the fuel!"

Someone in the crowd jostled me. "Hey, lady, you're holding up the line. We want to get paid ourselves," called one.

"That's what you get for thinking you can be a pilot, lady," jeered another.

"Yeah. If you'd had any sense, you'd have been the first one in here instead of letting the Cowboy get the jump on you. That's a pun, lady."

Someone yelled, "Take it like a man," and the crowd laughed. I stomped out in fury.

One glimpse of Guerd and my anger dissolved in a flood of tears. I had to say good-bye to him and think about flying east. I had to face Sunny Sundorph and admit that I hadn't a dime. I buried my head in Guerd's shoulder and cried. He tightened his arms around me. We stood without speaking. He was my trusted friend, my lover. He would have helped me if he could, but neither of us had the money to bail me out of this mess. I felt spent and drained, bitter and powerless. Anger began to replace the tears once again.

"Men are hateful, Guerd."

"I hope you don't mean all men," he said gently, cupping my chin in his hands. "Get a grip on your feelings, Edna. It won't do to be upset. I'd like to see you get started before you run into darkness at the other end. You've a long flight ahead of you and you shouldn't fly when you feel so angry."

"I'll run out of fuel before I run into darkness," I said, bitterly.

I kissed Guerd good-bye again and turned to climb into the Travel Air.

"We haven't had a chance to talk about the future, Edna," Guerd started, hesitantly. "Obviously, this isn't a good time...."

"No, it's a lousy time. I'll drop you a line from Newport."

"Good flying, Edna. Let me know that you've arrived safely, will you? I do care...a lot."

I taxied the Travel Air to Sunny Sundorph's, dreading telling him the truth. I rehearsed a few stories on the way, then simply blurted, "My jumper ran out on me, Sunny. He collected from the Hendersons, but he never paid me a dime. I'm sorry, but now I don't have any money to pay you."

Sundorph was congenial and gracious. "Don't worry, Edna. You go back to the hospital in, where is it, Newport, Rhode Island? Just send me money every month until your bill is paid."

I shook my head and looked down at my shoes. "He left me high and dry. I don't even have enough money to buy fuel to *get* to Newport, Rhode Island."

"I guess I'll have to stake you to that, too," Sunny said with a laugh. "Okay, pretty brown eyes. I'll tell you what. You take this money for fuel, I'll add it to your bill, and, then, can you send me something each month until...?"

"Until the bill is paid in full. Oh yes, I promise. And, I don't know how to thank you enough." I stood on my tiptoes to give Sunny a kiss on the cheek. I shook his hand and then, on an impulse, threw my arms around his neck and kissed him again.

I left as fast as I could get fueled for the trip. I headed for Springfield and the Barrington Mountains. The airplane hummed like a champ until we'd crossed the timbered foothills of the Barringtons and then, suddenly the needle on the tachometer gauge started dropping. The gauge, indicating the revolutions per minute of the propeller, dropped to zero although it was obvious that the fan was still out there turning.

Below, the tree-covered terrain was rugged, strewn with boulders—certainly not a good place to land. My stomach clutched and I stiffened. My hand tightened on the stick. I hung on every beat of the engine, every hiccup, every cough. It ran smoothly, yet I was edgy, waiting for it to quit. I finally found a grassy field that was long enough for a landing and a takeoff. I put her down, bouncing *hard!* The engine began to pop like a machine gun.

I gave her the gun a few times, listened to the pop-pop-popping. It *ran,* although the needle was still pegged on zero. I decided to push for home. After takeoff, the ruckus began to make me laugh. I flew to the next airfield where I could take on fuel and, like a World War I fighter pilot, clattered around the field shooting at an invisible enemy before landing and shutting her down. I hadn't enough money for a mechanic, so I simply filled the tank with fuel and headed for Newport.

The engine pop-pop-popped as I circled the field in Newport. Prolonging the fun, I grinned as I gunned at every imaginary Fokker or Sopwith Camel. When I landed, I "strafed" the field with the loud belches.

Clarence "Sonny" Nelson, our Newport engine man, took a look at the OXX-6 and found a cracked intake pipe and a broken tachometer cable.

"So what's new, Sonny?" I said wearily. "I arrived home here in Newport owing repair money and a borrowed loan to another 'Sonny,' Sunny Sundorph. Now I have to beg you to trust me for any repairs that you make."

"Did you like the Cleveland National Air Races, Edna?" he asked. "How did you do with a jumper?"

"The races were great. The jumper? An absolute louse. Instead of making expenses or, heaven forbid, making a little *profit,* I *owe* money to everyone on God's green earth, including you."

"Don't worry, Edna. You're good for it. Besides, I've got your airplane for collateral, don't I?"

It was time to get back to nursing and to park my airplane for a while. I could *earn* as a nurse. I *spent* money with aviation— a *lot* of money! I returned to nursing with a vengeance and hoarded all that I could from my paycheck. Most went directly to a monthly payment to Sundorph Aviation. When that dun was met there were payments to Sonny Nelson.

I received an invitation to attend a meeting of female pilots, Ninety-Nines, in Providence and I went—by car. That 1931 meeting was presided over by Amelia Earhart. It was held at the home of Louise Sisson in Rhode Island's capital city—the same year that Amelia astonished the country with the admission that she would marry George Palmer "Gippy" Putnam, her aggressive promoter.

Publisher G. P. Putnam, who profitted from publishing Lindbergh's *WE* and Admiral Byrd's *Skyward,* searched for a female pilot to exploit, one who would write about having been the first woman to fly across the Atlantic. Putnam made money and Amelia skyrocketed to fame in 1928 after the flight of the *Friendship,* the first of his many promotional schemes, but she was embarassed by the fuss made over her. She readily admitted that, although she held a pilot's license, she never touched the controls of the *Friendship.* She crossed as a passenger. She was quoted as saying, "When a great adventure's offered, you don't refuse it."

Amelia was then and continues to be the most widely known, most beloved woman pilot of the United States. A gracious, lovely lady, she more than vindicated herself in '32 with her outstanding solo success across the Atlantic and she tirelessly spoke on behalf of female pilots. After having met her, I looked forward to seeing her again.

I wrote to Guerd about meeting Amelia Earhart and the organization of women pilots, the Ninety-Nines. I told him that I had met Anne Morrow Lindbergh, that her Bird was hangared near my Travel Air. I told him, too, of the beautiful fall foliage of New England—the crimson, bronze, yellow, and gold that decorated the valleys and painted the mountainsides. When I discovered that they were looking for an instructor at Colonel Green's airport where the Travel Air was hangared, I wrote, "Please think about moving to Newport, Guerd. They want you to be an instructor of flying students and I have bragged about how good you are—in more ways than one."

10

Newport
and a
Fairchild

I 've over one hundred flying hours now," I wrote to Guerd. "I keep reading about lady pilots setting records at inside loops, outside loops, and rolls. I wish you would come east to fly with me, to teach me more. I really wish you were here."

Guerd answered my letters with good news. "I'll move east in January, Edna. Here's to 1932!"

Guerd arrived, bag and baggage. We rejoiced to be together again and we became inseparable in the hours that I wasn't nursing. He quickly made friends at Colonel Green's airport.

As his reputation as a pilot grew, Guerd was surprised to see Charles Lindbergh approach him. It was during the tragic days between the kidnapping of the Lindberghs' son and the discovery of the terrible reality of the child's murder.

"I have been told that my son might be a captive on a ship

off the coast of Newport," Lindbergh told Guerd. "Will you fly an observer who represents me?"

"I'm quite new in the area, sir," said Guerd. "If your man is familiar with the coastline, I would be happy to pilot him. I'd like to do whatever possible to help you find your son. We're so sor—"

Lindbergh nodded curtly, interrupting the conversation. He knew that people cared. He knew, too, an indescribable powerlessness. The anguish of the long vigil had etched dark circles under his eyes. His coat covered a rumpled suit and his hair was unruly as if he'd repeatedly run his fingers through it. Fame carried too dear a price—far too dear.

"My wife, Anne, is pregnant and unable to fly at this time or we would make the flight ourselves. We find activity to be essential. Take my observer in her Bird. See if you can establish contact with the ship."

"Do you know the type of ship or the size of it?"

"No. The message was sketchy, but we are following every lead. I've very little information, but I won't give up hope. It is discouraging when there is no reason to believe that this is any more accurate than any false leads we've followed. It has been two months. . . ." his voice trailed off.

Guerd flew Anne's silver and blue Kinner-powered Bird to search fruitlessly. Small ships are all but lost in the vast expanse of Atlantic Ocean off the coast of Aquidneck Island. It was May 1932, and almost simultaneously with Guerd's piloting of the Lindbergh biplane the tragic chapter ended when the child's body was found in a shallow grave in the woods near the family home.

Another chapter soon ended, too. Guerd had taken on several students between January and May of 1932 when Colonel Green abruptly decided to close the airfield.

"Edna," Guerd suggested. "The Vanderbilts own the grass field in Newport at Coddington Cove where we've landed so many times. What would you think of running that airfield together?"

"Do you suppose they'd let us operate it? That sounds like a great idea."

"I've done a little checking and there's a man named Dick Adams at Newport Realty Trust who handles the property for the Vanderbilt family. Let's talk with him and see if we can strike a deal."

The field lay on the west coast of the island edged by Narragansett Bay. There was only a small shack and a gas pump on the property, but Guerd and I grew more excited by the day.

"We don't need to have money change hands," Dick Adams told us, "But we'd consider it good business to have gas kept in the pump and an operator on the field."

"Yes!" I agreed. "Guerd, we're in *business!*"

"Luckily it is early summer," he said. "I am sure that will be the only time an airfield can turn a profit in Newport. We'll have to hump during summer's warmer weather and longer days to scavenge a flying trade..."

"...when high-society people have wealthy summer visitors," I finished.

"I'll live in the shack," Guerd offered. "We can fix it up a little bit and have an office as well. But, do you know another thing I really want to do? I want you to sell your Travel Air and buy a Velie Monocoupe. I saw one for sale on Long Island last week."

"Damn, Guerd. You've been thinking about this without telling me, haven't you? And now you want *me* to sell *my* airplane. That's real nervy of you."

"You remember Ollie Cole, don't you? The slender, brown-haired fellow that I was flying with at Round Hill? Ollie promised to put in some money with us to buy the airplane. Russ Simpson on Long Island picked the Monocoupe up in Brazil. It's a good one—has good buckboard gear—and it would be a smart move."

"My Travel Air isn't even all paid for yet. Why do you want me to sell it?"

"We want to build up flying students and sightseeing rides, don't we? How many sightseeing rides could we sell during the cold weather with that open cockpit Travel Air? Ollie..."

"Wait a damn minute! Are you talking about taking Ollie Cole in with us as partners on the airfield?"

"No, just on the Velie Monocoupe. I'll talk to him. He may not like the idea of sharing the cost of the airplane and not having a say in the management of the field. That might make him a bit owlly."

"Splitting it three ways sounds risky to me."

Guerd continued patiently, "Well, perhaps we'll swing the deal ourselves—buy the Monocoupe and manage the field. What do you say?"

"Well, I'm tied to sutures, needles, and bedpans. I can't quit nursing, so you're the one who'll operate the field. We'll need my salary, but it won't go very far."

"It'll help a lot. I'll operate the field, you stick with the nursing, and fly when your schedule permits. We'll cooperate with the owning of the airplane and its costs. If we start to turn a profit, we'll buy another airplane. I've got my eyes on a Curtiss Robin in a hangar in Charleston. I hear it has logged very few flying hours on its engine. We can both hop passengers and teach flying. Is that a deal?"

"Now you're beginning to talk some sense. A profit's easier with fewer people. You've got yourself a partner, Guerd."

One morning, after we'd been managing the airfield at Newport for a while, Guerd drew me to him and held me close. "Are you interested in negotiating the partnership further?" He kissed my throat, my cheek, my mouth.

"I'm learning to love you, my sweet teacher," I told him, encircling his neck with my arms. "I guess you know I think you're wonderful. Do you suppose all girls fall for their instructors the way I'm falling for you?"

"I haven't kissed and held very many of my girl students, so I don't know the answer to that."

"That's no answer. You never *had* any other girl students." I pushed him away playfully, then I frowned. "But, while we're on the subject, I sure resent that rich bitch that keeps riding her horse out here to see you."

"Hey, do I detect a green-eyed monster lurking behind your beautiful brown eyes?" Guerd's eyes twinkled with amusement. "She's not a student...yet."

"Miss Hoity-Toity prances around out here and her fool horse digs monstrous holes with its hooves, then drops its crap in bilious piles all over the place."

"She's got a name, Edna—Lorette Robson. It doesn't hurt to be friendly with her. She's worth a cool three million, you know."

"That's what I said, a rich bitch. When she isn't prancing around on that animal making eyes at you, she's cruising up in her classy Buick convertible with the top down and her snares out. You can't fool me. I know you two have been flying together."

"Who's trying to fool you? How many times do I have to tell you that I haven't eyes for anyone else but you? I'll fly with anyone who pays money for the privilege. That's what we're in business to do here, isn't it? I do like a customer with money and she has *money*. But you know? She seems happy to simply fly around. She doesn't want to be a pilot."

"God, men are such fools! How blind can you be? She wants you, Guerd. Can't you tell when a woman's in heat? Speak of the devil. Here comes Miss Fancy Pants and her Buick right now. I'm going to put some gas in the Monocoupe—anything to avoid *her*."

I gassed the Monocoupe, then found some valves that Guerd had set out as a project in the shack. I pretended to be well engrossed in wiping them and checking the O-rings, staying well clear while Lorette flirted with Guerd, but I steamed. Guerd might *say* he only had eyes for me, but how much temptation could he take? And she was worth three million? I couldn't even think in such terms. It was mind-boggling...and infuriating.

When the two of them climbed into an airplane and took off for a flight, I was the one who couldn't resist a temptation. From the piles of dried horse manure deposited around the shack, I gathered several lumps and shoved them into her Buick's gas tank. With a smirk of satisfaction, I dusted my hands together. That'd fix her. She'd never know what ailed her fancy rig. I left in my own roadster for the hospital.

The next day, a Saturday, grounded by a swirling mist of coastal fog, we turned to some of the maintenance projects that Guerd had started. I perked some coffee and, when we retackled the valve job, we sat shoulder to shoulder on stools pulled up to the workbench in the shack, both dressed in somewhat grimy white coveralls, cups of steaming coffee beside us. We set to work actually wiping the valves that he had ground, which I'd merely fingered the day before. Guerd told me that he'd had to take the gas tank out of Lorette's car. "She had a terrible time getting her car started and then it wouldn't run worth a damn," he said. He looked at me quizzically.

"Oh?" I feigned innocence.

"You wouldn't know anything about it, would you, Edna?"

"Me? Why would I know anything about the bitch's Buick?"

"Well." Now Guerd could hardly keep a straight face. "It does seem odd that there was horse crap in her gas tank. *Somebody* had to put it in there, don't you think?"

Ollie Cole opened the door of the shack. "Hello in there," he called.

"Good timing, Ollie," I said, with a smile. "Do you suppose the fog will lift soon?"

"Good timing? Am I interrupting you two?" His grin was wicked.

Guerd laughed. "No, darn it."

"The fog is interrupting us, Ollie," I told him. "Want to fly? I bet we could climb through it. It'll be sunny on top."

"No, I'm no hero. I prefer to fly when I've a glimpse of the ground, some idea of rightside-up. I came to show you an article from the paper, Edna." He handed me a clipping. "They are looking for a nurse who is a pilot, a Flying Nurse, to fly the same Bellanca that Clyde Pangborn and Hugh Herndon flew across the Pacific last year. They're planning a medical flight across the Atlantic Ocean. They want the nurse to be a copilot and, listen to this—the pièce de résistance will be to have her parachute down in Italy at the end of the flight. Are you interested?"

"Am I interested? That sounds fantastic!" The stool fell over as I jumped up. "Don't you think so, Guerd?" I looked at Guerd. He looked shocked and dismayed. I needn't have asked.

Characteristically, Guerd said nothing. He had called me impetuous more than once. Obviously, we'd have a lot to talk about tonight. When Guerd was opposed, he could be downright stubborn. Perhaps it didn't matter. We weren't engaged to be married or anything like that. On the other hand, he was my best friend and lover. Anything I did with an airplane was done better with Guerd's help and expertise. I might have to win him over.

I contacted Dr. Leon M. Pisculli, the doctor who would be the medical observer and arranged for an interview. Guerd reluctantly agreed to fly with me to Long Island, New York.

"At least we can listen to the plans for the flight, Guerd," I pleaded. "Just think. They've renamed the Bellanca from *Miss Veedol* to *The American Nurse*. Imagine the publicity that would come from such a venture! I can see the headlines now, "The American Flying Nurse crosses the Atlantic in the Bellanca that Pangborn and Herndon flew across the Pacific." Amelia Earhart herself said, 'When a great adventure's offered, you don't refuse it.'"

"All right, Edna. We can go listen to the man. But, I can't imagine the need for you to have to parachute out of the blasted airplane over Italy. That's just plain stupid."

"From what I understand, the purpose of the parachute jump is to commemorate Florence Nightingale's birth in Florence, Italy, more than a hundred years ago."

"And you don't believe that her birth can be equally well honored with a safe landing at an airfield? You've never parachuted in your life."

"I know that, but lots of women have. Look at Tiny Broadwick. She has plenty of parachute jumps to her credit."

"Then let *her* go in the Bellanca."

"Guerd, now you're being stupid. Tiny Broadwick is neither a nurse nor a pilot."

"Okay. Okay. Let's go see this Pisculli fellow and hear him out. But, don't expect me to be thrilled at the prospect of you, one, flying across the ocean and, two, jumping out of the airplane at the end of such a long, tiring flight."

"I can see you'll have a real open mind at this interview. You let me handle it, hear?"

Whenever we'd previously flown to Long Island, we generally skirted the coastline to cross to Fishers Island then island-hopped to Orient Point of Long Island. This time—to prove my daring?—we crossed more water. I aimed the Travel Air at Block Island and over the juncture where the waters of the Atlantic meet those of Long Island Sound. The fishtail-shaped tips of Long Island reached out into the wavy stretches of water and sunlight reflected from the tiny whitecaps that broke at the crest of each wave. Montauk Point slid beneath us with long white beaches. We crossed the sand dunes shaped and lapped by gentle Atlantic waves.

"See, Guerd?" I told him after we'd landed at Roosevelt Field. "En route to Rome, I'd simply be flying over a wider stretch of water than what we just covered. You can't pick up a paper these days without some mention of Amelia Earhart since she and her Vega safely soloed across the Atlantic last month. I could become as famous as Amelia."

"Or as dead as Nungesser and Coli," Guerd observed drily. "They tried to cross the Atlantic and haven't been seen since."

"Amelia and Charles Lindbergh *both* crossed the Atlantic and have been raised to hero status by the American people—thanks to publicity. Publicity is the fuel for the fire of fame, Guerd."

"Just don't let it consume you, Edna."

I clamped my mouth shut. Guerd didn't always get the last word, but this time I was quiet until we found Dr. Leon Pisculli. He told us that the proposed flight would be from New York to Rome and would carry a speaker on aviation medicine to the Academy of Medicine in Italy. He added, "William Ulrich will be the pilot-navigator, I will be the medical observer and you,

Miss Gardner, if selected, would be our copilot and medical observer, too. You have also heard of our plans to honor the memory of the great nurse, Florence Nightingale?"

"Yes, Dr. Pisculli," I answered, silencing Guerd with a quick glance. Then I smiled at Dr. Pisculli and added, "I've never made a parachute jump, but I can't see that as a problem. I'm sure I could do it. During the flight what type of medical observation would I be expected to do?"

"I envision a flying medical lab of sorts," answered Dr. Pisculli. "I want to experiment with pilot fatigue, carbon monoxide, blood pressure, use of strychnine for stimulating a pilot with fatigue, those sorts of things. I want to study the effects of long flights on pilot endurance. We will take some small laboratory animals along for tests. Have you a transport license?"

"No sir, but I would be happy to practice for the tests and get the license."

"I understand you are with the U. S. Navy. Could you get a leave of absence?"

"I'll check with the commander. They have been good about giving me time off to stunt airplanes in the Boston, Newport, and Providence areas and to drop a parachutist at the Cleveland National Air Races. This project sounds like something the U.S. Naval Hospital should support."

"Our research could be valuable," Dr. Pisculli added. "I believe I will check with naval brass in our nation's capital to see whether the government will allow you to travel from New York to Rome in the uniform of the U.S. Naval Nurse. That would add prestige to our project, don't you think?"

Guerd could stay silent no longer. He interrupted and asked, "Dr. Pisculli, what about the maintenance of the Bellanca? When Pangborn and Herndon crossed the Pacific, they arranged for the gear to drop off to lighten the drag of the ship. As I recall, Pangborn even had to climb out onto a wing strut to ensure that all of the parts were shed. Their landing in Wenatchee, Washington, was almost a disaster. With no gear, they belly-landed and the ship almost turned ass over teakettle."

I hadn't realized that Guerd knew anything about the *Miss*

Veedol. He never ceased to amaze me. I hadn't thought about the ship itself. I looked from Guerd to Dr. Pisculli, who answered, "You're right. Nine months ago Pangborn crash-landed the *Miss Veedol.* We've had mechanics working on all necessary repairs. I must admit that we are having difficulty at the present trying to get the rear fuel tank to feed."

Guerd turned to me. "Pangborn and Herndon had the airplane equipped with long-range tanks for that first flight from Japan to the United States, but having the gas aboard and getting it to the Wasp engine are two separate matters. Look at what happened to me in your Travel Air at the air races. There aren't any airfields for land planes between New York and Rome. And, while we're at it, did you see a whole helluva lot of publicity on the successful flight across the Pacific? The Orientals called Clyde 'Mr. Pan Bang,' which was a pretty astute name for him when you saw a picture of his belly landing. But, in our country, the flight went virtually unnoticed."

"They didn't have G. P. Putnam behind them." My voice was flat. I glared at Guerd. If he blew this for me, we'd be through.

Guerd turned to Dr. Pisculli again and continued, "Do you intend to drop the undercarriage in order to get all the way to Italy? And, if so, are you experienced at belly landings in airplanes that are generally equipped with wheels?"

He was ruining my interview. I ached for a chance at fame; this was my opportunity to *do* something. "We'll talk later," I hissed at him through clenched teeth.

I stood up and smiled at Dr. Pisculli, told him that I'd like to be the copilot in his venture. I fought for control of my temper and, in the most pleasant voice I could muster, promised, "I'll work toward my transport license," and said goodbye.

I stomped out to the Travel Air, shaking with anger. I had nothing to say to Guerd as we returned to Newport or for several days after. Men are such fools! Was this man going to keep me down, too? Did every man in my life have to shake my trust like a vicious dog with a rag in his mouth? All I wanted was a chance to *be* somebody.

Within two days, Dr. Pisculli telephoned me and said, "I'd like to invite you to be our 'American Nurse.' I believe we can forge a successful first for medicine," he said. Thrilled, I immediately planned a requested leave from the Navy, a month-long trip to New York then on to Rome. How exciting! I wondered if I should call the newspapers.

The next day Dr. Pisculli called again and told me that I would be required to *pay* for the privilege of being included in the flight. Why tell Guerd? I still fumed that he was so disapproving in the first place. I talked with my hospital patients, veterans who seemed to enjoy my tales of flight and flying. They generously raised a purse to help my project.

Dr. Pisculli called again a few days later. "Edna, I've been to Washington and have met with nothing but resistance. There is vehement objection to use of a military person in military garb engaging in any experiments or stunts. They refuse to give permission for you to make the parachute jump as well."

A government attorney and his wife took me to dinner. They reiterated the Navy's refusals and insisted that I either return to work at the naval hospital or resign from the Navy. The pressure was enormous to give up my golden opportunity. Dr. Pisculli dashed my hopes completely when he called to tell me that another nurse, oddly enough another Edna, had been selected to fly to Italy in "my" place. He said, "I'm sorry, Edna. We would have liked to welcome you aboard, but we have chosen Edna Newcomer to fly as copilot and have high hopes that she will do a creditable job." He added, "as we're certain you would have done," almost as an afterthought.

I was bitterly disappointed. "Let's fly to Waukegan and to Chatfield during your leave, Edna," Guerd suggested. "Perhaps some of your frustration . . ."

"Don't patronize me, Guerd. I'll go on a flight west, but you can bet that I'd rather be headed east in that Bellanca."

Guerd was quiet. It was becoming increasingly difficult to get rid of any anger that flushed over me when I was crossed or thwarted. It seemed like every man I knew wanted keep me down. Wisely, Guerd changed the subject. "Let's fly the Curtiss

Robin. We can visit my folks and your mother—have a vacation."

When we got back to Newport, Guerd was sensitive and unduly quiet when he held a newspaper toward me. He said softly, "You made the headlines in the Boston *Sunday Advertiser* after all, Edna. They say, 'Uncle Sam's "No" saves Navy Nurse from ill-fated flight from New York to Rome.'"

"Ill-fated?"

"Yes, my love. I'm lucky to still have you. The Bellanca carrying Pisculli, Ulrich, and Newcomer disappeared after nearing the Azores. It's gone—down in the Atlantic. I'm so glad that you weren't aboard." He read the article to me:

Miss Edna M. Gardner and Miss Edna Newcomer, two nurses with like first names were odd playthings of fate. Miss Gardner, well known to thousands of Massachusetts naval men as the 'Navy nurse,' had planned to fly the Atlantic on the ill-fated plane, American Nurse. But Uncle Sam stepped in and refused leave of absence to her. Her place was taken by Miss Newcomer. Yesterday the wreckage of the plane was seen off the Azores by sailors of a British steamer.

Guerd read another article aloud, by Rudy Arnold, the long-time official photographer of Floyd Bennett Field on Long Island. Arnold took photos of many persons who figured in aviation history and was the last to see Ulrich, Pisculli, and Newcomer alive. He wrote, "Miss Newcomer and the woodchuck, Tailwind, waved a rather pathetic farewell. Ulrich's minister wished him well and they disappeared into the eastern sky—forever."

"They must have made some dumb mistakes," I said. "I'll bet you anything, if I'd have been flying on that airplane it never would have crashed."

"I'm glad you have confidence in your flying ability, Edna, but you must realize that even the best pilot has no guarantees."

I earned my transport license in December, flying in a Monocoupe and also in the Bird airplane that Guerd and I completely rebuilt—a Bird with a sad fate. The Bird had a beat-up engine and the fabric covering was worn. We put a lot of effort into recovering it and rebuilding the engine. When we heard storm warnings for Newport, Guerd and I hastily dragged the Mono-coupe outdoors and tied it down. We put the Bird under cover, thinking the makeshift tee-hanger would offer it at least minimal protection. The wind howled. Rain pelted the roof and streamed across the window panes, driven by the wind. We huddled inside the shack in Guerd's living quarters until the storm was spent and, when the wind died down, we ventured outside. The Velie Monocoupe had strained her traces, but she was unscathed. The newly recovered Bird was a shambles. The hangar had been blown to bits by the wind, completely wrecking the airplane. We sold all the debris for a measly one hundred dollars.

"In the red for another month," I admitted dejectedly.

As if one mishap wasn't enough, Guerd was flying our Curtiss Wright Junior with a passenger in front of him and a pusher engine behind him—a three-cylinder Eagle. When it was all over, Guerd told me, "That engine put out too much power for its beef. It suddenly blew up. The throttle flew out of my hand and, honest to God, the engine wanted to jump off the mount! I couldn't reach the switch and I kept yelling for my passenger to shut off the switch! My hands were full trying to go straight ahead to the golf course. Cut the switch! Cut the switch!" I kept yelling and he finally did. We skidded to a stop and, sure enough, when we could look it over, it was a cylinder that had blown. Chunks of cylinder dented one of the steel longerons in the fuselage. Pieces also slammed into the throttle rod, snapped it right off! No wonder I had no control.

"I asked Sonny and a blacksmith to go out and weld the longeron while I flew another trip to Boston in another airplane. As I returned, I looked down at what I thought would be our Junior on the golf course and, Edna, there was nothing but a charred mess. Sonny and the blacksmith lit up a welding rod and the doped fabric burned like tinder. I'm not going to sell the skeleton, though. I think I'll rebuild it. That Junior has been fun to fly and I really like going duck hunting in it."

Guerd worked at a boiler factory during the winter and I, of course, stuck to nursing. The winter was death on flying—no rich customers and short, cold days. Even Lorette Robson stopped coming around. I heard she moved to Arizona or someplace. No skin off my nose.

We rebuilt the Curtiss Wright Junior and held the airfield together with our combined salaries and mutual efforts. By the following June, in 1933, I had about 250 flying hours, had stunted airplanes, taken passengers for hops over Newport, and tested my wings in a variety of airplanes; when I heard of an All Women's Air Race at Floyd Bennett Field, I was primed!

"The races are scheduled for June 4 and 5. I'll fly to Long Island, Guerd, race, and I'll be home at the end of the weekend. I wonder if the Robin is fast enough. Will you check the engine and help me get it to peak condition?"

With Guerd's tweaking, Robin NC 37H took me around the course for a fifth place in the race and I was hooked. "Guerd," I told him excitedly when I'd gotten back to Newport, "I'm going to enter every race that I can. That's more fun than anything I've ever done. I keep thinking about John Livingston, too. If I watch the starter's *arm* instead of his *flag*, perhaps I'll win as much as Livingston does. What a rush!"

"Did you win any money?"

"Not enough to pay for the fuel for the round-trip flight, but a little. That's not all bad. I'm bound to improve with experience. I'll start finishing in the money—the top three."

"Hey, don't be hard on yourself. Fifth place is good. It's great. But, be careful, my pretty. I'd hate to see you hurt . . . or worse."

"There will be a race and air show in Boston, Edna," Ollie Cole reported later that month.

"What dates, Ollie? I'll request leave from the Navy."

"The show is the fourteenth and fifteenth of July. I know of a fellow in Providence who owns a Fairchild 22. Would you want to borrow that?"

"Ollie! I'd love you forever if you could get that ship for me.

Do you suppose? Could we fly to Providence and talk with him, get me checked out?" I hugged Ollie around the neck.

Guerd watched us for a few minutes and then, in his quiet way, said drily, "And you didn't want me to fly with Lorette? Turnabout's fair play, though, is that it?" He winked at me. He was pretending to be miffed.

"You flew with Miss Rich Bitch anytime she wanted, so why can't I fly with Ollie? Especially with the chance to fly a Fairchild. That'd be great. Should I mention Miss Doris Burbridge, too? You certainly take notice when that lady appears out here at the field."

Guerd nodded. "You're absolutely right. I believe she's about the prettiest woman that ever looked my way. Can't deny that, I guess."

"See? Neither of us is ready to settle down yet, Guerd. I guess we've been trying to decide that for a while and haven't really faced it." Guerd and I stared at each other for a moment, then I quickly changed the subject. "Did I tell both of you that the Navy has issued me a parachute? The C.O. at Quonset Point Naval Station heard that a Navy nurse was stunting an airplane and decided that I should be protected. They've issued me a parachute and they'll pick it up and issue me a freshly packed one every thirty days. Isn't that great?"

I turned back to Ollie. "When could we go to Providence?"

Ollie laughed. "Let's go right now." As we started toward an airplane he turned to Guerd and asked, "Didn't you say that they used to call this lady a spark plug?"

"You don't have to tell me," said Guerd with a smile. "Why do you think I left Illinois to move to Rhode Island?"

Ollie and I flew to Providence and we worked out a deal to borrow the tandem, parasol-wing lightplane. I was checked out and proceeded to take it to altitude to practice some acrobatics and get a feel for the airplane. With its sleek fuselage and Warner Super-Scarab radial engine, I imagined that we sparkled like a firefly to the two men watching me from the ground as I tumbled the craft about in the sunshiny sky.

In mid-July 1933, I landed at Revere Beach in Boston to be

part of the weekend air show and festivities. Unlike Cleveland, this time I could park my airplane in front of the grandstand and feel proud to be a participant in the show and air races. I joined all of the fun—flour-bomb-dropping contests, acrobatics, and, the most fun of all, my first-place finish in a woman's air race.

In the air show, I rolled the airplane, did some steep flipper turns to stay directly in front of the hundreds of people in the grandstands, and then looped it three times. Wearing the Navy's parachute, snugged tightly into the cockpit, I finished my act by climbing high in front of the crowd. I chopped the throttle and kicked a rudder to spin the aircraft to the right. The craft spun well. Then it spun faster, still faster. I couldn't recover. What was the matter? I kicked the left rudder—hard. Slammed it against its stop. Nothing! The Fairchild spun around and around like a bullet shooting straight for the ground.

Oh God! I'll have to jump. It would be my only chance. I released the belt to pull myself up and forward. The craft nosed forward enough to break the stall. We recovered from the spin! I didn't have to jump—didn't have to lose this beautiful and *borrowed* airplane. Thank God!

The fright took its toll, though. As I skittered to a landing, my legs were rubbery and my hands shook. I touched the skittish airplane down, then whirled around and groundlooped to a stop.

People clustered around me and scolded, "Why in hell did you let that airplane keep spinning until you got so low?"

"You're crazy. Why didn't you stop spinning sooner? We thought you'd crash for sure!"

"My God, Edna, were you trying to prove that you are the most fearless pilot in the world?"

I wasn't trying to prove anything. Once the spins began, it was a matter of survival. The shift of not only my weight, but also the weight of that Navy parachute saved the Fairchild. Later I was asked several questions by the manufacturers, factory reps who traveled from Hagerstown, Maryland, to discover what I did to get into the spin and what happened that caused me so much trouble. A test pilot for a few anxious moments, I gave input so that subsequent 22s were given knife-edged additions to the wing leading edges, engineering that improved recovery techniques. I flew home to talk it all out with Guerd. He rejoiced with me in my air race win and my stunting. I told him the whole story of the prolonged spinning. He'd read about it in the papers anyway.

11

Disaster

at

Dayton

I logged flight time as an instructor pilot for the first time in August 1933. I'd hopped plenty of passengers, added almost three hundred flying hours, and tested every different airplane that I could con an owner into letting me fly. Newport itself, as well as our airfield, hummed with activity during the summer. Guerd and I put on air shows to draw even larger crowds. We taunted our engine man, Clarence "Sonny" Nelson, until he agreed to parachute jump for us. Guerd, the airfield manager, was in demand to speak to local groups, although he hated public speaking and was much happier to be in control of an airplane as an instructor and as a charter pilot.

Flight students began to ask for me as an instructor and I discovered that teaching was the best way to learn. I saw the common mistakes a fledgling pilot makes and quickly realized that a pilot who hasn't taught flying hasn't learned all there is to know. Later, Anna in *The King and I* would say, "When you become a teacher, by your pupils you'll be taught." As I explained flight, I began to understand.

I nagged Guerd repeatedly about publicity. "It can't *help* but further our flying business to have newspaper write-ups. How else will people be drawn to the airfield?" I insisted.

"It seems like bragging, Edna."

"Bragging, my foot. Would you go to the movies if you didn't know what was playing? We have to convince people to come out here and spend money learning to fly. If we let folks know about the contests and races that I'm entering and winning, they'll be excited. They'll think about flying, too."

In September of 1933 I won four first places at the Legion Air Meet in Springfield, Massachusetts, and my confidence soared. Naturally, I saw to it that it hit the Newport papers. Some aerial business came from the publicity. I was paid to "strafe" Newport's Third Beach looking for the body of a drowned person. I found nothing, but at least the public was beginning to discover uses for the airplane.

One day Ollie Cole showed me publicity for an aviation meet at Roosevelt Field. "Look, Edna. It says that the singer Kate Smith has put up five hundred dollars in trophy money for a women's air race."

"Five hundred dollars? Ollie, are you sure?"

"Read it for yourself," Ollie told me, holding out a flyer that announced the race to be held on October 8, 1933.

"Guerd! What kind of airplane can I scrounge? I want to be the winner. Can you get a line on something to borrow?"

Guerd found a Waco 10 that the owner agreed to let me fly. I hopped it around Newport a few times and then turned to Ollie and suggested, "Do you want to fly to Long Island with me and help me, Ollie?"

"What about Guerd?"

"The tourist season is over and he's back at the boiler factory and, anyway, someone has to mind the store. We'll never keep this airfield solvent if Guerd goes off everytime I do. Besides, I'd really like your company. What do you say?"

"Sure, Edna. I like the races."

"You like the airplanes and you like the ladies."

"So what's the matter with that? I'm just not sure you've got the order right." He grinned at me.

Ollie and I left Newport in the Waco 10. We flew over Fishers Island, watched Orient Point slip by below, and followed the fish tail of Long Island all the way to Roosevelt Field. Every inlet, stretch of beach, small town was familiar to me by this time. I landed and signed up to race in the Kate Smith Women's Race. There were about eighteen women competing in what thrilled me as a lineup of marvelous, modern, speedy airplanes.

Jacqueline Cochran was there. She had learned to fly in a short three-week period in 1933 and, with only forty or fifty hours of flying time, she was nervous about this, her first air racing.

"I'm scared to death," she admitted to several of us, huddled together in the shadow of one of the Roosevelt Field hangars. "I've never flown in a race before."

Each of us had a bit of advice for her, but not one of us wanted to see her win. We had our own interests at heart. We could be superficially cordial before we climbed into our airplanes, but once aboard with our seatbelts tightened, there were no holds barred.

Someone said, "Try to relax, Jackie. It won't do any good to build yourself up into a nervous wreck."

I added, "Pylon races are always flown in left-hand patterns. We race low, pass on the outside—to the right. If you go to the inside, you'll be disqualified."

"If not worse," muttered another, then said, "the spacing and overtaking are very critical. Stay away from everybody until you learn the ropes of pylon racing."

I finished, "Keep your eyes open and watch for the rough air behind other airplanes. But, you'll enjoy it once you've tried it. It's great fun!"

"Thanks," she said. "Well, here goes nothing."

"Good luck, Jackie," I said aloud, but, of course, I didn't want her to be lucky enough to beat me. I wanted to beat *every* lady pilot in the race—wanted to show all of them nothing but my tail. I went into every race determined to win. Why else would I be racing?

Ollie helped me tune the Waco 10 and, watching the arm of the starter, I was the first off, the first around the pylon. What a heady rush. There was no one ahead of me—no one at all. The ground blurred beneath me, the speed dizzying. I pinpointed each pylon out ahead and dove for it, rising slightly in the steep turn around it. As I circled, I sighted down the lower wing, then sliced down onto the short straightaways, always watching for the next pylon. There it was! The checkered flag! I glanced over my shoulder. I was first. I *won!* I climbed the Waco from the race course and wiped my sweaty palms, one after the other, along my thighs. My heart thumped in my chest. My legs trembled.

"I won! I won five hundred dollars," I screamed to Ollie, when he ran over, grinning widely at me after I'd landed.

I posed for photographs in front of the Waco 10, received the check from Kate Smith herself, and was filled with heady excitement, the adrenaline rush of winning. My picture was in the paper the next morning and I bought a few copies to take back to Newport with me. Guerd would be so proud of me. I knew he would. I'd have to send one to Mother, too. Perhaps even a report to the Chatfield paper.

Ollie and I took off early the next morning for Newport. In the cold dawn, mist poked inquisitive fingers along the ground. As we took off, fog thickened over Long Island. It snaked along creeks and inlets, rising above the marshes of the south shore. As we climbed, the sun climbed above us and, as if someone had pulled a fluffy cotton batting over the cold earth, fog obscured the ground. I could see a few church spires, a water tower or two, but as the clouds piled higher it became impossible to tell where the island lay and where the shoreline began. There was nothing to mark the land or the water of Long Island Sound or the Atlantic Ocean.

"We're in trouble, Ollie," I shouted to him. "We're in real trouble."

I wanted to press on. The skies above the fog provided better than adequate visibility, but, what if something happened? As Guerd had so often told me, stay where you know you have a safe place to land rather than pushing your luck and finding yourself stranded in an unknown place over unknown terrain. The Atlantic could be terrifyingly final in the case of an engine failure or a mistake. I'd heard about people getting disoriented in clouds and fog. Everyone knew of ships that had run aground. When visibility dropped to zero zero, you couldn't see the hand in front of your face, much less the hazards below.

"Ollie," I shouted again. "I'm going back. I'm going to see if I can find Roosevelt Field."

I turned the Waco around and headed toward what I believed was the center of Long Island, wishing I could see something familiar, wishing desperately that something would rise out of the white fluff to give me some clues.

"There it is!" I screamed at Ollie. "There's Mitchel Field!"

The orange-and-white-checkered tower of Mitchel Field loomed through the fleecy layer and I knew that Roosevelt Field was just south of that. I checked the sun to gain my bearings and ducked down into the dense soupy fog. As we crept lower and lower, the fog swirled around us. I remembered words of caution from pioneer aviatrix Katherine Stinson, who warned that, in dense cloud, you'd finally be unable to see even the wingtips of your craft. Fog was just that—a dense cloud resting on the cold earth.

Frightened, I pulled the nose up. "I don't dare dive any lower, Ollie," I yelled. If he had answered, I was unaware of it. All I could hear was the sound of the OX-5. At least that was still running. What would I do if...? Great Scott, Edna, I told myself. Don't make it any worse than it is!

"I'll pull up above the fog and try it again," I screamed. Was I talking to myself? It helped me come to grips to make my decisions aloud.

The Waco burst out of the white cotton fog blanket like a stunt motorcyclist bursts through a board wall—blasting out of the gray matter and scattering wisps in every direction. The sunlight was brilliant above, so brilliant that it hurt my eyes.

Once more, I pulled the power back and slowed the Waco to its slowest speed. I tentatively started down into the fog, reaching for the ground, hoping for sight of a familiar building or, most especially, the runway on Roosevelt Field. The lower the big craft crept, the harder my heart pounded, the louder the OX-5 roared in my ears. I couldn't stand it. I had no idea where the buildings were, where other airplanes were parked, where the runway or any portion of the grassy field could be found. I couldn't penetrate any lower. I yanked back on the stick and gave her the gun.

Up reared the nose of the craft. I could feel anxiety throughout my body, my back and shoulders tense and rigid—a stiffness in my arms, the tightness in my jaw and the shooting pains in my legs that told me that I was growing seriously close to panic. Again we plowed through the top of the murky white stuff, scattering sprays of it off of the propeller blades, slicing through it with the wings of the craft.

I leveled off the Waco and headed for a beacon in the soup, a round silver tower. "They can't build towers like that on the water," I yelled at Ollie. "We'll just circle here slowly until we run out of gas. Then, when we come down, at least we'll come down on land and not where we'd *drown!*"

We circled for about forty-five minutes. It seemed interminable. I peered first to the left, then to the right, straining for the sight of something that would give me a clue to the terrain below. When the engine finally quit, I braced myself, slowed to near stall and yelled, "Hold on, Ollie. We're going down!"

In the swishing silence, I talked the airplane down. "That's it, baby. Take it easy. Don't be in any hurry. You're gonna hit something, let's hit it as slow as we can. Take it easy, baby."

Whump! The left wing dropped, the nose sliced quickly down and the tail tried to throw itself over my shoulder. I was thrown, hard, against my seat belt. The airplane rocked up onto her nose, then settled slowly back down again.

"Ollie, are you all right? Answer me, Ollie. Tell me you're okay!" I yanked out of the seat belt, climbed free.

"I'm here, Spark Plug. I'm banged up some. I think you gave me a nosebleed, but, don't worry. I'm alive and going to live to fly again. It sounds as if you made it. Are you okay?"

"I'm not hurt. I'm just angry. Where do you suppose we are?" Out of the Waco, I rubbed some sore muscles. I was stiff and my back and shoulders ached.

From the dense, swirling fog, we heard a man's voice. "Yoo hoo?" called the voice. "Yoo hoo, can you hear me?"

"Over here," I hollered back. "We're over here."

"Keep hollering," said the man again. "Are you hurt?"

Ollie answered this time, "We're okay. We're damned lucky. I've nothing broken, anyway. Right, Edna?"

"Some aches and pains, but no broken bones, Ollie."

The man's voice said, "I'm trying to find you," just as a dark figure emerged slowly from the mist. He wore a dark suit with brass buttons. A policeman!

"I heard your engine," he explained. "You kept flying around and around and around. I knew that if I waited long enough, I could try to help..."

"You knew that if you waited long enough we'd eventually come down," I said, glumly. "What goes up has to come down, dammit. It would have been a helluva sight better to come down on an airstrip. Where are we?"

"This is the Woolworth estate," explained the policeman. "You're in Oyster Bay, Long Island."

Luckily, the wealthy Woolworths welcomed us into their huge home, concerned about us. I was braced for their fury that an airplane had landed and damaged their property. They even drove us to Roosevelt Field and later assisted with trucking the Waco from the rock garden onto which it had settled. The left lower wing was badly crumpled, caught by a low fence as we crashed.

There was publicity, of course. The newspapers ran the photographs of my five hundred-dollar winnings and told that I'd crashed on the way home. It came as no surprise to me later

Edna Marvel Gardner in the 1930s.

Edna, who was commissioned in the U.S. Naval Nurse Corps in 1929, poses in her uniform. She was sometimes called "The Flying Nurse."

A snapshot of Edna sunning in 1929.

Edna Gardner with her flight instructor and sweetheart, Guerdon Brocksom, in 1931

Around 1929 Edna Gardner Kidd with some of her growing collection of trophies.

*An on-pylon turn in
Edna's Aero
Commander 200.*

*More trophies for
Edna's collection,
including the
Outstanding Competitor
Award of the 1967
Cleveland National
Air Races.*

One of Edna's greatest pleasures is teaching young women to fly. Here she rigs student Donna Case with a parachute before aerobatic training in a C-152 Aerobat.

Edna Gardner Whyte among the more than 125 trophies that fill her home at Aero Valley.

Edna's home, on a taxiway at her Aero Valley Airport, with an attached hangar in lieu of a garage.

that the fellow who repaired the Waco charged—what else? *Exactly* five hundred dollars.

The cold clammy winter was depressing. Guerd grumbled about the lousy pay at the boiler factory. "Fifty lousy cents an hour. I hump all day for what? Four lousy dollars?"

"Don't complain to me, Guerd Brocksom. My nursing pay is seventy dollars a month. Figure that out to an hourly wage! I minister to the sick for $17.50 per week and, divided further, that's a measly $3.50 per day. You're a laborer and I'm called a professional!"

Winter brought few customers. I only added twenty-five hours of flying to my log book, although I did get some more practice in low ceilings, rain, snow, and temperatures that sometimes hovered around zero. Although I hated to admit it, Guerd was right to opt for an airplane with a closed cabin. When the wind blew and temperatures dropped to the bottom of the scale on the thermometer, who wanted to be flying in open cockpits?

When we tackled a maintenance project one morning, Guerd eyed the snow that covered the ground, draped precariously off the roof, and piled high on the cowl of each aircraft parked outside. He laughed and suggested, "Perhaps we should have looked for an airfield down south."

I'd been waiting for the right time to tell him what I'd known for a while. "Don't laugh, Guerd. I'm afraid I have news that deals with just that topic. I got some orders. The Navy is shipping me out, like any other sailor. I'm supposed to report in Washington, D.C., by April."

"Well, I'll be damned. Here we go again, eh?" He leaned back against the workbench and shook his head. He absently patted his left chest pocket with his right hand and drew out a pack of cigarettes. Cigarettes gave him two advantages, if you could call them that. The act of removing the cigarette, lighting it, and taking the first drag gave him a bit of time, while the narcotic calmed his nerves. He squinted as smoke rose to his eyes. "I guess I could follow you all over the globe, Edna, but I have been trying to put down roots. I want a career in aviation."

"That seems to be in conflict with what the Navy wants for me."

"*I* want you, Edna. Won't you consider resigning and staying in Newport with me?"

"Number one, without my Navy pay, where would we be here in Newport, Guerd? We haven't made a go of the airfield yet. I do care for you, you know that I do..."

"But, number two, you're moving to Washington. And, if I want to see you, I'll have to commute, right?"

"It won't be all bad, Guerd. I'll get acquainted down there and, who knows, maybe even find a better deal than this seasonal situation we have here."

"A better deal or a better man? If I know you, you won't be without one long. Oh, forget that I said that. I'll be all right here. I'll make it. I just talked with E. W. Wiggins last night. He wants me to go to work for him, says he's going to spring for a big hangar for me one of these days. I'll stay put and see what kind of an operation I can build here. I'm meeting lots of people, making contacts. Who knows? Aviation is growing. Maybe one of the airlines will hire me someday."

I couldn't keep the resentment from my voice when I replied, "That's a hope you can harbor. You're not a *woman!*"

At the end of March 1934, I was transferred to the naval hospital at 23rd and E Street in the nation's capital. I settled into nurses' quarters and a forty-hour, five-day work week. As quickly as possible, I traveled all around to check on the nearest airports. It didn't take any time at all before I was scheduling students to fly at Congressional, Beacon, and Capital airports, and at College Park in Maryland. I wangled my way into as many different airplanes as I could find: Travel Air, Fleet, Monocoupe, Challenger, and Aeronca. I borrowed airplanes to enter bomb-dropping contests, and won a women's race and a relay race in a Fleet and an OX-5 race in a Travel Air.

On sunny, clear, quiet days it was all I could do to pay attention to my nursing—on the psychopathic and surgical wards for veterans of World War I. I was beginning to earn more money as a flight instructor than I was as a nurse. And, no two ways about it, flying was out and away more exhilarating.

My name was mentioned time and again in the papers. News clipping became a regular pastime. In a Washington paper, Jack Parker wrote,

On June 1st there was a meeting of the Washington Air Derby Association. For the first time in the two and a half years of the Association's being, members of the fair sex were present.

At the previous meeting it had been decided by vote of the members present that women were eligible for active membership. Three local gals were invited to join...all three are pilots—all three are active in sport-flying—and (Hold your hats, boys!) all three are unmarried. Gentlemen—the Misses Edna Gardner, Johanna Busse and Helen Frigo!

Besides the preponderance of men, there were many ways to have fun flying in the Washington area. Chet Warrington, who later became the contest chairman for our Washington Women Pilots Association Women's Air Meet in October of 1934, devised an aerial golf game. His directions said,

Nine different airfields will be used. Every competing plane will carry, besides the pilot, a passenger to be responsible for the score. If the pilot is a man, he must take a girl with him and vice versa. You tee off (take off) from the College Park Airport to the first green at Congressional Airport where a can is sunk in the ground with a red marker nearby. There you drop one of your three golfballs attached to a small parachute, as near to the hole as you can. Land and play out the hole under the eagle eye of your passenger, counting the flight as one stroke. The green now becomes the tee for the next hole. Hop into your ship and repeat the procedure at Hydra Valley, Beacon Field, Capital, Queens Chapel, Hybla Valley, Congressional....

There was fun but there was also discrimination from arrogant male pilots. I've already mentioned the speed race in Baltimore in June of 1934 when I raced against eight men and *won,* fair and square. It still angered me to recall the difficulty with which I finally claimed the trophy and the money and the way they barred women from competing the next year.

I'd called Guerd and he had flown his Aristocrat J6-5 to Washington for me to race. He left it saying, "I hope you do well, Edna. But I do worry about you."

"Don't worry. Racing is the greatest thing I've ever done. Thanks for letting me use the Aristocrat. It's such a fast one."

Then, he mentioned a newspaper clipping that month that I hadn't seen. "A famous race pilot has been killed, Edna," he told me.

Guerd read the newspaper clipping to me. "A tropical hurricane hit Patterson, Louisiana. The millionaire, Harry P. Williams, lost all but one of his airplanes. Attempting to sell the remaining airplane, a Gypsy Moth, famous race designer and pilot, Jimmy Wedell, winner of the 1933 Bendix in his Wedell-Williams #44, took a prospective customer for a flight in the Moth. The customer panicked, froze on the controls. The Gypsy Moth nosed up, stalled, fell out of control, and crashed, slightly injuring the customer. For Wedell the crash was fatal."

"He wasn't killed *racing,* Guerd."

"No, he wasn't. Just take care of yourself, okay?"

"I'll be on Long Island later this month, Guerd. Will you come down to see me, to tweak the Aristocrat with me? I'll be there from June twenty-second to the twenty-fifth flying in the Third Annual Annette Gipson Race. What do you say?"

"I don't know if I can be there for the entire time, Edna. But I'll try to get down. Wiggins is building the big hangar here in Newport for me as he promised. I've a few irons in the fire. . . ."

"A few other women, Guerd?" I asked, strangely detached. He didn't answer.

It was almost intriguing to watch our romance cool as my love of racing heated up. I found the racing scene dizzying — exciting and electric. Mrs. I. J. Fox, wife of the prominent New

York City furrier, was to present the trophy to the winner. Edith Descomb, Suzanne Humphries, Frances Marsalis, Arlene Davis, Helen MacCloskey, and several other pilots joined me in the cockpits of our airplanes while none other than Amelia Earhart herself waved the flag to start us off. I would be watching the muscles in Amelia's arm—watching for the very first twitch of movement.

I'd practiced flying around the Roosevelt Field course, a good reason to arrive two days before the race. Like Guerd's cigarettes, it gave me time to settle down, get the pre-race jitters under control. It was important to fly the course, visualize the pylons, see the checkpoints that could be crucial to winning the race. There were racers that actually got lost on a race course. If I was out in front, I didn't want that to happen to me.

On the twenty-fourth, dressed in clean white coveralls, I started the Aristocrat. Guerd had her in prime condition. The J6-5 purred, I knew the airplane well and felt a part of the machine—intimately involved. When slim, athletic Amelia raised the flag, I didn't watch the wind tousle her full pantlegs and her short hair. I stared at her arm. My feet danced on the rudders. The engine revved, the beat constant. The instant that a ripple moved Amelia's long-sleeved shirt, I gave her the gun and off we roared. I was out in front. I zipped around the thirty-mile course in twenty-four minutes and won flat out.

The trophy, topped with a slim nude holding an airplane aloft, was so tall it extended from below my waist to above my head. When Mrs. I. J. Fox presented it to me, the newspapers captured my broad grin of pleasure. The check for five hundred dollars wasn't going to be spent repairing a bent bird, either. No more foggy takeoffs from Long Island. I reveled in this, my biggest win thus far.

In July, I had a chance to fly a Taperwing Waco. The Women's National Air Meet was scheduled for Dayton, Ohio, on August 4 and 5. If I was going to race the Waco, I wanted to know all about her. I practiced landings, but much more importantly, I practiced aerobatics including snap rolls, a sheer delight. On August 3, I left Washington, D.C., and flew to

Dayton via Wheeling, West Virginia. It took six hours and twenty minutes and I was thrilled to join the racing ladies, women I was getting to know, but with whom I felt guarded and competitive; among others: Jeannette Lempke, Gladys O'Donnell, Annette Gipson, Helen Richey, Frances Harrell Marsalis, Ellie Smith, and Helen MacCloskey. We often circled one another with feigned joy and a great deal of hugging, only to feel inside the wariness of cats.

On Saturday, pretty, blond Ellie Smith won and I was fifth to put my Waco closest to the line in the precision landing test. Knowing that one thousand dollars in prize money waited for the winner of Sunday's Fifty-Miler, I decided to hold back and nurse my engine through the Twenty-Mile Free-for-All. I planned my strategy. I'd watch the starter's arm, get away fast, and, although I wouldn't "sandbag," I wouldn't run all the juice out of the J-5 engine, either. Maybe I'd get lucky, get out in front, and win this prestigious race.

My Waco, NC-6930, was ready. My feet trembled with excitement, my hand was moist as I gripped the stick. I licked my lips, drew the helmet over my marcelled hair, and adjusted the goggles. The flag was up! I glanced to the left and right of the J-5 to clear the space before me, then glued my eyes to the starter. I wanted to win! Lord, I'd love to win every contest, every race. Off we went in a roar of the engines, a cloud of dust. I was airborne almost instantly, zooming straight and low, leaning forward in the seat—determined, my upper body tense.

I wasn't first as I raced around the pylons, scattering a bevy of ducks that had the misfortune of being on a nearby pond, but I wasn't bringing up the rear either. I kept one hand on the throttle, the other on the stick. I couldn't afford to have the throttle creep. My heart was synchronized with the thunder of the J-5. The craft and I were one. I saw a plane pass by, then another. Did I dare give her more gun? Would I have anything left to race with Sunday? Maybe it wouldn't hurt to let them blow their own motors. A little less competition tomorrow wouldn't be all bad. A few more passed to my right.

We landed and, in the official results, I not only didn't win, but I came in last—Tail-End Toni. Damn. I hoped I didn't have to listen to whining about being a sandbag. I raced. I just didn't race as well as I hoped I could on Sunday. The list of winners named Jeannette Lempke in her Great Lakes, Annette Gipson in her Aristocrat, Gladys O'Donnell in her Monocoupe and, down at the bottom, in the very last place . . . Edna Gardner, Waco.

Sunday dawned. I moved up some—came in third in the bomb-dropping contest, flour-bombing the target on the ground from our airplanes. Adding fifteen dollars to the five dollars I won in the landing contest, all I could think was, "Twenty is better than nothing."

But the big race was finally called—the Fifty-Mile Free-for-All. Helen Richey revved up her Eaglerock. The two Monocoupes of O'Donnell and MacCloskey spurted short puffs of smoke as they started. Annette Gipson fired her Aristocrat. I was ready, the fan spinning on my Waco, when I noticed Frances Marsalis climb into her Waco Cabin.

Frances was a well-known race pilot, famous for the endurance record for women she set with Louise Thaden in a Curtiss Thrush in 1932—they'd stayed airborne for more than eight days. A fine pilot and a true competitor, Frances had talked with me earlier. As two of the five flying Waco airplanes, we compared notes, seated on a bench. I reminded her of what a good sport she had been when I narrowly beat her at the National Air Pageant at Roosevelt Field—the Kate Smith race, my first national one.

"I should cancel out of racing today, Edna," she told me, shaking her head. "I've got my period. I've got cramps and I feel lousy. But, you know how it is. Once you get here you feel committed." Her generally bright hazel eyes were dull. She leaned forward and rested her chin on her hands.

"You're normally so full of spirit, Frances. It's obvious you don't feel well. Why do you think you have to race?"

She straightened up with a sigh. "I'm showing the Waco for the distributor, Ehlers. He told me to pick up this new Cabin model just north of here in Troy to display it for the crowds today. He's undoubtedly out there watching. I can't let him down. And that isn't the half of it. Bill and I are getting a divorce. This just isn't my day." She shrugged, "My month? My week? Hell."

"I'm sorry, Frances. That's tough."

She shook her head and took a deep breath as she stood up. She smiled wanly and, as we all revved up for the race, she gave me a salute as she climbed aboard her Cabin Waco.

My hands were balled around the throttle and my stomach tied into knots. This win would be a big one. Imagine! A thousand dollars! I felt for Frances, though. With three little children at home, going through a divorce? How sad for her. She shouldn't fly.

But fly she did. We all did. We polished the pylons, the ground a blur. I passed another Waco. We were very low. The pylons weren't tall enough. I could see my shadow on the ground, then two more. There were too many shadows, one on top of another. We were tight, too tight.

I glanced to my right. Someone was way too close. I instinctively veered away to the left, sliced lower through the air, tipped precariously onto the left wing and skirted a pylon. Around we went. I was in front and suddenly I saw nothing but a flailing airplane whirling through a barrage of dust.

"*No!*" I screamed, my feet beginning to vibrate with terror on the rudders, my eyes wide and fixed. The Waco biplane had flipped from Frances's control. It roared into a nose dive and augered straight into the ground, flipping over several times as the dust rose and billowed as if to cover and hide the horrible tragedy. "*No!*" I cried again, fighting panic, fighting the urge to burst into tears.

The ground was a blur as I brought the ship across the finish line first. I *won!* My usual euphoria was dampened to a grim smile of pleasure as I brought the Waco in for a landing, shaking with terror, afraid to confirm that someone I knew well was gone.

"What happened? What happened?" I asked the nearest person when I'd stopped my airplane and climbed out.

"Frances Marsalis is dead," I was told. I covered my face with my hands, sunk down to the ground, and sobbed.

Later, Victor Strahm, the race referee and a member of the contest committee found me by my airplane. "A violation has been filed, Miss Gardner," Strahm began.

"A violation? What are you talking about?"

"The Misses Ruth Nason and Annette Gipson filed charges against you. They contend that you passed on the inside, a clear violation of race rules."

"I know that overtaking airplanes are supposed to pass on the right. I've been racing..."

"I'm sorry, Miss Gardner, but we are upholding the protests and naming Miss Helen Richey the race winner and the recipient of the thousand-dollar prize. Your violation disqualifies you."

"No!" I screamed, spent with the horror of Frances's accident, drained of all energy. I moaned, "I didn't cheat. I wanted to avoid an accident."

The next day I filed a protest in return. It cost twenty-five dollars to file, but I hated being disqualified. I was flying a tight race. I veered to the left to keep from a mid-air collision. So I passed someone. I veered away for *safety!* I didn't cut off another racer—at least, not intentionally.

In light of Frances's death, the Women's National Air Meet ended in somber silence. My protest was so unimportant in comparison to Frances's fate. I formally rescinded my protest by writing the following letter.

U.S. Naval Hospital
Washington, D.C.
11 September 1934

Mr. F. Trubee Davison, Chairman, Contest Committee, N.A.A.
Dupont Circle, Washington, D.C.

Via: Mr. William Enyart, Secretary, Contest Committee, N.A.A.

Subject: Withdrawal of protest filed 22 August 1934 with filing fee of $25.00

My dear Mr. Enyart:

In the interest of true sportsmanship and my future standing in racing circles, especially among the women, I hereby formally request that the Contest Committee of the National Aeronautic Association withdraw my protest relative to the controversy growing out of the recent Dayton Air Races for Women.

Naturally it hurts me beyond expression in this regard as I conscientiously and firmly believe that under the circumstances I followed the correct procedure and tried to the best of my ability to avoid an accident. For this I have been disqualified.

However, after due consideration, my better judgment prompts me to withdraw and I trust that the Contest Committee will concur in this and grant my request.

> *Cordially yours,*
>
> */s/ Edna M. Gardner*

Loss of a race paled. I tried to put things into perspective by remembering that, unlike my delightful friend Frances, I was still alive to race again.

12

Congressional

and

an

Aristocrat

G uerd Brocksom let me call his Aristocrat my own. He flew it from Newport to Washington and left it with me to fly and to demonstrate to potential customers. Also I would sell a Waco 10 for him later. I'd never forget hearing that he had to be pried out of the frigid cockpit en route to New Orleans from Newport in freezing temperatures while he ferried that open cockpit biplane to me.

"Sell the Aristocrat if you can, Edna," he agreed. But, before it changed hands and went to somebody new, I thoroughly enjoyed knowing that I had an airplane at my disposal. I looked forward to 1935 with the same feeling of freedom that my own Travel Air had given me. No longer did I have to mesh my nursing hours with busy flight schedules or try to connive an airplane from someone else. Even better, no arrogant men could push me from a rental airplane and tell me that, rather than fly, I should be home doing diapers and dishes!

I was halfway to a thousand hours and, when I wasn't nursing, I was feeling as free as a bird. I'd come a long way from the woman with barely the required two hundred flying hours to take the transport pilot test in Hillsgrove, Rhode Island, in December of 1932. "You're the first Rhode Island aviatrix to receive this," they told me at the state airport. Now, I could see how much I'd learned; how teaching, racing, acrobatics, competing, and experience had honed my skills. I looked forward with promise to 1935.

Just after New Year's Day, I received a phone call and an engraved invitation from the German Ambassador to the United States. "Please come to the airfield," he said in his halting English. "Ve are pleased to velcome our own German aviatrix, Miss Elli Beinhorn, to the United States. Could you join Mrs. Phoebe Omlie in a delegation that greets her upon her arrival?"

Flattered, I said, "Of course I will be there. Thank you for asking me." I wanted to ask, "How did you know about me?"

He went on, "Und, after she is once comfortable, ve vish to include you at the showing of a motion picture."

"A movie?"

"Yes. Ve vould like to have you attend on January 2 from five to seven o'clock to see a film of the preliminary Olympic Winter Games at Garmisch Partenkirchen. An invitation has been issued to you."

Charles Lindbergh was reportedly impressed with Germany and her Luftwaffe. Was this my first exposure to German propaganda? I was pleased, nonetheless. I told him, "Yes. I received it. I will keep it in my scrapbook of aviation memories. It will be an honor to meet Miss Beinhorn with Mrs. Omlie and to attend your official festivities. Thank you. I'll be there."

I could scarcely wait to call Phoebe Omlie. The ambassador must have heard of me through articles in the newspaper. Guerd didn't value that publicity? How foolish of him.

After the reception at the German Embassy, I called Guerd. I told him about being with Phoebe Omlie. "Her license number is 199, Guerd. Isn't that something? She flew to campaign for President Franklin D. Roosevelt and she has just been put on his National Advisory Committee for Aeronautics. Eleanor Roosevelt suggested that women fly across the country seeing that air marking is accomplished for navigational aids. She recognizes the contributions that can be made by us women!"

Guerd chuckled. He'd heard me boast about the talents of female pilots hundreds of times.

"Oh, and Guerd, I'm going to fly to Florida in the Aristocrat."

"Oh?"

Like so many other northerners fleeing January's winter weather for Florida, I told him that his airplane and I were going, too. The motive was more involved with air racing and less with sunshine and warmth, although that sounded inviting, too.

"The All-American Air Maneuvers will be held in Miami, Guerd. I want to be there. This is the first year that they've offered races for women. I wouldn't miss that for the world."

"Sounds fine to me, Edna."

"I have a week off from the naval hospital. Maybe I can even find a buyer down there. A huge crowd generally flocks to Miami. The J6-5 engine should make me competitive, don't you think?"

Guerd replied, "I should think you'd do well with 165 horses. You have before. I hope she runs well for you. Fly safe and let me know how it goes, will you? I won't be joining you there."

I was relieved to hear Guerd say that. I hadn't told him that I'd met another man in Washington: Ray Kidd, a dark-haired, urbane writer for the United States Information Service. Kidd held promise of being *my* G. P. Putnam. "Gippy" Putnam may have had a corner on the publicity market and catapulted Lindbergh, Byrd, and Earhart into national prominence, but Ray Kidd could have been his second-in-command. A writer and a promoter, a glib wit and a charmer, Kidd and I had hit it off from the first moment we met.

Ray spent a good deal of time out of the country on investigative assignment for the USIS. I didn't expect to see him in

Florida, so it didn't matter one way or another if Guerd had shown up. It just muddied the waters a little to imagine both of them simultaneously arriving at the races to "surprise" me. Actually, once there, the races would absorb me.

It was great news that these seventh annual Miami All-American Air Maneuvers were open to women. First flown in 1929 as a mid-winter invitation to one and all to enjoy the fine weather about which Floridians bragged, the Miami events had always been limited to men. The famous Bendix Trophy Race, first flown in 1931, had been entered by male pilots only. In 1934 it was *limited* to men, reportedly because of a female pilot's fatal accident. Florence Klingensmith had died in a fiery racing accident with a Gee Bee and the men found in that an excuse to forbid entries from women. What irony! Were men excluded from racing after Lowell Bayles, Cecil Allen, Russell Boardman, even Zantford "Granny" Granville himself were *all* killed in Gee Bees?

I erased both Guerd and Ray Kidd from my thoughts as I left for Miami. I flew via Savannah, Georgia, and Orlando, Florida, and calculated a ten-hour flight, but it was lucky that I left well ahead of time. On my way south, I taxied into a drainage ditch and dug the propeller blades deeply into the dirt. I had to pay a mechanic for repairs and all he did was put the prop between two boards and pound it straight! A hole punched into the ground meant a hole in air race winnings, money I hadn't even yet won!

Once repaired, the Aristocrat and I headed south. The prop vibrated, I'd discover later, although it seemed to perform well after being fixed. We had to skirt a few showers, but winter storms were nothing like the ferocious, billowing thunderstorms that mushroomed over thirty thousand feet into the air in the muggy heat of summer.

As I flew into the overhead circuit around the airfield, the Aristocrat and I joined a bevy of airplanes like an errant goose joins a tail end of the V-formation of a gaggle. I waggled my wings and spun my head from right to left, watching other aircraft, jockeying for position. Below us, Army and Navy planes were parked in precise military lines. Small racers and showplanes crawled with activity as pit crews scrambled over their sleek birds like so many ants on sweet cake crumbs. Miami offered a stage for seaplane builders to showcase their airplanes, arranging landings and takeoffs from the serene blue waters of nearby Biscayne Bay. A few of them were airborne when I arrived and I watched one splash to a landing, the water spraying from the craft's floats. As advertised, Florida's flying weather was perfect—clear and sunny with the wind steady from the water, just riffling the surface.

Mine was no sightseeing jaunt, although it was hard not to appreciate the miles of gleaming beach, tongues of land reaching tentatively into the rolling, frothing Atlantic Ocean, hundreds of sky-colored lakes, and seemingly thousands of birds. I concentrated on the airfield. I wanted to memorize the approach, visualize the race course, see the pylons, and plan my racing strategy. I circled over the flat coastal ground, eyeing outstanding checkpoints, then coasted down to a landing on the gleaming white runway. The sand sparkled with brilliant diamonds as I taxied to park my airplane next to one that was familiar to me. It was the Monocoupe that belonged to Helen MacCloskey.

"Hi, Helen," I called. Helen was busily wiping the salt spray from her precious craft. "How is one of my favorite rivals?"

"Friendly rivals, right, Edna?" Helen asked, with a grin. She straightened up, shook the rag in her hands. "That was some air meet you and Genevieve Savage organized in D.C. last October. Helen Richey and I talked about it. We thought it was a howling success. She and I have been flying with Phoebe Omlie, Louise Thaden, Nancy Harkness, and Blanche Noyes with the air marking program. What a picnic! We're flying all over the place to paint major town names on rooftops—thousands of them. It ought to help all of us to stay on course when we fly cross-country."

"So I heard, Helen. I talked with Phoebe, too. We were invited to welcome Elli Beinhorn to the United States and to the German Embassy afterwards. It was really grand. And I know about you. You've not only been painting all over the country, you've been *competing* all over the country. Getting the Aero Club of Washington trophy must have been one of your highlights."

"No two ways about it, Edna. I was lucky! I liked seeing Melba Beard at your air meet. And Pancho Barnes—what a character! Nothing like her boots, that military jacket crisscrossed with leather, and a tilted beret." Helen laughed and shook her head. "She and Bobbi Trout traveled some distance to make it—all the way from California. Good for them!"

"That was the uniform of their California Women's Air Reserve. Pancho and Bobbi are great gals. They both can more than handle an airplane. I wonder how Pancho's Happy Bottom Riding Club got along without her for a few days?"

"All the Smith girls probably kept it humming." Helen smiled at me knowingly, then changed the subject. "How did you do in your meet, Edna? I've forgotten."

"I was second behind you in the race and third in bomb-dropping and acrobatics. Nothing to write home about."

"Nothing to sneeze at, either. Good for you." Helen's light brown hair brushed her shoulders. Her light cotton skirt flattered her stockinged legs. Always feminine and attractive, she was a crackerjack pilot and I knew I had my hands full in the race and in the acrobatic competition to follow.

"Well, good luck, Helen. Can you believe that they're actually letting the women race? Shall we shake on it?"

"May the best girl win," she said. Her grin was contagious. We laughed as we shook hands.

I snap-rolled, looped, and spun the Aristocrat to the best of my ability, but came in second to Helen's win in the Women's Acrobatic competition. I steeled myself to congratulate her afterwards and she said, graciously, "I watched your acrobatics, Edna, and I think you're getting better and better."

"Thanks, Helen. The race is next."

"Yes. I called for some fuel. Did you want some?"

"No, thanks," I told her. "I'm fine. I think that I've just about the right amount of gas."

She turned away to service her Monocoupe and I thought

about fuel. Races were won and lost on so many seemingly minor factors, well-calculated fuel consumption being one of them. Running out of gas would be stupid and dangerous, but there was no need to fill the Aristocrat, either. I knew we'd be faster with less of a load to haul around the pylons.

My strategy worked. I got off first, diving low and tight around the first of the pylons. "No *cutting*," I warned myself. My head swiveled, looking for other racers, then I concentrated on the course. I was out in front and I clung tenaciously to my lead like a rabbit being chased by galloping greyhounds.

I won the race! I could hardly wait to call Guerd. Once on the ramp, Helen and I hugged each other. Both winners, we could let competition rest for a while. "Hell, it's time to play now, Helen. We've done what we came to do. I'll get gassed up before I park the Aristocrat for the night."

As I taxied toward the gas barrels, the engine sounded rough. I'd run at ninety-eight miles an hour and, until the very end of the race, the motor hummed like a happy cat. Now, a mechanic checked and reported, "You've got a faulty magneto. Do you want it replaced?"

"Can you repair the prop, too?" I asked.

"You bet. You'd just have to repair the mag again if you don't get that prop straightened. It's gonna cost you some money, though—about three hundred dollars."

I hadn't much choice. "Do whatever needs to be done," I said flatly. "Keep the bill to the absolute minimum, will you? This isn't my airplane, but I have to pay for the repairs *and* get it all the way back to D.C."

Clipping newspaper articles for my scrapbook became more complicated all the time. Articles were naturally featured on the front page of Miami papers, but they appeared elsewhere as well. The Chatfield, Minnesota, paper wrote, "In the Miami meet, Miss Gardner won the first prize in the women's race and was awarded $250. She took second prize in aerial acrobatics. Races are open to all fliers." Mother sent the article.

What the newspapers didn't report was that, again, it cost almost all of the coveted prize money to pay for the fuel for my twenty-hour flight, my hotel rooms, meals, and, damn it, for the repairs that had to be done to the propeller and the magneto. Shades of Cleveland '31.

Before we parted, Helen MacCloskey and I gave each other a hug. Her trophy was packed into her Monocoupe and she was getting ready to leave Miami. She said, "Next week Genevieve Savage and I hope to try for a speed record in light landplanes. I think we can coax about 166 miles an hour from my 145-horse Warner."

"Good luck," I said, my voice tinged with the envy I couldn't hide.

"By the way," she continued pleasantly, "you know that our own Helen Richey has been hired by Central Airlines, don't you? She's the first female to pilot an airliner on a scheduled route. She's flying trimotors." MacCloskey leaned against the cowl of my Aristocrat.

"Do I ever! I'm so proud of her, and as envious as I can be. Johanna Busse and I went straight to the Central offices, trying to get our applications accepted when we heard. No luck, so far, though. How does Helen like it?"

"She just started last month, but we're all hoping that this is the big breakthrough for female pilots. She's a copilot, flying between Washington and Detroit, the rare times they let her go. It has to be sunny and clear. The bad news—there's an all-male pilots' union."

I made a mental note to contact Johanna Busse again when I got back to D.C. and back to work. I was still toying with giving up nursing. I knew I would give anything to be an airline pilot.

After a fuel stop in Charleston, South Carolina, and a fuel and overnight stop in Raleigh, North Carolina, I was home. To my surprise, a note from Ray Kidd waited for me. It warmed the chill of Washington. Kidd enclosed a copy of my picture from the *New York Times*. It was from one of the many contests I'd entered, one I happened to win. Instead of a pose in my usual white coveralls with an airplane behind me, this photograph portrayed a "society girl." A soft, silken collar rolled gracefully around the neck of the girl in the photo and her dark, gently waved hair was bobbed below the ears. Carefully penciled eyebrows arched over demurely lowered eyes. A hat cupped smartly over her head, tipped over one eye, jauntier than a beret, more modern than a cloche. The caption said, "SNAPPY—Miss Edna Gardner, Naval Hospital nurse and aviator, wearing the hat awarded by Miss Amelia Earhart." Could the person in the *New York Times* photo really be me?

Kidd's note said, "SNAPPY indeed. Here's to an accurate adjective and being together in 1935. Happy New Year!"

At the naval hospital, I had become the supervisor in charge of the wards. I made sick call with the doctors and saw to it that one of my nurses followed up with their recommendations; cleansing, medication, or whatever treatment was required. The laborious work was done by military corpsmen. The nurse with the neatest ward was awarded an E on the front of her door and I trained corpsmen to properly clean my ward so that I could claim the E more than my share of the time.

During off-duty hours from the hospital, I drove my DeSoto roadster to any one of the many Washington-area airports, sometimes with scheduled students waiting for me and sometimes just to be there in case a student came around—one of the hangar "bums." During some of those times our "hangar session" stories smacked of the unbelievable. Other times we genuinely helped one another, sharing what experience had taught.

My demand as a flight instructor was increasing. More and more students requested me and I hopped students and passengers all over the eastern seaboard. I flew the Aristocrat, Waco, Challenger, Bird—even rode in an autogyro at Bolling Field and for two hours in a Trimotor Stinson during the winter of '35. I climbed high for acrobatics in a Buhl Bull Pup, snap-rolling it and laughing out loud at the fun.

I entered any race that I could find, dropped parachute jumpers, popped balloons, and flew in aerial "Treasure Hunts" for the fun of it, to meet other pilots, and to watch the flight time build higher and higher in my log—six hundred, then seven hundred hours.

One day while I was seated on a bench in the sun at Congressional Airport near Hyattsville, Maryland, two Japanese boys sauntered in. A sign on the entrance to the airfield said, LEARN TO FLY FOR $49.50, and the foreigners plunked down the money to take advantage of the opportunity. We were using C-2 and C-3 Aeroncas, J-2 Cubs. Two male instructors were sitting beside me and they jostled one another with their elbows. "Those look like good students for Edna, don't you think?" one asked the other.

"You bet. Give 'em to Edna," the other echoed.

"Okay, you guys," I agreed. I taught the two to fly and soloed them, and they arranged for me to be invited to dinner at the Japanese Embassy. It was one of the most gracious, pleasant dinners of my life.

One of the Japanese students wrote later, "We've been sent to Rantoul, Illinois, for ground school and further flight training. After training we will return to Japan, where we will be instrumental in organizing Japanese pilots."

Building a Japanese air force was what they meant. They were polite and quiet, grabbing all of the knowledge and flight experience that was offered to them. It was '34 when I taught them to fly and it was '41 when they helped kill thousands of our men in Pearl Harbor. I haven't been able to forget that.

In May, unannounced, Ray Kidd arrived at the airfield. He smiled at me, his lips and a dark, thin moustache framing clean white teeth, his face tanned. Polished shoes shone beneath his nicely creased slacks. His white shirt was open at the neck. A heady rush warmed me as he leaned toward me and whispered, "How's my SNAPPY pilot been doing? Does she have time to take a flight with a friend?"

"Do I have time? If I didn't, I wouldn't be sitting here, I guess," I stammered, flustered. He smelled even better than he looked. His aftershave lotion must have been fashioned with him in mind: dashing, intriguing, and sexy.

"If I tell you about my time abroad on assignment, will you tell me what you've been up to for half the year?" he asked, casually putting an arm around me as we walked toward an Aeronca and pulling me to him. He was smooth. Very.

He swung his free arm toward the "flying bathtub," and added, "Or should I ask what you've been down to? It looks as if you can drag bottom in that little crate."

"It's pretty squat, I'll grant you that."

"The fuselage looks like the lower jaw of a Key West brown pelican. Hopefully it won't expand when we sit in it. It's been a long time since I got grass stains on the knees of my slacks or, in this case, my tail."

I laughed. "Don't worry. I haven't had to launder the clothes of any of my students or passengers yet."

"Do you promise that those two puny cylinders will be enough to take us up into the air and over any nearby trees or buildings?"

"I promise, as long as you promise to keep your legs still. They'll be pretty close on either side of me once we're in ..."

"That sounds inviting," he interrupted with a grin.

"...the cabin," I finished lamely.

"This sounds better than I'd imagined."

Kidd and I flew together for almost two hours. As Bob Martin had once showed me how to hold the stick and use my feet, I showed Kidd how to turn the Aeronca, how to climb, level off, then turn...up and over, reversing direction with a steep wing-over. Every few moments, I felt one or the other of his legs tense, rub against me. I was acutely aware of them, stretched past me. Although I could no longer get a whiff of his aftershave, his proximity was distracting. I had to force myself to pay attention to business.

Kidd, tall, good-looking, easy to talk with, well-groomed, and sophisticated, swept me off my feet. He had developed a smooth line as he cruised the world in the governmental information game.

After we landed, I climbed out first and waited for him in front of the wing. He unfolded his lean body from the scant rear seat of the airplane. He couldn't stand erect, but had to bend to crawl out from under the oversized but low braced wing. "This is a . . . ?"

"An Aeronca," I answered. "Sometimes, besides a 'bathtub,' it is called an 'Airknocker.'"

I saw his amused gaze slide down from my face, appraise my body. "Don't say it," I warned. "Don't even think it."

His smile was disarming. "Discretion, Miss Snappy Lady, discretion. I'm capable of it, sometimes."

"Have you flown before?" I asked.

"I've been in an airplane, but never with a lady pilot. That was a first. You surprised me."

"Surprised you?"

"You did a very good job."

I started to feel indignant, then softened. "I just had my pilot's license marked 'Flight Instructor.' I believe I'm one of the first in the Washington area."

"Good for you, Snappy. That name fits. And thank you for a wonderful flight," he whispered, leaning over to kiss me lightly on the cheek before he left. "We'll have to do that again, often." He handed me a twenty-dollar bill, smiled, and strode off. My hand inadvertently went to my face and I stood for a while gazing after him. I wondered if or when I'd ever see him again. I wavered between feeling defensive and flattered that I surprised him by doing a creditable job of piloting.

"What're ya holdin' your cheek for?" asked the maintenance man as he walked out of the hangar toward me. "Did you bump it on the wing?"

"No. Nothing," I answered quickly, yanking my hand away. "Not a darn thing."

"Are ya through with the Airknocker? She's got to be relicensed and, before we take her for that, I'd better give 'er a look-see, don't ya think? Got any complaints about her?"

"I can't think of a single complaint in the world right now," I answered with a broad smile. "But, don't take the Aeronca now. I've another student."

One of my most conscientious and regular students was a girl, a pretty blond named Sarah Livingston. Sarah would make a fine pilot one day. I truly enjoyed working with young women, coaxing them toward flying lessons, toward success with flying, perhaps even flying careers. The more I taught Sarah and the better I watched her become, the more convinced I was that teaching flying was what I ought to be doing for a career. I thought about resigning from the Navy. I sent an application, again, to Central Airlines.

Whenever new airplanes showed up at any of my favorite airfields, I wasn't the least bit shy about introducing myself to the pilots and owners, getting my foot into the door for the possibility of rides. I wanted experience in as many airplanes as possible and all the flying hours that I could get. I flew in a 450-horse Wasp-powered Grumman one afternoon during the middle of the summer. Then I checked out a Taylor Cub and a Porterfield. The Cleveland Air Races were in September and I decided to get familiar with the Porterfield and its LaBlond engine. Perhaps it would be competitive at the Nationals.

I flew the Porterfield every day between August twentieth and the twenty-ninth, then hopped from D.C. to the shores of Lake Erie for the big show. I marveled at how much more competent and comfortable I felt in comparison to the new pilot who'd carried Cowboy LaPierre aloft four years before.

Genevieve Savage, the girl who had helped me put on the Women's Air Meet in Washington and who set the speed record with MacCloskey, was competing with me in the Women's Race, a free-for-all. When we parked alongside one another at Cleveland, Genevieve said to me, "Don't you think it is fantastic that Amelia has entered the Bendix Transcontinental Speed Dash?"

"Well, she has Gippy Putnam's money behind her. . . ." I said.

"That's nothing new. He has been sponsoring the dickens out of her and helping her meet all sorts of goals in aviation. It's almost as if everyone has to have a sponsor to help them in an expensive endeavor like a transcontinental race. But what *is* new is that this is the first year that a woman is even entering in and *flying* the Bendix. That's what I find fantastic. We're getting more and more accepted, Edna."

"I hear you, Gen. Amelia is really trying to help forge new

avenues for women in aviation. She's such a nice person, too. If only that dratted Putnam..."

"She needs him," Genevieve said simply.

"And he needs *her!*" We both smiled at one another—wry smiles—and turned to think about our own projects. It was going to be a free-for-all and, as usual, I hoped no one would see anything but my Porterfield's tail feathers.

The end of summer in Cleveland brought changeable weather, warm sultry days that ballooned Lake Erie clouds into monstrous towers of billowing, churning white. I watched a Travel Air, Fleet, Waco, Aeronca, and Great Lakes arrive, vying for the Ruth Chatterton Sportsman Pilot Trophy. This wasn't limited to women, nor was it just a race for the fastest, it was a test for precise navigation and accurate flying. Ruth Chatterton, a movie star and pilot, put up a purse of five thousand dollars and pilots handicapped themselves. I could enter something as expensive as the Bendix, I thought to myself, if I had a sponsor like Gippy Putnam or Floyd Odlum. Hmm.

The free-for-all brought Genevieve Savage, Melba Beard, Peggy Remey, and winner Edith Berenson into the field with me. We were all closely matched; only thirty-four *seconds* separated the first from the last! I came in third behind two Birds piloted by Berenson and Beard. Genevieve's Great Lakes and Peg Remey's Travel Air were behind me. We bunched together and whizzed around the course like so many drones coveting the queen bee.

I loved racing. I loved the surge of power, the fight to stay low, fast, close to the pylons, yanking and banking in the turbulent air. I loved winning, but at the very least I wanted to finish in the money. My share of the purse was only $187, but I was happy to see it. I went over to see Sunny Sundorph on the other side of the field, just for old times' sake, then I flew back to Washington, D.C., and to a big change in my life.

Ray Kidd, masterful man that he was, rushed into my heart and life and, in a flurry of surprise and secrecy, we married in a ceremony on a friend's yacht, romantically floating on the quiet swells of the Potomac River. I resigned from the Navy and we spent an idyllic month in and around Norfolk, Virginia. We flew together in various airplanes—Fleet, Fairchild, Stinson, Waco, Ryan—and we flew to various places. Our destinations weren't worldly and exotic, but short getaways to College Park, Maryland; Plymouth, North Carolina; Elizabeth City, North Carolina; and Virginia Beach. It was a whirlwind romance, a whirlwind of travel. Witty and clever, forward and brash, Kidd gave hints of the airplane promotions that he could bring to our lives.

"The USIS has given me another overseas assignment," he told me. "But, before I go halfway across the world, we can have a wonderful time. Together we can see this old year of 1935 out and the new year in. You choose where you would like to go, where you would like to live, Edna. When I return, I'll join you. I just want to be with you."

We flew together, we loved together and then, suddenly, with the start of 1936, Kidd had to go. I remained in Norfolk for a while. They had interesting airplanes to fly and seemed to want me to teach students and fly passengers. I kept my maiden name, kept my secret. Who really needed to know?

One of the Norfolk airplanes, a J-5 Ryan like the one flown across the Atlantic by Lindbergh in 1927, could carry four passengers in the back and a pilot up front—in this case, me. I loved barnstorming, opening the door on the left side to let passengers climb in and opening the door on the right to let them out. I'd take young boys, eager flight students along as helpers and, on busy days, when carload after carload of people parked for a ride in "Lindbergh's plane," one boy opened the doors, the other took the money and sold the tickets. We'd barnstorm from a peanut patch, a dirt road, or any available field. We barnstormed northern North Carolina, east of Roanoke Rapids, down by Edenton on the Chowan River—all around the lush, green countryside. I recall one particular day.

"Get a dollar from each person in the crowd and load them up, boys. For God's sake, don't let anybody go near that spinning propeller, you hear? I'll give them one circuit."

When passengers were in the seats, I'd open the throttle and take off with one wing held low. I'd put in full aileron and we'd climb into a turn as soon as the wheels left the sod. As quickly as possible, I'd circle the field and come back for a landing, sideslipping to a halt. The faster the circuit, the more money we made.

"Get on in, folks," I'd call over my shoulder. Away we'd go again, one wing low, a complete circle in just under four minutes. I was giving folks perhaps their first ride in an airplane. I was keeping them moving.

Suddenly, one of the boys ran up to my window and said, "Edna, you've got to stop. The people are complaining. They want their money back. They say, 'That woman doesn't know how to fly. She can't keep her wings straight.'"

I had to change to fly more smoothly and keep my wings more level and flat. It took me ten minutes to get around that way, but at least the customers stopped complaining.

The customers had no corner on the complaint market. My friend and airline pilot, Helen Richey, had a great deal to complain about, as did another woman pilot, Johanna Busse, and I. Johanna and I were rejected flatly in our applications for copilot positions with Central Airlines. Although they had hired Helen, she was limited to fair-weather flying and allowed to fly only a dozen trips or so during the entire year of 1935! In the final straw, she quit after having been refused by the all-male pilots' union.

After flying events were cancelled for women because of strong winds, Annette Gipson had been quoted in the New York *American*:

It's not fair. The officials at Miami's air show have advertised and ballyhooed events for women for months and now, with some flimsy excuse, the officials tell us that there won't be any races for women. Unfair! All we can do about it, apparently, is squawk. It's not at all fair!

I thought about Genevieve Savage telling me that "we're getting more and more accepted." I wondered if Helen Richey and Johanna Busse would agree with that. It seemed to me that the harder we tried, the greater the stumbling blocks placed in front of us became.

13

Shushan and a Maid

The wind tugged my hair, occasionally whipping locks across my cheeks as I drove out of Norfolk, Virginia, in 1936. I felt free and I sang with joy. It was late February and I was headed, like a decade before, for warmth and sunshine. Anticipating a complete change—no naval nursing, no military transfers, no need to bake ingredients of my kitchen into a cake — I stopped along the way, bought meals, slept in hotels, stretched my legs, and answered to no one but myself. My earthly possessions filled my DeSoto roadster and the highway led to New Orleans, Louisiana.

I was a stranger in New Orleans, but that wasn't important. I had heard the "Crescent City" was full of fun, a place for lovers; a delight for shows, dancing, music, Cajun cooking, Mardi Gras, fantastic coffee, and jazz. I'd easily become acquainted with people everyplace else that I had lived. Why not

New Orleans? After all, it had Shushan Airport. What more did I need?

At the Miami Air Maneuvers, I'd listened to pilot after pilot rave about Shushan.

"It is the most modern airport in the country," said one.

"It isn't only modern," said another, "it's downright beautiful."

"Besides that," insisted a third, "how could any air racer go wrong in that part of the country? Nearby Patterson is the home of those winning Wedell-Williams racers."

The brilliant Jimmy Wedell's design and engineering combined with sponsorship money from multimillionaire lumberman Harry P. Williams had resulted in several famous raceplanes! New Orleans enjoyed their fame; first-place winners in the Bendix in 1932, 1933, and 1934; second place in the Thompson in 1931 and 1932, and first in 1933 and 1934. Although I would have loved to get my hands on a Wedell-Williams racer, I arrived too late. In 1934, Guerd had told me about Jimmy Wedell's fatal crash in a Moth. Walter Wedell was tragically killed in a crash in '35 and, soon after arriving in New Orleans, I was shocked to read that "Mr. Harry" died in the crash of a Staggerwing Beech on takeoff from Baton Rouge.

I turned my interest to the famous Delgado Trades School on Shushan which, like the Wedells, built raceplanes. Perhaps a women's speed record was not completely out of my grasp. Ray Kidd had suggested that I find a place to live. New Orleans, full of air racing spirit, held promise. It was Mardi Gras festival time when I arrived and, in the midst of the joie de vivre, I wished Ray were there to make merry with me.

Shushan Airport was dedicated in February of 1934, exactly two years prior to my arrival, at the height of that year's Mardi Gras. As a portion of the Shoreline Beautification Program that dated back to the teens, Shushan was authorized to be built on Lake Pontchartrain as early as 1928, but had taken a great deal of planning. Pilings and footings had to be anchored to support concrete poured onto reclaimed lakebottom acreage.

The year that Shushan formally opened, air races on land

and over the lake were flown. The racing planes were christened by beautiful debutantes. (New Orleans was filled with beautiful women. They, like women the world over, were attracted to airplane pilots, especially dashing air racers and daredevil acrobatic pilots. I lived to rue that.) At the dedication, racers and aerobats performed while hoopla—band concerts, drill team exhibitions, parachutists, military demonstrations, and political speeches—added to the fervor of the Mardi Gras and filled the agenda. That year, Jimmy Wedell set an unofficial world's speed record—266 mph—in his Wasp Sr-powered Special #45 and Steve Wittman set a world's record for airplanes weighing less than 441 pounds—137 mph.

I'd known so many of the famed racers: the Wedells, Harold Neumann, Steve Wittman, Lee Miles, Art Chester, Gordon Israel, and Art Davis. I'd heard, too, of the money the men earned and knew that their purses from a single race dwarfed my meager winnings from any women's races. But, perhaps by 1936, as Genevieve Savage had hoped before she, too, was tragically killed in an air crash, things would improve for females in aviation. I thought about Genevieve and hoped that she would be long remembered. She and others gave the ultimate— their lives. Yet, I knew she had not only promoted herself, but *all* women when she participated in the aviation that she so loved.

Figuring that my first priority was to get a job as a flight instructor, I drove to Shushan. I could apartment hunt once I'd landed a job. It was early afternoon when I parked by the airport administration building and walked around it. What an architectural delight, even more of a work of art than it had been rumored to be. At a cost of sixty-five thousand dollars in 1932, I was sure that it bettered by far any other terminal in the country, at least any I'd seen.

The day was soft with a wash of warm wind from the gulf, a breeze that riffled the silken skirt around my legs and tossed the wide collar of my white long-sleeved blouse up around my neck. I straightened it a few times, pulling it from around my face, as I strolled around the outside of the impressive building. Scattered, puffy clouds cast moving shadows across the walls and walkways and sultry humidity lingered in the air—air scented with honeysuckle and pungent shoreline odors.

The outside of the building wore magnificent sculptured panels—bas relief that followed the development of aviation. I took my time, enjoying the structure and its coastal location, becoming acquainted with what I hoped would soon feel like home. Once indoors, I caught my breath. Shushan Airport was gorgeous, bedecked with aluminum- and bronze-trimmed tile, marble and terrazzo. The sheer drama of the massive waiting room, vaulting two stories into the air, drew my eyes to the marvelous balcony above. The mezzanine balcony surrounded the entire room as did a remarkable sculptural frieze, an ornamental band that encircled the room, a portrayal of the development of the airplane. I would have to run up the stairs and investigate that later. Or take the elevator. What a remarkable place. It made me chuckle to think of the little shack Guerd and I'd enjoyed at Newport. I'd have to tell him about this. What a contrast!

Marble decorated the walls, warmed by color in tones of red, cream, and beige. But, most striking and elegant was the giant compass in the midst of the terrazzo floor. Around its border were the names of cities of the world, their direction and the airline distance to each. I was entranced. I walked around its perimeter twice, memorizing the distances, imagining the flights.

Corridors led to wings from the massive central room. I investigated the lower floor and climbed to the balcony and upstairs wings. Eight lovely murals were painted around the balcony walls. The dining room and the roof garden were more elegant yet. The building was a veritable museum and art gallery and it was my kind of art—paintings of aviation and airplanes.

On the roof there were various levels to the roof garden and observation decks and, towering over all, the magnificent all-glassed octagonal control room. Its gleaming, pristine glass was formed with heat resistance and glare proofing for those who would inhabit the glass house to assist aviators within their view. Even aircraft directly overhead would be visible through the sparkling glass roof.

From the observation deck I could imagine approaching Shushan Airport in an airplane. I looked down at the blue expanse of Lake Pontchartrain, the wide concrete runways and waterways for both land- and sea-plane arrivals and departures—facilities that made most other airfields pale to nothing more than overgrown pastures or gravel trails. For night operations, there were floodlights, eight sets of three twenty-four-inch beacons that promised to illuminate the night runways to the brightness of day. I could hardly wait to start flying. As magnificent as the area was from the ground and from this lofty perch, I could scarcely imagine the beauty of the entire watery region from the air.

As I left, I saw a coffee shop, a news and cigar stand, an infirmary with rooms for a doctor and nurses, a post office for the airmail, and even hotel rooms. Now, if I could only land a job at this exciting airport.

In the hope of making New Orleans the hub of the southern air network of the United States, Shushan Airport wooed commercial operators like John Maynard, an airline pilot who also flew the mail. I'd longed for a chance to fly the mail. I discovered that Maynard flew from New Orleans southeast to Pilottown to link with ocean steamers and cut the delivery time of overseas mail by several days. He owned, as Hobley-Maynard, a flying operation for flight training and charter flights and, as I approached his office building, I couldn't help but smile at the Taylorcraft and Aeronca airplanes parked on the ramp. I might have been unfamiliar with Shushan and New Orleans, but I was more than comfortable with those airplanes. It buoyed my spirits to see the row of perky taildraggers and I confidently entered the office to apply for a job.

It was March 1, 1936, that John Maynard and I flew together as he checked my skill in Aeroncas. He hired me.

"I can't start flying students immediately," I explained to

Maynard. "I've a chore undone in D.C., an airplane that I have to pick up and fly down here to Shushan. But, I'll be ready in a couple of days, if you want to schedule some students then."

It was Guerd's Aristocrat that hadn't yet been sold. I traveled by train to D.C., then flew south to Shushan, seeing from the air what I'd pictured from the observation roof of the administration building. What a lovely area. Surely a buyer could be found in New Orleans. In the meantime, with "my own" airplane nearby, I was ready for any race, cross-country flight, an aerobatic demonstration, any contests, or a sale. I called Guerd to tell him so.

Once back in New Orleans, I lost no time starting to work for Maynard. By the end of March, I'd flown many people during the day and had well tested the remarkable Shushan night lights. After sundown, New Orleans sprawled in twinkling splendor beneath my wings and I had my share of flight students and passengers for sightseeing flights over the city I was learning to love.

The Mississippi River curves in a crescent around New Orleans, cupping the city and Lake Pontchartrain in its palm and giving the city its nickname. It flows almost directly east before turning south to drop much of its sediment in the delta and lose itself in the immense Gulf of Mexico. With so much water — canals, bayous, lakes, and rivers—I found it remarkable that such a profusion of tall cedars and cypress trees could find foothold for their roots. However, they looked magnificent: stately and green, liberally bedecked with draping Spanish moss. I became well acquainted with my new surroundings and I shared places of interest with those who flew with me. Like a barker in a carousel, I called back over my shoulder to show the mighty Mississippi, the waterways of the city, the pumping stations on each canal, the thirteen-million-dollar Huey P. Long Bridge, and the eleven-million-dollar spillway created between the Mississippi and Lake Pontchartrain. I especially loved night flights and the beautiful and changeable city light patterns that flickered brilliantly, reflected by so much water.

One day, airborne in a Taylorcraft, I was instructing a young man named Buddy Classie. We headed for a thick, billowy cumulus cloud and, before it became illegal for a pilot adhering to visual flight rules, I challenged him. I said, "Buddy, I'll bet you can't fly into that cloud and keep your bearings, keep the wings straight and level, and come out of the other side."

Buddy took my challenge and aimed the T-craft for the thickest portion of the cloud. He had no idea how confused he could get once he lost sight of the ground. With vision obscured, no other bodily senses help to tell which way is "up." Buddy was too new to the airplane to know what the instruments might tell him and "blind" instruments were still new to many of us.

Buddy dove into the foamy, blinding cloud. I was ready. I predicted that he would lose control of the airplane and he did. We came spinning down out of that cloud and I laughed aloud until I glanced at Buddy's face. He was terrified! His eyes were clamped shut with terror. His hands yanked back on the stick, holding it to him in a viselike grip.

"Let loose on the stick," I yelled at him. "Let *loose!*"

We were spinning around and around. Buddy's eyes stayed shut, his lips curled slightly, baring his teeth. He clung to the stick. I had to wrest control from him or we faced sure death! He was aggravating everything, tightening the spin!

I hit him, but still he held on. I yelled again, "Buddy, *listen* to me. Let *go!*"

I whacked him as hard as I could on the side of the head with my elbow. His head snapped back and his grip loosened. I grabbed the stick, kicked the rudder hard, pushed the stick forward, and eased the airplane out of the dive. We came out of the spin to straight and level. Buddy came out with a black eye. Later, flying Grumman Widgeons for the state of Louisiana, Buddy undoubtedly pursued his training to obtain an instrument rating. He probably never forgot his first experience with thick clouds and a spin.

I had the dubious honor of teaching one of the local gangsters to fly. His goons drove him to the airport in a limo and stuck around while I taught him the fundamentals of flying. He was dour and taciturn, generally grunting his understanding when I asked him a question. On the day that he soloed, I told him to take the plane around the traffic pattern a few times. He legged his way out of the cockpit afterwards, scowled at me, and, in the only comment I'd ever heard from him, said, "That was the first time in my life I've ever missed a woman."

During my moves from Newport, to D.C., and to New Orleans, my brother, Dean, and I kept in touch by telephone and letters. Dean had married his second wife, Helen Walsh, in 1932, and had became the proud father of two little boys, Wally and Larry. I received a letter from Dean in 1936. He wrote, "I've been trying to make a living with the Skelly Oil Company station in West Concord, Minnesota, Edna, but I'm barely scraping through. Last winter was a killer—extremely cold with almost continuous snow storms and blizzards. The driveway had about two feet of snow each morning and, after I shoveled every day, snow piles towered six or seven feet high. Sometimes I'd get the entire lot shoveled and not see a single car to service all day. It is hard on Helen, too. Wally is two and a half years old and Larry is almost one. Do you suppose you could find work for me in New Orleans?"

I asked Mr. Hobley, the silent partner with Maynard's Air Service and Gulf Manager of Luckenbach Steamship Company, if he could use my brother on the waterfront. He offered to interview Dean, so Dean, Helen, and the babies moved south. Dean was hired as a waterfront clerk. With a pay of $125 a month, life began to improve for them, but only temporarily. Helen, like our mother, got tuberculosis. In an effort to help, I purchased a five-acre lot for them near Covington, across Lake Pontchartrain. Pine trees covered the plot and, since ozone from pine trees was reportedly healthful for those with TB, we thought it a good place for the Gardner family, a good investment. Dean worked in New Orleans all week and returned to Covington each weekend.

Personal outrage, tragedy, and professional disappointment marred my otherwise challenging existence in New Orleans. I thought the lighthearted spirit of Louisiana, where so many cheery folks hailed *"Laissez le bon temps rouler!"*, would epitomize my days, but it wasn't to be.

Initially, I built a hearty list of flight students and filled my days with flying. Within a year the student business had grown to the point that Maynard added to his fleet of Taylorcrafts and C-3 Aeroncas to handle the load.

At last, Ray joined me and we rejoiced to be together, to behave like newlyweds all over again. Eventually we discussed our own business on Shushan. I suggested, "Ray, if I can bring students to fly with Maynard, why can't we make a success of a flight school of our own? Can you help me promote, manage it?"

"Baby, I'm nothing if I'm not a helluva organizer. You name it, we'll get it. We'll start a money-making flight school, if that's what you want to do."

With my yellow DeSoto as collateral, we borrowed and paid money on a Piper Cub. We found an office on Shushan from which to operate and opened the Southern Aviation School. Our brochures read: "Ray L. Kidd, Business Manager, and Edna Gardner Kidd, Chief Instructor." Many of my former students came with me as I left John Maynard and we gradually added other airplanes to the single Cub. Kidd was a promoter and a half! He could talk his way into more deals than we could handle. We soon had a fleet of nine airplanes and a few other pilots.

I still had Guerd's Aristocrat and, after he had told me over the phone that he had a Waco F for sale, I'd made a deal for its sale. He'd deliver it, so we'd have to meet. I knew a confrontation was inevitable, but I dreaded introducing him to Ray Kidd. I called Guerd and told him, "I've found two buyers. They're both sharing the cost of the Waco, Guerd. Will you fly it down here?"

"You bet, Edna. I'd like to do that. It's plenty cool up here in the northland. Would I find it warmer in New Orleans?"

I didn't answer. Not with me, he wouldn't. I didn't quite know how to break it to him. I avoided the question and said, "Uh.

I think you'll like these fellows. They work on an oil drilling rig on a floating platform in the water. I'm teaching them to fly."

Guerd was interested. "I've heard that they are doing exploratory drilling in places we never before would have dreamed we'd find oil. Is it a long distance off shore?"

"No, they tell me it's in still, shallow water. They said that you could go out to the floating platform with them and the good news is that they agreed to pay cash for the airplane."

"I'm almost on my way," promised Guerd. He started off toward New Orleans, but called me on the telephone from Greenville, North Carolina. "It will be a while, Edna. I lost a cylinder. A rocker arm support broke and the top of the cylinder popped off. I'll have to wait here for a new one to be shipped from Chicago."

When he arrived, he walked through the door at Southern Aviation School. He walked toward me with his arms out, but I stepped back and said, "Uh, Guerd? This is Ray Kidd."

Guerd's arms dropped to his sides. He looked at one after the other of us, then, with obvious self-control, held out his hand. Ray took it vigorously and said, "You have that Waco F outside? Edna's collected all the money for you. That's a rarity in these days, although I guess the worst of the Depression is behind us. We hope." He laughed lamely, but Guerd wasn't looking at him. He was staring at me.

"Well, I can't say this is a surprise," he said to Ray, his eyes never leaving my face. "But I won't say that I'm especially pleased to meet you, either."

He added, to me, "I guess I'll take that money and meet the men who want the airplane. Are they around?"

"Yes, Guerd. They said they'd like you to see their Texas Company drilling operation."

"Well, the day has been a hell of a surprise. I trust you haven't arranged for a windstorm to come up while I'm on the water."

"Don't be silly. We weren't engaged. You knew that."

"Yes. And I knew you'd not be long without a man. I just don't understand...."

"Come on, Guerd," I interrupted, "I want to show those boys the Waco. I'll fly one of them in it, then you can go out to their drilling platform with them."

"I can hardly wait," he said drily. "Okay, Edna. You're calling the shots."

He and Ray came to the front door to watch the flight demonstration. Guerd distanced himself from Ray, lit a cigarette, and leaned back against the building, one hand in his pocket.

I walked around the Waco with the buyers, then directed one of them into the three-place open cockpit airplane. Normally powered by a Kinner, Guerd had mounted a Warner engine into it. I taxied out and lined up on Shushan's runway for takeoff and, wham, just after liftoff, the airplane snap rolled and we crashed into the ground! Before I could kick a rudder or straighten the wings, before I could even *think*, it turned into a heap that was barely recognizable as having been an airplane.

Guerd rushed out onto the field. Kidd stayed behind, his thoughts on the flight school office. He undoubtedly could see me safely climb out of the wreckage. I brushed myself off and checked the student, who miraculously wasn't hurt either. Guerd said, "Are you hurt, Edna?"

"No, damn it all. Just my ego. What in hell happened? I wanted to make the machine look good for the buyer. I lined up for takeoff and, next thing you know, she was in a heap! Was it the damned wind?"

"I'd say you popped it off the ground too fast and she rolled on you, Edna. I came very close to doing the same thing in a Monocoupe when I was horsing around in Waukegan once while I was learning to fly. I threw the power to it and yanked it off the ground before she was really ready to fly. She snap-rolled. The wing didn't touch the ground though."

"I wish I could say the same."

At least Guerd had received all of the money for the purchase of the airplane. I had the Waco delivered to Parks Air College in St. Louis, Missouri, for repair and restoration. It was another expensive lesson.

Before he left, Guerd said, "You know, Edna. I used to think that we'd be an unbeatable couple. I always liked it that you were as enamored of flying and airplanes as you are. You always said, though, 'Men are such fools.' I guess you've finally gotten that point home to me."

"Guerd..."

"You are one helluva strong-willed lady. I think you have faced an uphill battle in your life and you're damned determined to succeed. I wish the best for you."

He returned to Newport, Rhode Island, and, four years later, married a schoolteacher, Dot Taylor, who became the mother of his two children. We remained long-distance friends. I sold his Aristocrat for him and we kept in touch with one another over the years.

Guerd was right about me. I was determined and strong-willed. I knew that I could succeed if I applied myself. I wasn't about to let anyone keep me from being a winning air racer— even the holder of a speed record, if I could manage it.

I arranged to meet racer designer Byron Armstrong and the personnel at the Delgado Trades School on Shushan. An instructor in the aviation mechanics classes, Armstrong was a longtime friend of Jimmy Wedell. Students at the school collaborated to build the fuselage of one of Wedell's racers as well as two racers of their own. As soon as I heard about their air race projects, I was itching to get an opportunity to fly their highly touted *Delgado Maid*. With a Curtiss Conqueror 700-horsepower engine, the sleek, black *Maid* wore race #6 on her fuselage.

I asked if there'd be a chance for me to win a landplane speed record in her when I heard that N.A.A. officials would be meeting at Shushan to time Art Davis as he attempted to establish a speed record for men. It was agreed that I could fly to try a speed record for women. My big chance!

Whenever possible, I hung around to watch the building process at the Delgado Trades School and even arranged for a sponsorship from the Jax Brewery. As the *Maid* was readied for the 1936 National Air Races, one pilot, Clarence MacArthur, tested her. After speeding to over 310 miles an hour, Mac-

Arthur landed, his feet blistered and burned, scorched by the heat of the powerful engine. New baffling was added to the firewall and the last-minute tweaking of the fast ship was completed.

Art Davis replaced MacArthur and I was in the crowd that watched him climb aboard for his record-breaking attempt. I was dressed in white coveralls and shoes with heavy leather soles with my gloves ready. My heart pounded. It would be my turn as soon as Davis was finished and he'd brought the ship back to me.

What happened is best described by Art Davis himself. He wrote:

> This was the last flight before the 1936 National Air Races. Below, the timers stood with stop watches on the marked course. I had put the ship in a thirty-degree climb, then I turned left for about a mile and a half.... In 19 years of high speed flying, racing, stunting and smoke writing, I have never flown a better handling high speed ship of such power. Suddenly the whole trim little racing plane was enveloped in a thick blanket of heavy black smoke! All visibility of the instruments, ground, and sky closed out.

Those of us below watched with horror as the beautiful *Delgado Maid* turned a half roll, vibrated, then, with an explosion, shot Art Davis out like a cannon ball. His parachute flowered and he floated down. The airplane augered into the soft muck of the Industrial Canal, the twenty-two-foot fuselage of *Maid* nearly out of sight in the swamp. "No!" I screamed aloud. My hopes of making history were dashed into the same millions of pieces as the landing gear, ailerons, rudder, and wings of the *Maid*. Damn! *Damn!* I felt completely helpless, drained. I'd held such high hopes.

Art Davis went on to successfully fly the Wedell-Williams #92 and that airplane became a movie star in 1938. Helen MacCloskey had been suggested as a pilot for the same airplane for a Bendix race but government officials said, "No lady pilot." Then, in bitter irony, the racer "starred" in *Tailspin,* a movie by Twentieth-Century Fox about a group of female air race pilots. It starred Joan Davis, Alice Faye, Constance Bennett, Nancy Kelly, Jane Wyman, and Joan Valerie—but *not* talented pilot MacCloskey! Probably all the flying scenes were flown by bewigged male pilots. It wouldn't be the first time nor the last!

The *Delgado Maid* didn't make it to the National Air Races, but I did. They were held at Mines Field, Los Angeles, California, and eight women were invited to participate in the Amelia Earhart Trophy Speed Race. I was honored to be chosen to compete with Henrietta Sumner of Akron, Ohio; Jennette Lempke of Bay City, Michigan; Melba Beard of Altadena, California; Martie Bowman of Medford, Oregon; Gladys O'Donnell of Long Beach, California; Genevieve Savage of Coronado, California; and Nancy Love of Boston, Massachusetts (who later would create the WAFs—the Women's Auxiliary Ferrying Squadron.)

Ed Porterfield, builder of the airplane in Kansas City that bears his name, called and told me, "Edna, I've just put a larger engine in my Porterfield. I'd like to have it in front of the crowd and I'd like you to race it in California for me. Can I count on you?"

"Ed, it won't have a chance at winning. The field includes a Staggerwing Beech, Gladys O'Donnell has a fast Taperwing Waco..."

"I don't care if it wins, Edna. I just want it out there so that the crowd can see it."

It was a far cry from the *Delgado Maid*, but at least I was racing and an airplane and all of my expenses were provided for me. I was fifth out of eight in the race, but the long cross-country was exciting and participation was lots of fun. I met skilled, wonderful people; I added to my newspaper clipping collection; and my trophy collection grew—it now numbered about twenty-five silver and bronze cups for the walls of my home.

Back at Shushan, though, it didn't take long to discover that, although I'd made many friends, I'd also forged an enemy. Maynard was angry that I'd left his employ and that Kidd and

I were competing with him with our Southern Aviation School. He confronted me and said, "You took my student trade. I'll break you if it is the last thing that I do."

Maynard was close with Dale Dalton, a government inspector who served Shushan Airport. The two wined and dined together and were fast friends. It seemed to me that they followed my every move, watched my operation just to pounce on any mistake they could find. They made it almost impossible for me to breathe.

One day, one of my students flew a Continental-powered A 40 Taylorcraft to Callender Field, down the Mississippi River a distance. He ran off into the grass and tipped the T-craft over onto its back. I went to the field; we righted the airplane and looked it over closely. I didn't see anything wrong with it, so I flew it back to Shushan Airport. Maynard turned me in to the feds for flying an airplane that had been flipped upside down.

Another time I was airborne in a Lambert Monocoupe and Maynard, in a Warner Fairchild, was flying beside me in the traffic pattern. I saw him rock his wings at me. "Well," I thought to myself. "He wants to see which one of these airplanes can leave the other in its dust. Why else would he rock his wings? He wants to race!" I gunned the Monocoupe and shot past him, a wide grin on my face. I loved to feel that surge of power. Maynard turned me in to the Feds for "racing in the traffic pattern." I was in trouble again.

The third time involved a three-place Stinson 108. I hired a pilot to carry passengers in it and, one day, it tilted to a stop in the middle of the airfield with a flat tire. Two men went out with a new tire and one man used his back as a lever, a jack, pushing against the bottom of the big wide Stinson strut. He raised the aircraft, the tire was replaced, and, unfortunately, he flattened the strut. I called the Stinson Factory to order a replacement, but continued to fly the bird before the new strut arrived. Maynard turned me in for flying a damaged airplane.

My license was revoked, a dreadful blow financially and emotionally. Southern Aviation School had grown significantly and the overhead costs were staggering while the lawsuit and re-voked license kept me from earning wages. It took a court of law, attorney fees, a great deal of money, and several weeks of time before I was finally exonerated, my certificates returned. The blow went deep.

Rather than wage a continuous war with the other operators on the lakefront airport, we decided to move, to dump the Southern Aviation School that we'd started. We opted to get off Shushan completely.

We bought a lease on some property near the Huey Long Bridge—the old Wedell-Williams airport. Work would erase whatever despair the lawsuit and fight with Maynard had caused. A new flying school, the New Orleans Air College, be-came my dream and my fulfillment. I'd build it up to even bigger size than the Southern Aviation School had been. I'd show John Maynard and any other bastard who wanted to keep me down. I'd get something going that would succeed and have some happy times doing so. The threat of a world war was sounding throughout our nation, directly affecting aviation. Government contracts were being let. I'd get a Civilian Pilot Training Program (CPTP) contract for courses at the Wedell-Williams airport. I'd get something going at Patterson, too. Didn't I hear that they needed seaplane piloting down there?

14

Wedell-Williams and Tragedy

On Sunday, May 23, 1937, New Orleans, Shushan Airport, and I received a unique treat. An unexpected radio call from an aircraft over Plaquemine, Louisiana, announced the intentions of a landing at Shushan. The radio transmission from a Lockheed Electra bore an unmistakable female voice. Immediately news was "leaked" so that a large crowd, newspaper reporters, and photographers with Moviegraph equipment could gather to greet the landing of the Electra and its famous pilot, Amelia Earhart. As I joined the gathered crowd, I couldn't help but envy the much-publicized Amelia. She was flying the silvery twin-engine airplane that was provided by Purdue University, where university authorities established a research foundation for Earhart, which included the airplane as a laboratory. What a lucky woman! Although, I would be the first to admit she worked hard for her "luck." At that moment I'd no idea that she would give her all.

Amelia, on a testing mission prior to a second attempt on her abortive around-the-world flight, was accompanied by her navigator, Fred Noonan; her mechanic, Bo McKneeley of nearby Patterson; and her husband, G. P. Putnam. This Electra was familiar to me. It was the same Lockheed with which Amelia and one of my friends and mentors, Helen Richey, had flown to a fifth-place finish in the 1936 Bendix race. That race ended at the Nationals at Mines Field in Los Angeles, where I raced the Porterfield in the Trophy Race dedicated to Amelia. I saw Amelia and Helen come in fifth in the Bendix cross-country race. I also saw Louise Thaden zoom across the finish line of that same race in her beautiful blue Staggerwing Beech! It was our turn to gloat! Men had been so sure that a *man* would win the coveted first-place prize that they benevolently offered a smaller (much smaller!) purse for the first *woman* to cross the finish line. Louise won them both! Amelia and Helen told me that they weren't thrilled with a fifth place, but all of us rejoiced for Louise. She beat all the men! It was great to see the pretty, brown-haired, vivacious Louise on the winner's stand accepting the huge trophy from Vincent Bendix himself.

As she started westward to circle the globe, Amelia ground-looped this Lockheed in Hawaii in March of '37. She'd flown from Burbank, California, and her disastrous takeoff toward the mighty Pacific resulted in smashed landing gear, a crumpled right wing, a damaged motor mount for the right engine, and bent propeller blades from plowing the Hawaiian runway. The ship was returned to Burbank for extensive repairs and, now, in a series of practice flights taking her eastward to Tucson, New Orleans, and Miami, Amelia and her crew were testing the big airplane before attempting a restart of the around-the-world flight.

Amelia, in dark slacks and a long-sleeved checkered shirt, its pointed collar open at her throat, waved as she climbed out of her airplane, smiling broadly. Her hair, customarily short and windblown, was further tousled by the New Orleans breeze. When she saw my familiar face in the crowd, she came straight toward me, her hand outstretched.

"How are you, Edna?"

I put my arm around her shoulders (reported by the *Times-Picayune* as "mannishly"—Rubbish!) and took her hand. "Amelia! It is wonderful to see you. I'm fine, but I was sorry to hear that you'd had some trouble getting started on your *big* flight from Honolulu. How is your airplane performing?"

"We're still flight testing. But, tell me about you. When I saw you at the Nationals, I guess you said that you were in New Orleans, but I still place you in the Northeast."

"I've got my own flying school here, Amelia. I resigned from the Naval Nurse Corps to make aviation my career."

"That was bold."

"It isn't easy."

"No. It isn't easy. I've said before, women run into stone walls and heartaches. But you know I'm all for women succeeding in aviation. Good luck, Edna."

"You have such *courage*, Amelia. Do you have plans to continue your world flight?"

"This is a shakedown," said Amelia. "The airplane was repaired in Burbank. Instead of continuing to fly around the world toward the west, I felt it better to make certain that all systems are in apple pie order."

I smiled. "You've added test pilot to all of your other ratings."

"Literally. We had to douse a fire two nights ago. The engine overheated and, just after we'd landed at Tucson, it backfired and burst into flames."

"Do I dare say anything as trite as 'Never a dull moment'?"

Amelia smiled. Before she started back toward her pressing crowd of admirers, she said, "We'll be staying at the Shushan Airport inn and having a dinner there tonight. Would you care to join us?"

I was flattered and told her so. I wouldn't have missed that dinner any more than I'd miss any air race for which I could scare up a racing plane. We ate together and, though they never admitted that her "last flight" was to start from Miami in just over a week, it was the primary topic of conversation. They debated and discussed data germane to the arduous flight. I heard them mention her radios, especially the trailing antenna provided by Paul Mantz. (I read later that she left the antenna behind in Miami, to Mantz's horror!) As rude and short-tempered as Gippy Putnam was toward her that night, I wondered if she wouldn't relish being off and away on the greatest adventure of her life.

Amelia Earhart's visit to New Orleans was front-page, big-headline news. But, prior to the publicity by George Putnam that catapulted her to become the most beloved, highly touted aviatrix in American history, Laura Ingalls was accomplished in aviation. Has anyone heard very much of her? Ingalls was a beauty, a dancer who gave up a stage career to fly. Before Earhart was reported to have flown to Mexico City, Ingalls completed a seventeen thousand–mile flying tour of Central and South America. She was the first woman flier to cross the mighty Andes Mountains alone, a remarkable feat when one considers the unsupercharged radial engine in her open cockpit Lockheed Air Express and the lofty altitudes of the Andes! Directly from that enormous undertaking, Ingalls entered a Lockheed Orion in the world's longest air race, the speed dash over eleven thousand miles and twenty-one countries between England and Melbourne, Australia. Ingalls copped intercity women's records and records in consecutive loops and rolls. She was named as the Outstanding Woman Flier of the International League of Aviators. She deserves the kind of recognition offered only to Amelia. So *many* female pilots do.

As the Lockheed Electra taxied for departure from New Orleans, I turned to Ray, "She's terrific. She really wants to help women to succeed in this 'man's field.'"

"I know another lady pilot who deserves some credit for that." He put his arm around me affectionately.

I frowned. "Don't you think it's a shame that all the honor and glory has to be bestowed on just one? You recognize the fantastic power of publicity, don't you?"

"You bet I do. That's what I do for a living!" After Guerd's reticence, even reluctance to subject himself to media promotion, it was comforting to know that Ray agreed with me. Experience with the USIS convinced him of the importance of wooing the press, attracting attention. His arm tightened around me. I relaxed against him. It was comforting, too, to have more than just moral support.

When Shushan Airport had opened in 1934, the old Wedell-Williams airport built by Harry P. Williams, approximately nine miles west of Shushan, closed. The property was jointly owned by Eastern Airlines, led by World War I flying ace, Eddie Rickenbacker, and the Illinois Central (I-C) railroad. After closure, it lay idle for two years while the I-C sought a manufacturer to build on the acreage, seeking to profit from lease of the property as well as from the shipping that would be done by the manufacturer.

In 1936, Ted VonRosenberg reopened Wedell-Williams with a fixed base operation (FBO) through a lease from Eastern and the I-C. He flew rebuilt Keystone Loening amphibians to transport supervisors of the Texas Company around the marshes and swamps to offshore drilling rigs, delivering them more efficiently than had their previous speedboats.

I often flew students to VonRosenberg's FBO for practice at takeoffs and landings. Occasionally I would solo a student at that field and, while the student was flying, VonRosenberg and I talked about the expenses and income of the field, owning the FBO, and the requirements of the railroad lease.

One day Ted VonRosenberg said, "I'm going to take a job crop dusting. There's an outfit that uses Travel Air biplanes and I'm going to give that a go."

"Would the lease for Wedell-Williams be available, then?"

"It sure would."

VonRosenberg had planted a wonderful idea into my mind. I climbed into the aircraft with my student and, when we got back to Shushan, I told Ray about VonRosenberg's departure. "This is just the break we've been looking for, Ray! We don't have to remain on Shushan."

Still demoralized and financially hurt by our legal problems with the operators at Shushan, we jumped at an opportunity for change. We purchased the twenty-year lease from the Illinois-Central, closed our Shushan operation, and moved to Wedell-Williams. Although it took time and effort and some of Ray's talent for raising money and obtaining airplanes, we created an FBO: the New Orleans Air College.

I continued to enter races and air shows. I flew charter customers, instructed students, and sold and demonstrated airplanes. As a Culver dealer, I ferried new Culver Cadet airplanes for customers from the manufacturers. In our expansion, one of the talented women that I'd taught to fly, Mary Dickey, joined our team. Mary reached her goals—commercial license, transport pilot, instructor rating—and began to teach with me. She proved to be a good friend and a wonderful flight instructor.

I had accrued so much flying time (2,888 hours) in 1938 that, when *Look* magazine did a survey of the flying hours of female pilots, I topped the list of American women. I was proud to lead an auspicious group of nine under the headline, "America's Top Women Flyers." The list continued with Phoebe Omlie, named by Eleanor Roosevelt as one of the "10 most useful women in the U.S.," and, third, former stage dancer Laura Ingalls. Amelia Earhart would have ranked next with 1,794 flying hours, had she not disappeared on her round-the-world flight in 1937. Her fourth place was taken by Janet Knight, a flying instructor at San Francisco. Fifth, Edith Foltz Stearns, a pioneer pilot of the Pacific Northwest, was a flying instructor in Salem, Oregon. Jean La Rene Foote, sixth, was the holder of an endurance record. She had learned to fly when she was thirteen. She taught and helped manage a flying school with her husband in Dallas, Texas. Seventh was Aline Rhonie Brooks, known for the history-of-flying mural that she painted at Roosevelt Field, Long Island, New York. Eighth was famed Louise Thaden, the first woman to win the Bendix, who also won the Harmon trophy for the most outstanding flying achievement in 1936. Last, but far from least, Betty Lund, stunt flyer from Hollywood, California, showed 1,398 flight hours according to Department of Commerce records.

Despite my flying schedule, at race time I cast about to find an airplane that would be competitive at the Miami Air Maneuvers of 1939 and 1940. In 1939, I flew the 90-horse Lambert-powered Monocoupe of Clare Bunch, Monocoupe president. The race was handicapped, which means that a handicap in miles per hour was given to each aircraft based on the known piston displacement of the engine and expected speed performance. The score was based on elapsed time and a final score was achieved by subtracting the handicap speed of each airplane from the average ground speed of that airplane. Although three other women raced against me and all of them actually flew faster speeds than I, the airplane with the highest score is the winner. I won the tall K. K. Culver trophy and a huge bouquet of long-stemmed roses.

In the Miami newspaper, my picture was featured with such speed and acrobatic greats as John Livingston, one of the winningest air racers; Jimmie H. Woods, famous for creating, with his wife, Jessie, the Flying Aces Air Circus; and Vincent "Squeek" Burnett, an aerobatic pilot par excellence, former stunt pilot with the Flying Aces Air Circus, and later famous for his contribution to the safety of pilots flying the Martin B-26 Marauder bomber.

The record crowds at Miami that year topped eighteen thousand. Like an actress who finds glamour in the applause, whistles, and calls of "Bravo!" from an audience that comes to its feet en masse, it was heady to be singled out to receive an armload of silver and flowers before such a huge gathering of clapping, waving, whistling racegoers.

In 1940, knowing that the Lambert-powered Monocoupe was inadequate for the win, Clare Bunch and stunt pilot Mike Murphy fixed me up with the Clipped Wing. This was the race after which Tex Rankin blurted, "Edna Gardner flies like a man!" I just flew, that's all. I flew the straight-legged, stubby-winged Monocoupe and got it around the pylons *first*. That's what I was there to do and it felt great!

Since the late thirties, the rumblings and preparations for war wrought changes in aviation. In Louisiana, we recruited students for our New Orleans Air College, some of whom followed me from Shushan and some who were lured by the rumors of military mobilization in Europe. A war effort began in our country and air racing, balloon-bursting, flour-bombing, and spot-landing contests began to wane.

President Franklin D. Roosevelt was quoted as having said, "Our existing (air) forces are so utterly inadequate that they must be immediately strengthened." Procurement programs for airplanes and airmen were instituted. Our U.S. Air Corps numbered a paltry 26,000 in comparison to 100,000 Brits and 500,000 in the Nazi Luftwaffe. Our aircraft inventory tallied 800 modern planes to the 1,900 of the British and the Luftwaffe's astounding *4,000.*

Although there continued to be charged arguments against preparation for war from isolationists, followers of the doctrine of air superiority focused on aviation. The prophetic Billy Mitchell—a man born ahead of his time!—put the spotlight on the contributions that could be accomplished by military aircraft and aviators.

As soon as the opportunity arose for civilians to teach the military pilots, our New Orleans Air College garnered a governmental contract for the Civilian Pilot Training Program (CPTP). The first group started training on June 15, 1940, as England became beseiged by Hitler's forces and the Battle of Britain began. Our air college was one of nearly seven hundred centers throughout the United States, Alaska, Hawaii, and Puerto Rico at which the structured program commenced. Certificated by the Civil Aeronautics Board (CAB), we were required to offer a seventy-two-hour ground school course and thirty-five to fifty hours of flight training. With a national quota of forty-five thousand new pilots to be trained at a rate of fifteen thousand every four months, we knew that, despite an initial monetary outlay, a flight school would profit handsomely.

Did *most* Americans think we could practice isolationism? In an impassioned plea to the generally apathetic public, a female pilot, and leading member of the Ninety-Nines, Nell F. Behr, of Anderson, South Carolina, stirred fellow Americans. She wrote:

The important question today is, "Is America ready today to defend herself?" and the answer is, "No." Congress has given almost unlimited power to our president to re-arm our country. They have finally admitted that our defense is air power, that WINGS ARE A NECESSITY IN NATIONAL DEFENSE! The time has come when we need every available engineer and mechanic working twenty-four hours a day turning out defense planes. While these are being manufactured, we must recruit without delay every qualified boy to train as an airplane pilot...[to receive] advanced training in handling fast pursuit ships and bombers...[and in] machine guns and the use of bomb sights. All this sounds cruel—to teach our son John during peace times—but it is the only safe insurance and assurance of a continued peace.

An emergency is at hand.... We must act quickly to strengthen our wings to equal that of four powers in Europe who now seem to have the upper hand.... Our first and most important step is air defense. There is a program underway to train pilots under the Civilian Pilot Training Program. This will be free to the trainee and will include any boy from the age of eighteen and twenty-five who has at least one year of college training and passes a rigid physical examination. The ground school course is to be given at various institutions and the basic flying course given at local airports. The quota of students is sixty, fifteen to each instructor.

The outlay of cash comes from the operator who handles the program. Little does the public know that it is a big job and an expensive one, too. The school must be approved and the operator must invest thousands of dollars in insurance, equipment, planes, mechanics, parachutes, and has to hire instructors. Instructor pilots are at a premium now as only C.A.A. re-rated instructors can teach on these programs. Bookkeeping for one of these courses requires the full time of a competent stenographer. Currently, the costs are absorbed by operators; but, with war getting closer to our shores hourly, it is pretty certain that Uncle Sam will soon appropriate funds to furnish this equipment and the training will be done under the direct supervision of Army officers in order to speed up our emergency defense. Let's train our American youth to fly, furnish them with the best planes in the world and ensure that our winged strength can better that of the opposing powers of Europe!

Behr was right. We bore the considerable expense of organizing our CPT Program, purchasing three Taylorcrafts, three J-3 Cubs, a Ryan STA, and a Cessna Airmaster. I used the T-crafts and Cubs for primary training, then transitioned students into the Ryan and Cessna for cross-country navigation and advanced training. Women were included in the program, although most of the students were men. I followed in the footsteps of the admirable Stinson sisters who, more than two decades before, had taught men to fly for World War I. What irony that I, a complete stranger to combat flying and, as a woman, strictly prohibited from it, was found qualified to prepare men to fly in combat for the United States in what proved to be World War II! I didn't waste time feeling bitter. There was money to be made in the CPT Program and we stayed busy. Success buoyed my spirits, helped me to recover from the disappointment of having warred with the other operators at Shushan, and, I was soon to discover, one of my life's ravaging heartaches.

In 1940, I wrote to the Civil Aeronautics Division to request a reissuance of my student permit with its original number, #4013, which had expired August 27, 1929. They wrote, "It is regretted that this number cannot be assigned to your commercial pilot certificate of competency since the numbers assigned to student pilot licenses were issued from a different series of numbers." I also requested that they reissue my pilot license in my married name—Edna Gardner Kidd.

That, I discovered, was wasted effort. The ink was scarcely dry on my new certificate when Ray dealt a staggering blow. He faced me late one evening to tell me that our five-year-old marriage was over.

"Why? What on earth is the matter, Ray?" I asked, incredulous.

"I've..." he stammered. He frowned and breathed a heavy sigh.

I waited, increasingly agitated by his evasiveness. I began to think of his unexplained late nights. I recalled nights that I'd spent away with our airplane business, nights that I'd tried to call but had received no answer. I remembered having seen a flicker of a smile cross his face when I'd tell him of plans to be away at an air show, in an air race, ferrying airplanes, teaching night flight to students, or flying cross-country.

"Oh, that's no problem, honey," he'd said magnanimously. "You do what you have to do."

And there were furtive phone calls that I'd occasionally interrupted. How could I have been so blind? So *stupid!*

"It's another woman, isn't it?" I straightened, tensed. Anger made my stomach knot, my voice quaver. My mouth was suddenly dry and I felt strangely spent, dead inside.

"Edna, you're busy all the time. She's...."

"She's what? An empty-headed beauty? A hussy who can't keep her hands off of you?"

"She isn't empty-headed at all. She attends Sophie Newcomb...."

"Ye gods, a *college* girl? Half your goddamn age? Was she a student in our Tulane-Newcomb civilian pilot course? Christ! Don't even tell me. I don't want to know!"

"She *needs* me. You're so capable, Edna. So strong..."

"You son of a bitch. How else could we have existed in this business if I wasn't capable? I *have* to be strong. Don't you understand that? Don't you know how impossible it is for a woman to succeed in aviation at all?"

"There's more, Edna. She's pregnant...." Hs eyes met mine briefly. He shrugged. "I..."

"You bastard! You good-for-nothing bastard! Don't bother

with the lurid details. Just get out. Get out of this house. Get out of our business." My voice rose to a scream, "It's *my* business now! Get out of my *life!* I don't need you. I don't need any man."

I grew as cold as ice. I shivered, staring at him as if he was a complete stranger. As he gathered his clothes and hastily threw them into two suitcases, I watched with strange detachment. I wondered why on earth I'd married him. I wondered if I had ever loved him in the first place. As he left, I slammed the door—hard.

Our marriage was dissolved in divorce and I began to put the pieces of my life back together. I knew that, rather than spend the rest of my lifetime worrying about the fidelity of a mate, I could go it alone. I could probably manage even better without him. I erased every mention of his name on any newspaper clipping that I could find. I regained my identity as Edna Gardner and swore that no man would ever be in the position of getting me off track again. I was going to make a living in aviation. I was going to make a name for myself and nobody would ever get in my way again!

The stress of confrontation with other operators on Shushan and the devastation of divorce combined to fuel the energy and determination that it took to succeed in business. I believe that any person who is hurt or angry can react positively to better a situation and to grow. Instead of crumbling with despair, drowning my sorrows in alcohol, or sleeping with any man who wanted me, I forged a burning need to succeed in aviation, to succeed with life. I made my CPT programs fly!

Yet, hurts continued to accumulate. Some of my students came with tales of having been hired by the airlines serving New Orleans—some with barely two or three hundred hours to my three-thousand. I had been turned down by Central Airlines, but five years had gone by. I still yearned to be an airline pilot and figured that if they would hire my *students*, why not me? I put in my application and went for a physical examination. The airline refused me because of my height. The weak excuse was that I was too short. I stood back to back to measure myself against two young men who had been hired, those who had learned everything that they knew about flying from me. I was as tall as one and a half-inch taller than the other.

What was it my mother used to repeat to me over and over again? "Rise above it, Edna," she would tell me when I was discouraged. "Rise above it."

At least I could still fly—still *loved* to fly! I followed up on some rumors I'd heard about seaplane flying in Patterson. I'd heard there were lumbermen down there who needed repeated float trips in and out of the bayou country. That sounded like a lot of fun. I met millionaire Thayer May, owner of a prosperous lumber company and a close friend of Harry P. Williams, who lived on the Bayou Teche near the Patterson airport.

Thayer May invited me to check him out in his beautiful white Staggerwing Beech. Once that was accomplished, I taught his wife, Pat, to fly it. The Mays, interested in having their logging supervisors licensed as pilots, invited me as an instructor and extended an invitation for me to stay at their mansion on the Bayou Teche. A Taylorcraft and a Cub on floats were moored in the water in front of their stately home. I obtained my seaplane rating and spent many hours splashing down in the bayous, teaching the four May Company supervisors to fly.

Some of the flying was done at the Patterson airport. A famous landmark at Patterson was the tall watertank attached to a beacon tower. On warm, sunny days, when students were few and far between, I'd climb halfway up that water tower to sunbathe in the nude. I never knew until much later that some aerial eyes spied me there.

One day, my flying cancelled because of rain, I drove to Covington to visit my brother Dean and his wife, Helen, still frail after her bout with TB. To supplement their income, Helen and Dean raised chickens on their small piece of property. Dean had been invited by Mr. Hobley, King of the Mardi Gras Krewe, to attend a formal pageant. Amazed that he would don a tuxedo, I wanted to hear all about it. While I was there, Dean said that he and Helen had some broilers that they wanted to deliver to New Orleans. They asked me to stay with their small boys.

I said I would—the most tragic decision of my life. No sooner had Dean and Helen driven away when Wally and Larry begged to be allowed to go swimming in the river. I stayed nearby as they paddled and played in the shallow water. Then, for just a moment, I left the boys alone while I went into the house. I returned to the river to find others standing over an inert little figure on the sand. Larry had slipped under the water and drowned. He was gone. Dead.

I burst into tears. Wally was crying and I wrapped my arms around him and held him tightly, swaying with his small, sob-wracked body. There was nothing on this earth that I could do. Larry was a beautiful little boy and now I had to live with the biggest hurt of my life. Even more devastating, I had to tell Dean and Helen when they returned from New Orleans. None of us would ever recover from this tragedy.

There is salvation in staying occupied and busy. Dean and Helen shortly left Covington and moved to New Orleans. We sold the place and, although Larry's loss would never be forgotten, we all tried to silence the pain with concentrated effort toward other goals. I plunged deeper into aviation; continuing to teach students, barter airplanes, and participate in air shows in the New Orleans area. I formed a three-ship formation with Culver Cadets to show off the airplane and to advertise its virtues: on just 75 horses the Cadet cruised at 120 miles an hour.

I continued to fly passengers as a charter pilot. One black night I lost the engine in the Beech Staggerwing I was piloting. I headed for an off-airport landing. We were going down. I just had to hope that, aimed for a large black stretch away from twinkling lights of a small town, the dark hole represented a field and not a morass of mud, a swamp, or a shallow marsh. I was lucky. The airplane wheels touched firm footing. We rolled to a stop and, though arrangements had to be made to send my passengers on by train, at least they made it. We all made it.

I made my third and final attempt to be hired by an airline. I'd written to Texas several times, submitting my qualifications to Braniff Airlines only to hear, "We aren't hiring." One day I flew a customer to Houston in a Waco cabin plane. It was a good chance for me to apply for an airline piloting job in person. I knew that Helen Wheeler had been hired as a pilot for Braniff, although, admittedly, she had a connection. She was married to one of the Braniff sons. I thought, if they've hired a woman once, perhaps they'll hire me.

I said to the secretary, "I have my application in and I'd like an interview," and was directed to a chair in the waiting room. Two men waited ahead of me. The secretary invited each man, singly, to enter the airline official's office. Two men entered after I did and she called one after the other of them. I sat for what seemed an eternity. "What's the matter with me?" I began to wonder. "I arrived before the last two."

When the room was empty, I asked, "What about my turn? Must I sit here all night?"

She hurried into the official's office and then held the door open to me. "Miss Gardner?" she said, briskly.

I entered and the Braniff employment officer invited me to sit down. He said, "I've looked over your qualifications, Miss Gardner. You have an impressive number of hours and variety of accomplishments in aviation."

"Thank you."

"Unfortunately, I don't believe we have a need...."

"I'd really like to fly for Braniff," I interrupted.

"No. Uh...Miss Gardner. I've given it a great deal of thought."

"Couldn't I at least have a check ride, get a chance to show you...."

"Miss Gardner, let me be frank. Think about it. Do you really think that people would climb aboard our airliners if they saw a *woman* pilot in the cockpit?"

"I can't imagine what you mean! I have a thriving flight school in New Orleans. People climb aboard airplanes with me several times a day, every day of the week."

"I'm sorry, Miss Gardner," he said coldly. He stood up and managed a tight-lipped smile. The interview was over.

I returned to the Wedell-Williams Airport, shouldering about all the discouragements that I could take. If it weren't for the success of my New Orleans Air College and the friendship of Mary Dickey, I'd have wondered what life was all about.

A message from the U.S. Navy waited for me. The Navy expressed an interest in buying the Wedell-Williams property and the government was willing to pay twice the money I had spent to obtain the twenty-year lease. That was good news. Although there had been some wonderful times, I had had more than enough pain in New Orleans. I was ready to start anew someplace else.

"Mary, what would you think about going to Fort Worth, Texas, with me?" I challenged my flight instructor, Mary Dickey.

"Fort Worth? What's there, Edna?"

"I've heard about a Spartan School in Tulsa, Oklahoma, where they are hiring flight instructors to teach instrument flying to the military."

"We don't have instrument ratings—neither of us."

"*That*'s what's in Fort Worth." I laughed.

Mary joined my laughter. "Aha," she said.

"We can go to Meacham Field, obtain our instrument ratings, and then go together to Tulsa and get jobs with Spartan. We could share the expenses of apartments in both towns and get the ratings we'd like to have anyway. Agreed?"

"Agreed! That's really a good idea."

After arranging for the sale of Wedell-Williams and my fleet of airplanes, I packed my belongings, bade sad farewells to Dean, Helen, and Wally, the Thayer Mays, and others. Saying good-bye to friends is eased for a pilot, though, by knowing that our highways in the sky would probably cross many times.

15

Racing—
the
Throttle to
the Wall

Mary Dickey and I landed at Meacham Field, Fort Worth, Texas, in 1941. Enrolled for instruction at Aircraft Sales, owned by air racing pilots Les and Marty Bowman, with whom I'd competed, we added instrument ratings to our tickets.

We were as shocked and furious as all Americans when the Japanese bombed our fleet at Pearl Harbor. I told Mary, "Our country helped to train some of those sneaky bastards to fly. I'm ashamed to have had even a tiny part in it. I even flew a Jap to the shrimp platforms on the bayou in Louisiana to buy barrels of shrimp. I had no idea that large quantities of dried shrimp from *our* fisheries would end up feeding warmongers!"

Mary and I joined our country's war efforts. For three years, we taught instrument flying for the War Training Service (WTS), readying military pilots at the Spartan School of Aeronautics in Tulsa, Oklahoma. We taught flight by reference to instruments and radio navigation in Spartan Execs. I'd take to the air with one in the front cockpit beside me and three men in the rear for each mission. To give each man a turn at the controls, we'd slide the seat back for two men to swap positions, crawling over each other. I made every effort to see that the young men that I trained were fully competent before being sent into battle.

In 1944, when General Henry H. "Hap" Arnold decided that the quota of military pilots had been met, military training stopped immediately. The government axed the program so promptly that Mary and I went to work one morning at 7 A.M. and were paid and finished by noon. With the abrupt end to WTS, Mary moved to the Pacific Northwest and continued to flight instruct. I entered the Army Nurse Corps and spent the last two years of World War II overseas.

When PEACE in four-inch-high letters headlined every major newspaper in the United States, I rejoiced. President Harry S. Truman was quoted as saying it would be possible to release about five million men from the Army. Magazine articles predicted that thousands of general aviation airplanes would have to be built to satisfy the demand of the many returning GIs and interested civilians who had discovered the thrill of flying. Writers figured that returning wartime pilots would want to keep on flying and that the government's G.I. Bill would open a floodgate to persons who wanted to learn to fly and would have governmental financial aid to do so. It looked as if aviation was about to boom and I wanted to be part of it.

In 1946, I returned to Fort Worth and was hired by Roy Taylor as a flight instructor at Fort Worth's Meacham Field. He was establishing a flight school under the auspices of the Veteran's Administration for, among others, students who could utilize their G.I. Bill benefits for flight training. In addition to flying students, I also started ferrying airplanes from factories to dealers—Stinsons, Aeroncas, and Pipers.

Finally, the rage and humiliation over Ray Kidd had paled and, along with it, bitterness toward love. As I interviewed prospective instructors for Roy Taylor's school, a tall, dark-haired former Marine approached. He smiled and I felt chills. I soon was involved in a relationship with George Murphy Whyte. In a whirlwind courtship, Murphy and I fell in love and decided to marry. Wed in August 1946, we moved into our first home in Fort Worth.

Murphy held civilian flying licenses for single- and multi-engine piloting, flight instructing, instrument flight instructing, and A & P—airframe and powerplant, the aviation designation for an aircraft mechanic. A caring man, he proved to be completely supportive of my passion for air racing. If an engine ran rough, Murphy tweaked the timing and checked the spark plugs. If a canopy needed to be modified, Murphy found a way to fashion a new one. I worked alongside him. If polishing an aluminum aircraft meant that the craft would run a few miles an hour faster, we scrubbed every inch to a high gloss. We figured new and better ways to get intake air to flow smoothly past the engine to reduce drag and we sealed any surface gaps to reduce friction. With Murphy's help, I entered every air race I could find and raced grooves into the sky.

A mere six years after the Wright brothers proved that man could sustain powered flight, the world's first air race had been held in 1909 in France and was won by Glenn Curtiss of the United States. After a hiatus during World War I, air racing continued in one form or another throughout the entire pre-World War II "golden era of flight." I first raced in that 1930s era, although I extended my own "golden era" well into the sixties, seventies, and eighties.

If people insist that they've been "bitten by the aviation bug" upon learning to fly, imagine the ravages of the contagious disease that is called *air racing!* Racers share a relentless quest for speed. As I zoomed low—close around pylons, close to the ground, close, too close to the other racers — I breathed in quick gasps. In the heat of competition, my heart pounded and sweat dripped from my body.

Racing is much more than a mere battle of wits; it takes strength to handle the control stick. Turbulent air caused by the wind tumbling past physical obstacles could yank the stick from sweaty palms. Violent burbling wash behind all of the planes that plunge around the course, their highly revved propellers churning, could arc an aircraft out of control. Twirling vortices have been known to kill.

In the heat of a race, the "G" forces of a tight, banking turn sucked me down into the seat, more than doubling my weight. My hands and arms were suddenly leaden on the stick and occasionally my eyes were rolled back into my head. A rush of adrenaline spurred me on and racing produced a heady thrill that lingered long after the race was run. To *win* was electrifying.

After the Second World War, piston-engined and jet military planes were purchased by civilians and the National Air Races started anew in 1946.

Early the next year, I said, "Murphy, look." I read a brochure that featured the Cleveland Air Races and told him, "They're offering an AT-6 race for women, the Halle Trophy Race, at the National Air Races. Oh, God, how I'd love to get my hands on one of those to fly at Cleveland. Will you help me?"

In one of the first of a long list of airplane acquisitions and mechanical improvements for my racing, he gave me a hug as he agreed. "Sure, baby," he said. "I bet I can scare up an AT-6 from some of the people I know from Columbus Air Force Base. I'd get a kick out of having one—not to race, just to poke holes in the sky. I'll even get it shipshape for you if you'll do something in return."

"What might that be?" I leaned against him. I thought I knew what he he had in mind.

"Keep my pretty baby's body from getting hurt. Pylon racing in AT-6s sounds hazardous. If they're in stock configuration, they'll all fly at the same speed."

"What speed could we coax out of one, Murphy?"

"Well, I'd imagine it'd be around 200 miles an hour. The dangerous part is that you'll *all* be circling those pylons at between 200 and 210 miles an hour. That bunches airplanes up on the pylons. Promise me you won't try to eat another woman's airplane alive?" He held me to him until I promised. We kissed. I was lucky to have a lover, a husband, and a friend all in one. That he was a pilot and a mechanic was icing on the cake.

One morning when I landed after having been flying with a student pilot, Murphy asked, "Do you want to help to modify the AT-6?"

I threw my arms around his neck. "You found one! Is it here? Did you really buy it for me?"

"Well, for you to race and for me to fly, too. I could use it with students. It'll have to earn its keep."

"How about air race earnings?"

Murphy snorted. "You gotta be kidding. I haven't seen an air racer yet who *made* money. Oh, yeah. They talk about those big purses for the winners, but it takes a huge purse in the first place to ready an airplane and get it out onto a race course."

Murphy whittled the rudder to help me coax more speed from the sleek silver bird. "If we remove the step on the side of the fuselage," he explained, "some drag will be gone."

"Anything extraneous can come off as far as I'm concerned," I agreed.

Murphy put all of the controls into the rear cockpit. "You'll fly from the backseat. Everything will be within your reach except for the plumbing and piping for the hydraulic release for the gear. That is going to be critical, Edna."

His face grew serious as he added, "You'll have to get airborne, clear the runway, and then lean forward to the handle in the front cockpit."

"The seat belt won't let me slide that far forward, Murphy."

"That's the critical part. You'll have to take off without your seat belt and reach all the way up past the left side of the front seat. It's going to be risky."

"I hope the C.A.A. isn't examining too closely. They'll disqualify me if they catch me without a seat belt. But, I can't race with the gear hanging down, either."

"Not if you want to be competitive."

No one had to mention competition to me. I must have been competitive from the day I was born! "I don't just want to be competitive, Murphy. I want to win! I'll just have to take some practice flights and learn how to manage the gear. It's as simple as that."

Murphy lowered the front cockpit four inches and measured my sitting height to fit a newly fashioned canopy to one inch above my head. I had minimal room for any maneuvering. We bought a large sheet of plastic, heated it, forced it over a mold, and weighted down the edges.

When I flew a practice flight after it was mounted, I discovered that we had distortion in the front corners of the bubble canopy. I selected some tall poles on the ground as practice pylons and, when I arced around one, fifty feet in the air behind that growling R-985 engine, I suddenly saw several poles. I learned to focus on the pylon way out ahead of me and keep it in sight until I'd passed it. I swore, "No pylon cutting for me."

All air race pilots amass a helpful crew from their lovers, employees, and friends. As my one-man pit crew, Murphy did a masterful job of tuning my engine. Grace Harris, the talented pilot who finished second in the 1947 Halle Trophy Race at Cleveland in front of my third place, gives credit for her ability to "polish the pylons" to race pilot Bill "Pappy" Ong.

In order to learn successfully the racehorse start for closed-course pylon racing, she wrote in her autobiography, *West to the Sunrise*:

Three AT-6s were on the line. I took the center one with Pappy [Bill Ong] on my left and our Chief Pilot, Wayne Miller, on my right. Clarence Diggs was the starter, standing on the field before us.

Pappy said, "When Diggs makes a circling motion with his hand, rev up your engine and hold the brakes hard. He'll raise his arm as the starter at Cleveland will raise the flag . . . then drop it. When he does, release the brakes and sock the throttle open—fast. Watch the torque—I'll be only 75 feet on your left."

With idling engine, I glued my eyes on Diggs. He made a circling motion above his head. I jammed on the brakes and advanced the throttle as much as the brakes could hold. On either side of me the roar of Wasp engines filled my ears. Then Diggs dropped his arm and ran toward the side of the field. I shoved the throttle open and the ship lurched forward. Pappy and Wayne seemed dangerously close as we tore down the field. They were on my wings as we took off to circle the airport and land.

That's exactly what it was like. We women lined up at the Cleveland Air Races in front of the grandstand filled with cheering race fans. My eye was focused on the starter, the arm he held high. "Lordy, don't let the ship drift due to torque. You'll kill yourself and maybe someone else, too," I thought. The latter would almost be worse. Is that where we come up with the fool idea, "Better dead than embarrassed?"

Grace trained in the art of on-pylon turns with Pappy Ong, too. He cautioned her not to wait too long and not to make steep climbing turns. She recalled Pappy's advice: "The secret is to establish your bank early enough, gradually increasing it as you approach the pylon. Then, with back pressure, you can complete the turn with low Gs and very slight loss of airspeed."

Grace and I were joined by two other AT-6 pilots: Ruth Johnson of California, who taxied up in her gleaming military trainer, and a curvaceous Hollywood starlet whose craft was powered by a 450-horse inverted Ranger engine. Grace wrote:

> Pappy said, "We've got a 4th place airplane. I think about all you can do is hold the throttle open, remember the things you've learned, and try to keep from getting run over. These lady race pilots..." and he shook his head frowning. I knew what he meant, for in 1946 we had witnessed two female pilots, Kaddy Landry and Dot Lemon, actually scrape wings on the home pylon in their fierce battle for the lead.

Murphy was equally solicitous. "I know you're aggressive, Edna. Just remember that those other cats are, too. The speeds are going to be very close. Keep your eyes open."

Our speeds were close, as Murphy had predicted. Ruth Johnson won at 223 mph, Grace was second at 215 mph, and I took third place at 210. When Murphy gave me a post-race hug, I told him, "Wait till next year. I bet we can lighten the airplane to get her going faster."

In 1948, Murphy, the AT-6, and I returned. Racers, crews, families, and friends congregated at the Cleveland and Carter hotels, where parties were hosted and revelry lasted long into the nights. I loved the social side of racing—the camaraderie with racing greats. I learned racing tips and found it exciting to belong.

Before race day, I sized up the women racers. I became reacquainted with Ruth Johnson and Grace Harris and met Betty Clark, Bella Heineman, Helen McBride, Doris Langher, Kaddy Landry, and Dot Lemon. Landry and Lemon were still locked in fierce competition, primed for another go. A former Powers model, gorgeous Nancy Corrigan, was a rookie. She had more than her share of help from eager men. I dismissed her as a threat during the race. It must be a jealous streak that makes it so difficult to take a beautiful woman seriously.

At one cocktail party we attended, Murphy held a glass in his right hand, a cigarette in his left, and listened to me tell of having talked with Doris Langher. "I bet I could do what Doris does, Murphy. She's a Link instructor. What do you think? We could buy a trainer and use it with instrument students."

Murphy was well acquainted with the Link, a small, hooded ground trainer that pivots on a unique vacuum pump and simulates straight and level flight, climbing, descending, and banking.

"It would be a large initial expense, Edna."

"But, it would cost students far less than flying in an airplane. I'm going to go for the rating. That and my multiengine rating, too."

He shook his head. "Here we are, supposedly relaxing before a big race and all you can think of is biting off more to chew. You're a driven woman, Edna." He laughed gently. "Why not just enjoy the party?"

But, the next day, when it came time for the race, Murphy was as "driven" as I. He said, "This is getting to be serious business, Edna. There are ten ships that will all be racing flat out. Watch yourself!"

Well, I didn't have to watch out for Grace Harris. She was way out in the lead. That three-bladed prop of hers (and whatever else she and Pappy Ong had done) sped her around the pylons at a fantastic 235 miles an hour. She finished nearly nine *miles* ahead of the rest of us.

After the race, I told Grace about my wacky gear retraction method. She laughed and bettered my story. She told me that she was watching the starter. His hand was raised and circling. A couple of C.A.A. men climbed onto her wing and saw that her shoulder harness wasn't connected. She'd tried to fake it, but they kept shaking their heads, shouting at her. She never gave an inch. She smiled sweetly at them as if she couldn't hear them above the sound of the engine. Then, when the flag sliced down, she poured the coals to it and the two men went ass over teakettle off the wing.

Grace was excited after her dramatic win. She said, "That was some start. We thundered across the turf, hell-for-leather."

"The rest of us snarled like fighting tigers, but you just left us in your dust," I said to Grace. To Murphy, I later added, "I think they should prohibit the use of that damned three-bladed prop."

Race rules did scratch the use of that propeller in 1949. Harris's pit crew removed the power section of her Warp engine and beefed it up with a 14-to-1 blower. There she was again, on the winner's stand getting flowers and a trophy from none other than the handsome movie star Jimmy Stewart himself.

Air racing proved to be downright addictive. I raced in pure speed contests. I entered handicap speed races, even exhibition races, fuel efficiency, and pre-race estimated speed races. Any excuse to race was a good excuse. I liked to climb into a strange airplane and open it up to find out what the sucker could do with a wide-open throttle—diving, screaming through the air. In the fifties and sixties, when organized national air racing slowed a bit—the air racing at Cleveland stopped abruptly in 1949 when Bill Odom flew Jackie Cochran's P-51, *Begin the Beguine*, into a house and killed an innocent young mother and her baby—Murphy helped me with racing airplanes and I entered a slew of cross-country races sponsored by the National Aeronautic Association (NAA) and the Ninety-Nines, the International Organization of Women Pilots.

"You're going to a lot of meetings, aren't you, Edna?" Murphy asked me one day. I was packing my suitcase again.

"I joined the Ninety-Nines in 1931, two years after it was chartered, Murphy, and long before I met you. It's a great group. They offer so many opportunities. I'm getting somewhere with them, too. I'm moving up to the board of directors and have a chance to be the president of the whole thing."

"I'm not surprised. That would really get you acquainted with the doers in aviation and give you a little clout."

"That's not all. It gives me a circle of people who share what I like to do—flying. You get a lot of tips from other pilots. You know that as well as I do."

I didn't list all the attributes of the organization for Murphy, but it pleased me to belong to a group that sponsored hundreds of aerospace educational workshops for teachers, gave airport tours for school children, aviation talks to service clubs, courses to alleviate flying fears in apprehensive airplane passengers, flight instructor revalidation courses, and, right down my alley, encouraged races to upgrade piloting skill and proficiency. As a nurse, I applauded that Ninety-Nines transported cancer patients and blood for the Red Cross.

The Ninety-Nines continue these projects to this day and also continue the airmarking projects started by Phoebe Omlie in the forties, painting huge compass roses on runways across the nation. They serve on local, state, and federal aeronautics commissions and give airplane rides by the thousands to interested youth groups whose young people will be inspired to be tomorrow's pilots. I was thrilled to be elected to serve as the president from 1955 to 1957.

Murphy knew that the Ninety-Nines have been involved with

many racing events like the AWTAR (All Women's Transcontinental Air Race), which was flown from 1947 to 1977, and the Air Race Classic (ARC), which started in 1977 and continues. For years, I entered women's long-distance races like the one Will Rogers parodied as the "Powder Puff Derby" of 1929. His name stuck. When the International Air Race was flown between Canada, the United States, and Central America, we became "Angels" and, again, the name, Angel Derby, stuck. The name was born when racing pilots had poor weather upon arrival in Monterey, Mexico—mist, clouds, and rain. As one after another of us staggered in through the murky skies, the Mexicans exulted, "Another angel has come down from the sky."

A beautiful young mother took it upon herself in 1935 to champion the cause for women to be allowed to fly during pregnancy. Officials had decreed that a pregnancy might cause a woman to have trouble at the controls of an airplane. She confronted the men of the CAA, which created headlines that read, "She'd License Stork to Fly!" There were even those officials who claimed that women shouldn't fly at all when menstruating.

Air racers, on the other hand, have always flown in either condition. Women pilots have been avid air racers since 1929, when the first women's cross-country Air Derby was flown and the Ninety-Nines was chartered. The Ninety-Nines have organized women's races all over the country—speed dashes, closed course races, and efficiency contests. The AWTAR became one of the largest women's aviation sporting events in the world. The first race in 1947 saw one entry and two women participating, but by 1959 it had grown to 66 entries and 129 pilots. Few other races were as demanding in terms of planning, aircraft knowledge, chart reading, weather analysis, and piloting skill.

The Powder Puff and ARC are long-distance races, roughly twenty-five hundred miles in length. Flying per race could more than double that distance, however, with flight to race starting points and home again at the completion of a race, effectively doubling the cost of racing as well. Some pilots fly practice courses that could triple or quadruple the distance and the cost. All Federal Aviation Regulations apply and the race is to be flown in daylight, in visual reference to the ground at all times.

After one particular race, I marched through the door to our home in Fort Worth in a foul, black mood. I was the president of the Ninety-Nines at the time and I was disqualified after an incident in Dayton, Ohio.

Murphy knew better than to even ask a question. He could tell by the fire in my eyes that I was in no mood to speak. I finally simmered down sufficiently to admit, "Damn, you can't race as much as I do without making mistakes and some enemies. I guess trouble is to be expected."

"Do you want to talk about it, Edna?"

"The chairwoman and the others in charge voted to disqualify me from the race. They said I took the wrong runway. They accused me of endangering another pilot. Murphy, *nobody* was hurt! We never scratched a girl."

"And the airplane?"

"Neither airplane was damaged. You know that I borrowed that Mooney airplane from Al Mooney and that the last thing I wanted to do was hurt it. I wanted to win so that he'd get the publicity for his airplane. I hate telling him that I not only didn't win—I got disqualified! The women voted that I took the wrong end of the runway to give myself a time advantage."

"What is your version of the story?"

"At takeoff, I took a glance at the wind sock. I taxied to the end of the runway that I thought favored that wind. I swear the wind shifted! Just as I took off, another lady pilot was headed straight toward me—landing. I thought, Maybe *she* chose the wrong runway. She pulled up abruptly. I banked hard. There was no damage done. Anyway, at the end of the race, when the fur quit flying, that was that. I was out. Not only that, they said they'd rather that I didn't fly their race again for a while. Fat chance I'd want to!"

Jackie Cochran, well known as brash and overbearing, was

no slouch in the temper department and neither was I. Hell, a shrinking violet wouldn't last a day in a career in aviation. If the men didn't browbeat her to death, the other women would.

"Could you have been wrong, Edna?"

"Oh hell, Murphy. Sure I could. But you know that those women doing the timing and observing at all the airports along the route have their likes and dislikes, too. I can hear the comments now. 'She's the president of the Ninety-Nines. How could *she* do such a thing?'"

Murphy put his arms around me.

"I didn't *mean* to cheat, Murphy."

He drew me close. Thank God for George Murphy Whyte. When we sat down at the table for dinner together later, I told him another story from the race. A little lovemaking did wonders for the disposition and I was even able to laugh.

"I heard that at another women's competition, the winner of the race was sponsored and, at the end of the race, the sponsor and his wife showed up to greet the racers. Rumor has it that the sponsor's *wife* was angry with the winning pilot because the pilot refused to sleep with the sponsor. Can you beat that? The wife thought the winner 'owed' it to her husband."

Murphy grinned and shook his head. "This racing does bring out some doozies!"

"Don't blame it on racing!"

"What did the winner do?"

"She called her mechanic at home and said, 'I don't care what you do or how you do it, but you get down here and make it known that we're a 'thing' and help me get this guy off my back. The creep thinks that, since he put up money for me, I owe him something and his wacky wife agrees with him.'"

"Who knows?" Murphy said. "Maybe he was lousy in bed and it took the wife off the hook for a night."

"That doesn't sound like something a *man* would say."

Murphy grinned. He was a pretty confident fellow.

Having disappointed Al Mooney, I was loathe to ask him for another Mooney to fly. When the next race was scheduled, it required strategy. I knew that in many of the races that I entered the airplanes were handicapped. All conceivable entries were assigned a par speed—a speed based on the manufacturer's promises or, more fairly, on repeated test flights to determine expected speeds. The race winner would be the pilot of the aircraft that averaged the highest *ground* speed in relation to the published par speed. Times were tabulated after all racers had arrived at the destination airport. The plane with the highest score was the winner.

Many racers would analyze the handicap sheet published for a given race, then go find a few different models of an airplane that featured a plus. They'd rent (beg, borrow, steal, buy) the cleanest, fastest, nicest airplane that they could get their hands on. Those who already owned a specific model had no choice and often went along for the fun of the racing, knowing ahead of time that they hadn't a competitive ship.

No airplane was supposed to be modified, but almost everyone found ways to get around that. Murphy helped me considerably. On my Cessna 120, my winning little two-placer, he faired the wings and kept the engine highly tuned. It also helped that, from 1955 to 1969, I worked as a saleslady for Harry Pennington, the owner of Electricoating, a company that promoted ChannelCromium, the chrome plating of cylinders. I was often sponsored in races by my company. My deal with Harry meant that he would pay all my expenses for my race if I would spread the word about his chroming process.

In 1960, when I won the International Air Race (IAR) to San Salvador, we had a southeast wind—a headwind. I dipped low to skirt the driftwood on the beach to get out of that headwind. I won the race in my C-120 at an average groundspeed of 126 mph! Murphy and I choked and chromed my barrels. Chroming is considered a legitimate option for racing and there was no way to prove that, during the chroming process, the cylinders weren't being bored or altered in some way. We changed the angle of the wings slightly when I recovered them with fabric, lifted the rear trailing edge, lifted my ailerons about an inch, and put washers on the stabilizers so that, when the throttle was wide open, the airplane would fly level and *fast*. In a normally rigged airplane, when you open the throttle, the tail goes up and the nose goes down. You don't get *speed*.

Another friend of mine, Margaret Callaway, also worked for a company that chromed cylinders. We both contended to all that would listen that we opted for chroming because the more efficient the engine, the better the performance of the airplane. No one could prove otherwise and we competed like the two AT-6 pilots, Kaddy Landry and Dot Lemon—like women possessed. We ran circles around everybody else for years.

"You know?" Murphy philosophized. "Many might accuse you and Margaret Callaway of being too competitive. I wonder, do they realize that it's your *job*—that you have to be?"

"Murphy, do you know what I heard? I heard that on one of the IAR races, Callaway ran out of gas short of the airport and landed in a field. Some other racers flew overhead and saw her on the ground. They were on the radio frequency with the tower and heard her telling the tower controller, 'I'm on the ground, so you count my time as now.'"

"She *has* to make the airport to prevent being disqualified, doesn't she?"

"You bet she does, Murphy. I was disqualified for going the wrong way. You bet she'd be disqualified if she's in a field someplace! She was just trying to stay in the action. It has always bothered me that when a man cuts corners, takes an advantage he's thought of as shrewd. When a woman does it, she's considered a bitch."

It was interesting to watch a female air race, though. At the start, each woman acted like a winner. Each one insinuated, 'I'm the best pilot,' or 'I'm gonna win this race.' If you asked, 'How'd it go?' *during* the race, you never got an admission of truth. The standard answer would be, 'Fantastic, absolutely fantastic.' A woman might have screwed up royally, but she'd never admit such a thing. Some argued along the way with timers in an effort to coax two minutes here, five minutes there. There were girls who argued over thirty *seconds*. Then, when the race was over, there was only one possible winner. All of the others found their placement down the list and it took the stuffing right out of many of them."

"All actresses to the bone?" Murphy suggested drily.

I agreed with him and nodded.

"Some gals could be your best friends before and after the race, but during the race they act as if they hardly *knew* you. I guess I'm guilty, too. Winning is so damned important."

"And, once that starter flag goes down, you're on your own!"

16

Meacham

and

Pivotal

Turns

I entered hundreds of competitions and, if flying was the joy of my life, racing had to be the passion. Many times I entered the International Air Race, the "Angel Derby," and took first place in four. Continuing to race assuaged the pain of having been excluded from the AWTAR, however brief it was.

Invitations were extended to me from those who managed the long cross-country races; requests to let bygones be bygones. Some of the most experienced female pilots of our nation enjoyed air racing and though there was strong camaraderie, there was fierce competition among them as well. Many women entered with winning uppermost in mind. Others said, "Come on, Edna. Join us. These races are supposed to be fun."

I considered it, but the handicap list had to favor whatever airplane I'd be able to race. When—as a race car driver puts the pedal to the metal—I shoved the throttle to the wall, I wanted *speed* and I didn't want to be handicapped out of the winner's circle. Perhaps racing was supposed to be fun, but, to an intensely competitive person, winning was the fun and I enjoyed socializing with the racing crowd, as well.

In the fifties, living near Aberdeen, Mississippi, where Murphy taught Air Force aviation cadets in AT-6s and T-28s at Columbus Air Force Base, I taught primary and commercial flying to civilians.

One evening, Murphy suggested, "I saw a twenty-eight foot travel trailer for sale. Let's buy it. We've both been working pretty long hours and it isn't doing our marriage any good. Let's take some time off."

"Other than racing, I don't believe I've ever had more fun than I had teaching floatplane flying on the bayous of Louisiana, Murphy. What would you think of heading for the lake country of Michigan and teaching in seaplanes?"

"Let's give it a try, Edna."

In Flint, Michigan, we introduced ourselves to Ed Dalton, the manager of the Flushing Airport. He hired us and we started anew, deep into student flights and, for Murphy, civil aviation mechanics. He was a mechanical genius, I believe—a highly technical man with a dedication to doing repair and restoration as diligently and correctly as possible.

Murphy was exacting about flight training as well. I heard him say to a young instructor one day, "You just started that student yesterday, are you are doing nothing but takeoffs and landings today?"

"Yes," said the young instructor, taken aback.

"A student pilot needs plenty of time in the air. Until a novice is accomplished in flying at altitude, you've no business going around and around in the traffic pattern, close to the ground."

I also heard Murphy chastise a young man whose father had plunked down all the money for his flight training. The boy was spoiled rotten. He would play all night, arrive at eight in the morning for ground school, then nod off to sleep. Murphy refused to baby him. He said, "I can't drill a hole in your head and put the information in. I'm giving your dad back his money. You are wasting your time and mine." He was adamant and, despite pleading from the father and son, Murphy wouldn't budge. The boy may have gone on for training elsewhere. Perhaps Murphy pushed that young man to take initiative. I have often said that the best pilots, male or female, were those who made their own decisions in life.

I enjoyed teaching flying in Michigan. In the winter we replaced floats and wheels with skis on the Piper Cub, Cessna 120, or Cessna 140 in which we taught. "I'm going to land my student on the frozen lake today, Murphy," I announced as we grabbed a bit of breakfast one morning.

"Watch out for the fishermen. I was over the lake yesterday and I counted several small ice-fishing huts. The wind might drift the airplane right after touchdown if you aren't on top of everything."

"I've landed on the ice. I know it's entirely different from land or water. You don't have to tell me."

"I'm not criticizing, Edna," Murphy said quietly. "But, there's quite a wind today. It just occurred to me that the combination of ice and crosswind might slide you into some poor fisherman when he least expects your company."

"I get competition in air races, Murphy. I really don't think that you and I have to compete, too." We both left the house, stony-faced and cold. Murphy had my best interest at heart, but it made me angry to receive direction.

In the early summer, one of my advanced girl students and I took off in an Aeronca Champ on floats. "Wow, this has power," she exulted.

I laughed aloud. "You bet. We've been flying in 65- and 85-horsepower Cubs. I thought you'd get a kick out of this 90-horse Airknocker. Do you want to fly to Traverse City? Didn't someone mention a cherry festival?"

"Great."

"And, Bea Trimble flies out of Traverse City. If we run into her, I can tell her that I'm selling my Cessna 140. She teases that I do too much air race winning. Maybe she'd like to buy one of my winning airplanes."

After we splashed to a landing, we climbed into the shallow water of the bay and pulled the Aeronca up to moor her. A policeman drove up and stopped nearby. I frowned. Were we in violation? Damn.

"Have you had a piece of cherry pie today?" he called to us.

"No," I answered, still frowning. My student shook her head.

"Come with me. I'll have to take you to jail. Unless, of course, you eat a piece of cherry pie." The husky, ruddy-faced man, at his second mention of cherry pie, broke into a cheerful grin.

Delighted, we climbed into the backseat of his police car for a regal escort to the center of Traverse City. The main street had been roped off. A parade was organizing to march along the route and, along the full length of the street, within sight of the gently lapping waves of the Grand Traverse Bay, a long table had been set, filled to overflowing with homebaked cherry pies. Locals greeted us and smilingly saw to it that we could escape jail. They served each of us a piece of pie that featured Michigan's famous black cherries. We didn't see Bea, but she later bought my C-140 and, best of all, we didn't have to do time in the jail.

While I enjoyed cherries, floatplane flying, and the watery wonderland of Michigan, famed Jackie Cochran was persuading her wealthy husband, Floyd Odlum, who owned the company that manufactured Sabre Jets, to allow her to fly a jet. Lucky lady! Although it took two years for her persuasion to succeed, Cochran did fly a Canadian Sabre and captured several speed records. In May of 1953, she was the first woman to break the sound barrier.

I wrote a letter to Jacqueline Cochran, December 28, 1956. I was the Ninety-Nines' president and had been entertaining a house guest, Countess Coudenhove-Kalergi of France and Switzerland, who had been active in European aviation as early as 1911.

"Dear Jackie," I wrote. "The countess wants European

women to recognize their potential in aviation. She plans to organize a flight from the U.S. to Europe with an entirely feminine crew. She has a sponsor and the rest of the arrangements are well underway. For women qualified in large aircraft, the consensus of opinion was that you are the most eminently qualified of our 99 pilots. She wants you to be the aircraft commander."

Jackie Cochran answered a month later from her ranch in California. She asked several questions about the countess's idea and expressed her interest in the venture. Unfortunately, that particular Atlantic crossing, like so many other dreams, never came to be. Naturally, had there been an all-woman crew organized, I would have gone to all lengths to be part of it.

While we were in Michigan, Murphy received a surprising letter from his ex-wife. An alcoholic, she had, in the rage of a drinking stupor during their marriage, peppered Murphy in the legs with shot from a gun. They had not communicated with each other since their split; the divorce had been bitter. She had kept Murphy from corresponding with their daughter, Georgeann "Ann" Whyte, too.

He had told me about the shooting when we married; his legs were badly scarred. It must have been a horrible scene. Their little daughter, Ann, was witness to it; only five years old, she had been holding onto her father's leg during the shooting. Murphy knew that Ann had nightmares of the terror long after the shooting itself.

"Ann was clinging to me when the gun went off," Murphy said now, the letter in his hand. "She remembers the jar of my leg as I was hit and her striped dress, spattered with blood. It was a miracle that she wasn't hit, too."

"I can't imagine a mother doing such a thing with a child so close. What does she want now? That was a long time ago, wasn't it?" I asked Murphy.

"She wants us to take Ann."

"To take her? Have her live with us?"

"She needs a good home, needs the stability..."

"Are you asking me to stop work, stop flying? Stay home with a child?"

"She's in high school, Edna. She won't need to be cared for like a baby. In fact, perhaps we could even teach her to fly. I'll bet she'd enjoy that. After all this time, all the efforts that I've made to get in touch with her, I'd certainly like to have her live with us."

"With you, you mean."

"No. Don't tell me what I mean. I'd like to have her live with *us*. I'd like to give her some idea of normalcy...."

"We're in a twenty-two-foot trailer, Murphy."

"My mother isn't getting along very well in Fort Worth. Perhaps Ann could even be of some help there. We'll move back to Fort Worth and..."

"But, Murphy. I told you that I've just heard from the VA and they approved my G.I. Bill request to take my helicopter rating. I'm scheduled to go to Providence, Rhode Island."

"That's no problem, Edna. You go ahead and take that course. It ought to be challenging—I can just see you handling the cyclic and the collective. Once you've received your helicopter rating, you can join us in Fort Worth. By the way, will you see your old friend from Rhode Island?"

I shook my head. Guerd Brocksom was no longer in Rhode Island. By this time, he, his wife, and two children were living in Bogotá, Colombia. I said, "Guerd is a career airline captain flying for Avianca Airlines. So, for that matter, is young Fred Stripe. He flies for United, I hear." I was still bitter about not being allowed to fly for an airline.

When Ann arrived with her suitcases, mine were already packed for my training course in Rhode Island. We were together a short, testy time. It wouldn't be easy for either of us, I could see that.

Eager to be the tenth U.S. woman to obtain the helicopter license, I left for the East. Murphy and Ann climbed into the car and towed the travel trailer from Michigan to Texas. They stayed with Murphy's mother until they could locate a home to buy. I wondered how large that home would have to be for three distinct individuals to live harmoniously. There was already competition between Murphy and me. I wondered if we'd be like three caged lions, circling one another warily.

"Who knows?," I thought. "Perhaps Ann would like to learn to fly as Murphy had said. Perhaps she'd even want to accompany me on some long cross-country racing flights. That'd be interesting—mother and daughter fly together. I can see the newspaper articles now."

I obtained the helicopter rating and returned to Fort Worth. Murphy and I both flew with Ann, training her to become a pilot. She soloed and, when we flew an Angel Derby in 1956, a *Life* magazine writer and photographer flew part of the race with us. We flew from Ontario, Canada, to Buffalo, New York, and on to Cuba. This was before the rise to power of Fidel Castro and a subsequent end to our mutually beneficial relationships with Cuban officials who had warmly welcomed the *competencia,* the *carrera aerea para mujeres,* and pictured the *trofeos* that were awarded to the winners.

By that time I had 12,000 flying hours and had earned 26 air racing trophies. I was the president of the Ninety-Nines, flying in as many air races as I could, and getting the headlines to prove it. A newspaper in Holland wrote of me in Dutch and, when the days of photographs gave way to videotapes, my interview was taped for a German television program. All I understood from international articles was my name, the numbers of my flying hours, and the growing group of *trofeos* that cluttered the bookcases, mantel, bedroom dressers, and the counter in the kitchen.

Ann attended Birdville High School. She took flying lessons from both her father and me and learned to pilot an airplane before she could drive our family car. She would have made a dandy flight instructor had she been interested, but she was eager to leave us and get out on her own as soon as high school graduation was over. She said, much later, "I learned to fly. I soloed. But, I didn't want to pursue it. I'm married to a man who thinks that if God had intended us to fly, he'd have put feathers on our arms. So it probably is just as well that I let it go." Once Ann's babies started to arrive, I had a new name— "the Flying Grandmother."

I plunged into long-distance flights to represent Harry Pennington's outfit. I put much of my salary into stocks and bonds, trading with a broker when I was at home in Fort Worth. Murphy opened an FBO on Meacham Field—Aero Enterprises— which he managed for the next twenty-four years. We were apart a good deal. We struggled with competition and, though I taught flying for him at Aero Enterprises and he bought me a Link Trainer so that I could teach instrument students in the ground environment, I opted to keep my aviation apart from his as much as possible.

"Murphy, you don't ever let up about my flying," I complained. "You criticize...."

"Constructively, Edna."

"Oh, I know—you want me to improve. But, damn it, that's condemnation in itself. You must already think you're a better pilot than I if you feel compelled to change me."

Resentment smoldered. We agreed, when it appeared impossible to tolerate each other on flights together, to fly separately. I preferred to work for someone else. I was convinced that Murphy thought I was a terrible pilot.

My lust for racing flamed as my marriage cooled, although I continued to depend heavily on Murphy for race tactics and his superb mechanical abilities. I generally called him every night when I was away on a race. I'd tell him about the current weather observations, the forecasts, the predicted winds aloft. I'd even call him again in the morning, if the wind forecast changed. He'd suggest altitudes based on his assessment of pressure patterns. I wasn't ashamed to admit that he was my brains. I loved the recognition and publicity that went along with the racing. I loved the speed, the freedom that I found in the air. I also valued Murphy's suggestions and the tips that he gave to help me win.

He always asked, "How is the airplane performing? What kind of speed are you getting? Is the engine running smoothly?"

Once I sent a wire to Murphy from Philadelphia. Murphy had just ground my valves, tightened the seals, and tuned my engine. I knew that he wanted to know if the airplane was leaking any oil, staining the lower fuselage. When I found the Western Union office, I dictated the following message to the clerk. "Murphy. Arrived safe. Good flight. Belly's clean. Love, Edna."

The clerk looked at me, puzzled. "'Belly's clean,' lady? Are you sure that's what you want to say?"

I laughed aloud, enjoying the special language of the aviation world.

"Go ahead and send the wire. My husband knows what I mean."

While cross-country racing helped me carve the sky from one end of the country to the other, from Canada to Mexico, the Bahamas, Cuba, Costa Rica, and San Salvador, nothing surpassed the thrill of banking steeply around pylons in closed-course racing. For me, that was air racing at its very best.

In the 1960s, several female racing pilots formed the National Woman's Pylon Racing Association, originally conceived by commercial pilot Irene Leverton. Once organized, the NWPRA was led by tall, slender, and attractive Judy Wagner, called by many the 'greatest female race pilot of them all.' I was voted vice president; Pat Arnold, executive secretary and later director; and Virginia Griggs, treasurer. We had a list of active members: Dorothy Julich, a good friend and capable pilot who was unfortunately killed on a later cross-country air race to Mexico; Elaine DuPont Loening, married to the son of Grover Loening, designer of the famous amphibians that bore his name. Elaine later married air racer and plane designer Nick Jones. She was a talented sculptor and died tragically in an auto accident.

Dorothy Anderson, Jill McCormick, Hazel Sigafoose, Dr. Mary Roscoe, Gini Richardson, and Cheryl Barrett joined our NWPRA, but the most active racers were Berni Stevenson, Mary Knapp, Dot Etheridge, Mara Culp, and Mona Coons, in addition to Wagner, Arnold, Julich, Loening, and me.

As with all other aspects of females in flying, there were

barriers against us. Originally, the Professional Race Pilot's Association (PRPA) refused to allow women to race. Judy Wagner incurred considerable expense getting the Woman's Association off the ground and Pat Arnold carried on an extensive letter-writing campaign to the PRPA and to the National Aeronautic Association (NAA) in Washington, D.C. She asked that the women's organization be recognized as an affiliate of the NAA with the same status as PRPA, so that women would no longer have to endure the rebuffs of the male pilots' group.

She delightedly reported later in a newsletter that the executive director approved the formation and affiliation of the NWPRA with the NAA. "Our organization flies!" she exulted.

She also noted that we officers attended PRPA meetings and decided that it would be a serious mistake to affiliate with the men's organization. In the newsletter, Arnold explained, "There is internal trouble in PRPA between the various class divisions, especially concerning the distribution of prize money. If we remain separate, we could give all members a fair and generous share of the purse rather than subscribe to the men's purse divisions. Also, the PRPA wants the women's races to be handicapped and we don't advocate that. Even worse, we would be liable for a lawsuit in the event of an accident."

We made progress! We raced a women's stock plane class at every major race in the United States, we increased the purse money, we hammered a set of workable stock plane racing rules, a rough draft of bylaws, and achieved national recognition through the press. We'd had mentors—Louise Thaden, Amelia Earhart, Jackie Cochran. But, even Cochran herself had unwittingly deterred us a bit when she doused perfume over the entire grandstands filled with thousands of people at the '64 National Air Races at Sky Ranch in Nevada. A manufacturer of beauty products, Cochran opted to announce her newest fragrance in what she considered to be an innovative way. She rented a Cub that generally treated crops for insects. Her stunt—liberally spraying perfume over those who had come to Nevada to watch air racing—infuriated many, yet one couldn't help but laugh to imagine the creative excuses that would go home with some of those men whose suits suddenly reeked of perfume.

To accentuate our female racers' plight, Pat Arnold wrote:

You will find this shocking, but because of the 'horse-and-buggy and women's-place-is-in-the-home' attitude of PRPA, the USA is the only country in the *world* that does not permit mixed competition in air racing. Our goal is to end this unjustified discrimination! Even back in the thirties and forties women raced along with men.

Our safety tips for closed-course racing began with a necessary warning:

"IF WE HAVE ONE ACCIDENT, WE ARE FINISHED. THERE ARE MANY WHO ARE JUST ITCHING FOR US TO MAKE ONE MISTAKE. THE LITTLE MONEY AT STAKE IS NOT MORE IMPORTANT THAN YOUR LIFE OR MINE, NOTWITHSTANDING THE TRAGEDY OF IT ALL. IF IN DOUBT—DON'T!"

Added to that serious challenge, our standards continued:

TAKEOFF: Set your altimeter at zero and cage your gyro instruments. Be sure you have enough gas, that you have selected the proper tank. If another airplane is crowding you, give way. Maintain a straight line, correcting for wind drift, and don't get into another's way.

RACE COURSE: Keep alert. Swivel your head. Do nothing abruptly without looking—don't sharply turn or climb or dive for another aircraft might be closer than you know. Pass on the outside only. If you get "boxed in," REDUCE YOUR THROTTLE! Try to maintain altitude in turns. Avoid the prop wash of other airplanes. If you can't, maintain strong back pressure on the stick and ride it out. Keep track of the laps flown. Watch for flags—a white flag for start, a black flag tells you to remove yourself from the course, a red flag means exercise extreme caution, and a black and white checkered flag signifies the end of the race. There will be 8 laps and a 9th 'safety' lap.

LEAVING THE COURSE: Fly the safety lap, straight and level down the course. Don't make a pull-up until after you pass the pylons and leave the race course. This procedure is the same in the event of an emergency.

PILOT MEETINGS: These are absolutely mandatory. Nothing preempts it. 10% of your prize money will be docked for each late at a meeting and each meeting missed.

A Cleveland paper wrote that an entirely new class of piston-engined speed planes for closed-course racing were being considered by the PRPA. Pat wrote to me, "This worries me. It sounds like the men are thinking of ways to get in on our act. Keep your ear to the ground."

Our stock plane racers zoomed around pylons at Cleveland, at Reno, Nevada, and at Frederick Municipal Airport, Maryland. At Cleveland in 1967 there were forty thousand cars filled with fans and a gate of fifty thousand dollars. Our own Dot Etheridge performed aerobatics in a Piper Cub. Famed Bob Hoover, called by some the "greatest pilot in the world," performed in his P-51 Mustang. To this day he leads the aerial start at the popular Reno Air Races and, as the big Unlimiteds snarl down from over the mountains west of Reno, his phrase, "Gentlemen, You Have a Race," has become legendary.

Gentlemen. They may all be men, but gentlemen? Ask Joann Osterud, rejected from flying the big Levelor-sponsored methane-powered Sea Fury in 1988. She would have been the first female to pilot one of the unlimiteds, the *Big Iron*. By 1990, the first woman finally made it. Erin Rheinschild competed in the unlimited category. Perhaps the race starter was forced to say, "Pilots, you have a race."

In 1966, I bought a thirty-four-thousand-dollar Rockwell Aero Commander Model 200 for $23,000. The company gave me almost eleven grand as a discount for public relations and advertising. I wrote to many different aircraft companies to scare up just such a deal—a fast competitive airplane with which

I could race in exchange for the publicity that the manufacturer would gain. My 200 was pink and blue with baby-blue leather upholstery. In it I won second place in the stock plane class and was named outstanding competitor and best sport at the Cleveland Races of '67.

I flew my 200 in various cross-country races; the Angel Derby, Dallas Doll Derby, and around pylons at Cleveland and Reno, among other places. My new craft wasn't ready in time for the Frederick, Maryland, races in 1967, but the company arranged a substitute 200 for me to fly. Borrowed from the foreman for the Colonel Sanders Fried Chicken company in Thomasville, Georgia, his plane had been sitting in a hangar and hadn't been flown for a while. I picked it up in Georgia and flew toward Maryland. Suddenly, the engine faltered. I switched fuel tanks and the engine seemed to run perfectly well for a while, then the tachometer showed a drop in revs and the engine would choke and falter. We limped to Maryland as I flipped from one fuel tank to the other, coaxing the gasping, intermittent engine until a mechanic could check it.

"What could the problem be?" I asked a mechanic on the field at Frederick.

"It sounds as if the tanks aren't venting properly. There's a vacuum in your fuel tanks."

"It isn't fuel starvation."

"No," he said with a smile. "It's mud daubers." By this time the mechanic had gotten a good look at the fuel vents and found that wasps had attempted to build a mud nest. He used a piece of wire to pull the caked mud from the vents and, to my relief, the engine began to run well. I dreaded the thought of wrecking someone else's thirty-thousand-dollar airplane. Times had changed dramatically since the five hundred dollars that I won on Long Island was sufficient to pay for any necessary repairs.

In 1967, I raced my Commander in the "Celebrity" Race from Fox Field in Lancaster, California, to Reno to coincide with the National Championship Air Races. Several Aero Commander pilots were sponsored by the company to fly with movie stars who were also licensed as pilots. A Hollywood-style bash was thrown the night before we took off. I flew with Conlan Carter, the star who played the medic in *Combat*. He sat in the left seat, the pilot-in-command position, and was not only a fine person, but could fly that airplane well, too.

As we chased one another across the mountains and the desert, Conlan and I followed in fourth place behind James Franciscus, the celebrity who won the race. Beautiful Susan Oliver finished second. Cliff Robertson, who currently owns a Spitfire and five other antique airplanes and continues to actively support aviation, was third.

It was exciting to be with Hollywood's stars, fun to race for long distances, but I preferred pitting my airplane and my wits against other racers in pylon racing. I could compare pylon racing with wrestling. In tight turns and bounced by windy, turbulent air, there are as many twists and jolts that make a racer sweat and strain as any wrestler finds on the gym mat. Tough and dangerous, pylon racing held the threat of mid-air collisions, takeoff and landing accidents, blown engines, sheared wings, and a potential of dreaded fire that lured the somewhat bloodthirsty race crowd and kept the excitement level at fever pitch among racers and fans alike.

Tragedy wasn't limited to air racing. Just prior to the start of the Cleveland Air Races of '67, eighteen sky divers left a converted B-25 Mitchell bomber. They were over a cloud cover that obscured view of the ground. In a horrible mistake, they were told by a controller, who was tracking their course on radar, "B-25, you are one mile west of the field." The jumpers left the airplane. Instead of being over the field, the aircraft was over Lake Erie and, with only two spared by a safe landing, sixteen sky divers drowned in the lake.

Tragedy was personal, too. My mother, Myrtle Hander, died in 1965 after having lived with Murphy and me for several years. She was a wonderful woman, loving and congenial. She and Murphy were fast friends and they enjoyed one another's company fully. Mother flew with me in a few races, especially the Dallas Doll Derby, an efficiency race for stock lightplanes. In one of the biggest mistakes of my life, I'd uprooted Mother from her home, believing that she shouldn't live alone as she entered her eighties. I discovered that until the day she died she regretted leaving and looked forward eagerly to each flying trip when I would take her to see her friends and relatives in Minnesota.

A scant two years later, in 1967, George Murphy Whyte and I squared off in divorce court. I was flying all over the United States—to California, Oregon, Nevada, Washington; to Winnipeg, Toronto, Montreal; over the beautiful waters of the Bermuda Triangle; and to Mexico and Central America. Murphy was probably justifiably tired of having an absentee wife. Well aware that our marriage was through, we faced a bitter, ugly ending to what had started so lovingly in 1946.

"I want an airport of my own, Murphy," I told him, although I knew that he wouldn't leave Meacham and leap into the herculean task of building a new airport with me. He had spent twenty-four years building Aero Enterprises, had many good friends, was involved with a Big Brother organization in Fort Worth that assisted homeless and troubled kids, and had found another woman, a lady named Pat McDade. Worst of all, he was sick. Years of cigarette smoking had caught up with him and cancer was ravaging his body. The leg that Andrea had peppered with shot so many years before eventually had to be amputated and Murphy was unable to put his energies toward a new airport even if he had wanted.

We split our assets, divided our lives. I sold my Aero Commander 200 to a medical doctor in New Mexico. I sold the house in Richland Hills, Fort Worth, which Murphy and I had shared, and bought property in Roanoke, Texas. Eventually I bought twenty-two acres of land.

I moved to a mobile home on the empty Roanoke field that had raised excellent cotton and Murphy visited me several times. Even as our marriage dissolved, Murphy helped me, although he had discouraged the project at the outset. I was sixty-seven years old and he was afraid that the construction and management of an airport would be too great an obligation. When he discovered that I was adamant, he began to see the virtue of my own home on my own airport. He advised me on the use of a contractor, the access roads, site elevations, the weight-bearing requirements of runways—the hard, cold facts of building an airport.

Murphy died in 1971. His daughter, Ann, was with him for the last weeks of his life. She wouldn't let me in to his hospital room.

"I want to see Murphy," I told her.

"The cancer has gone through his stomach, Edna. He is in a coma from a stroke. He can't talk to anyone and he is tangled in tubes, a life support system. You can't do anything—nobody can."

Just as Murphy himself had said, "And, once that flag goes down, you're on your own!"

$\mathcal{A}ero$ $\mathcal{V}alley$— a $\mathcal{T}axiway$ to $\mathcal{M}y$ $\mathcal{D}oor$

F or two years after our divorce, I searched for property on which to build an airport. In what seemed to be a remote, rural location, I purchased twenty-two agricultural acres in Roanoke, Texas, in 1969 and, within a year, had added an adjacent ten acres. Several warned that I was settling too far from the flying public.

The busy highway I-35 sliced from Canada to the Gulf of Mexico directly west of the site and the Dallas–Fort Worth International Airport was to the east. An enormous IBM complex was erected to the southeast and, to the southwest, H. Ross Perot opened a large and lucrative airport for aerial freight operations. My once rural, sleepy location was surrounded by burgeoning growth and rapidly rising property values.

I retired as a saleswoman for Channelchrome, but not before

I enjoyed a great deal of publicity as one of the few women who could discuss cylinders—bore, choke, rings, oil, and compression ratios—with the best of mechanics. I'd flown hundreds of miles swapping poor cylinders in return for Electricoating's nicely restored, chromed product and had talked to hundreds of customers. The advent of jet engines saw a rapid decline in piston-powered aircraft manufacture and I realized that I'd enjoyed the heyday of the chrome cylinder business.

I applied for a loan to underwrite the building of my airport and was denied. Bank officials implied that I was too old to build an airport. I'm certain that they thought of airport management as a man's job. Since childhood, when faced with denial or rejection, my typical reaction was to increase my determination to succeed. Rejection mobilized my efforts to carve Aero Valley Airport from my cotton field myself.

In the spring of 1970, Kelly Bryan entered my life. When Kelly, an electrical engineer with General Dynamics in Fort Worth, first arrived, I had a 2,200-foot-long gravel runway and one large hangar already constructed. I had sold my house in Richland Hills and three airplanes to raise cash and had borrowed money from as many persons as I could find. I had promised, "If you will pay for your flight training in one initial payment, I will guarantee that you receive the training necessary to obtain your license," to many prospective pilots in an effort to obtain cash for the runway and hangar. I was living in a small trailer on the premises.

Kelly wanted to be checked out in his Beech Bonanza. He said, "I hear that, once I've flown with you, I'll be sorry that I didn't get my primary training with you."

I laughed. "Well, you'd have a longer lobe on your right ear if you did. I've a reputation for grabbing that earlobe to hammer directions home when flight students don't seem to be listening. It does make them sit up and take notice."

"I've heard about the small megaphone that you take into the cockpit with you, too."

I laughed again. "My reputation seems to have preceded me."

With two partners, I had decided to build tee-hangars to rent to airplane owners. I traded flight instruction for Kelly's help with electrical repairs and avionics installations.

From that day on, Kelly made himself more than at home on Aero Valley. He wired the tee-hangars, the first of the money makers that have more than fulfilled my financial expectations. I was elected to the Texas Women's Hall of Fame for my economic acuity, and the airport, the runway, and those first tee-hangars set the stage for that honor. Kelly helped wire my big blue hangar and the apartment in the rear of it—a small bedroom, bath, and kitchen. I sold my trailer, moved into the hangar, and lived there for the decade of my seventies.

Student pilots began to enroll and people rented my hangars to base their private airplanes on my strip. I operated on a shoestring and Kelly helped with more than electrical and radio expertise. He bought stock in my operation, paid for several hangars, and bought three airplanes—two Cessna 150 trainers and a Mooney—for my flight school use.

He lived and worked in Fort Worth during the week, then lived and worked with me during the weekends. He handled the scheduling for oil changes, 100-hour inspections, the hangars that I continued to build—became a partner in my affairs. Kelly had been a confirmed bachelor all of his life and our relationship was mutually comforting and affectionate. To this day we need and depend on each other.

Aging toward my eighties didn't slow me down. I started my days at the crack of dawn and left many a younger person panting in my wake. I gassed and oiled airplanes, flew with daytime students, taught night flying to those who needed flight time after dark, taught aerobatics in Kelly's C-152 Aerobat, conducted ground school classes, and administered F.A.A. written exams. I often had a student fix a peanut butter sandwich for me to carry along during a noon instruction flight rather than take time to eat properly. I borrowed more money on promised flight training hours and bartered my way to a viable operation—the runway, a large school hangar, several rows of rental hangars, and, finally, when I could afford it, a home with the taxiway between the now hard-surfaced runway and my front door. I always promised that I'd find an old ladies' home to which to move, if I could find one with a taxiway to my front door. I didn't find it, I built it. I moved in just prior to my eightieth birthday.

Aero Valley Airport—my former cotton field—grew to house more than one hundred businesses, numerous hangars, subdivided plots for homes, a restaurant, an office building, and many, many aircraft. I sold much of my stake in it in April of 1980.

I have regrets over several occurrences in my life, but I relish glorious memories of some delightful, fruitful years. I only wish that men had been as kind to me in the early days of my flying as they are being today.

Kelly told me, "Edna, concentrate on the good. You have been elected to four halls of fame; you received the Charles Lindbergh Lifetime Achievement Award with such prestigious aviation greats as Bob Hoover and Paul Garber, and you are the first woman to be elected as an honorary member of the famed Order of Daedalians. Be happy with your honors and, best of all, that this recognition comes while you can enjoy it. You are still flying, still having droves of young people arrive at the door for a flight with you, your name in their logbooks. I'm so proud to be part of your life."

I have a message for senior citizens. I'd like to encourage them to enjoy their age by staying active until the very last minute. I'd like to tell them, "Don't give up. Keep a passion for living in your life."

To the youth, I say, "Watch your health. I never wanted anything to hinder my flying—not cigarettes, not alcohol, not dope!"

Lately, whenever I fly a race, reporters and photographers line up at the end of the race to watch me climb out of my plane. Forewarned that an old lady is piloting in an air race, they wait, certain that I'll fall out of the airplane on my ear.

I have fallen a few times, in a manner of speaking. I had a few accidents—once in 1985 when a male student and I pranged a Cessna because we hit an inch-wide cable suspended between two telephone poles. I hadn't seen the cable until the last minute of a simulated forced landing. I broke my nose and had four stitches. My student was bumped and bruised and the airplane was totaled. It wasn't the little airplane's fault. It was nobody's fault but mine.

Another time, I belly-landed my Comanche 400 when I had failure of my gear extension system. It cost a pretty penny to get the airplane back into the air. Also, I ran off the end of a runway in Fond du Lac, Wisconsin, and damaged a four-place Piper. I had to buy a car to travel home to Texas. I arranged for the Cherokee to be shipped back for repair. I discovered that an accident can be amazing. You don't realize what's happening until it's all over. I just thank the Lord that I've lived through so much.

I've often wondered, what is it about my childhood that made me accept such enormous challenges as building my own airports, borrowing large amounts of money, racing airplanes? People ask, "Where did you get the courage?"

I answer, "Flying. Flying makes you a different person. It gave me confidence to live. Those old words, 'Nothing ventured, nothing gained,' are so true. If I hadn't ventured, I'd be in a county home somewhere."

I was offered a chance to fly in a T-37 at Reese Air Force Base and I jumped at the chance. How many can genuinely say that they've flown from Jennies to Jets? I went through egress training, was fitted with a parachute, "G" suit, helmet, and boots and given indoctrination training with a group of shiny-faced young men. After doing loops and rolls in the jet with a handsome young Air Force captain, he paid me the ultimate compliment of my life. In front of the crowd gathered for the fancy dinner he said, "I flew with a lady who is over eighty years old. Edna Gardner Whyte, I could make a fighter pilot out of you." No words ever sounded sweeter. I'd like to keep that fighter pilot attitude. I don't *want* to stop flying. I want to fly until I'm 100.

As early as 1961, twenty-five women were tested for qualification as astronauts. Although thirteen passed, the testing was kept secret and it was determined that women would detract from the program for men and might deter America's race into space. Now, when I read that Captain Beverley Bass led seven women, an all-female crew, in a commercial flight of a Boeing 727 and that women have achieved the rank of captain in every major airline, when I note that women are an integral part of the U.S. space program; when I see that female U.S. Navy aviators land Buckeye jets on aircraft carriers; and when I discover that hundreds of women are flying military aircraft, I cheer progress. I hope that I've made some contribution to that progress. I hope that I have helped hold open the door to that sky so that every woman can "rise above it."

$\mathcal{B}ibliography$

Bilstein, Roger E. *Flight In America 1900–1983, From the Wrights to the Astronauts.* Baltimore, Md.: The Johns Hopkins University Press, 1984.

Buffington, H. Glenn. *Air Race Classic-Reflections.* San Diego, Ca.: Negenesch Printers, Inc., 1986.

Christy, Joe. *Racing Planes & Pilots.* Blue Ridge Summit, Pa.: Tab Books, 1982.

Davis, Art. "How It Feels to Explode in the Air at 420 MPH," *Home Pylon News,* Wendell-Williams Memorial Aviation Museum of Louisiana, Patterson, La., 1987.

Dictionary of American Naval Fighting Ships, Vol. II. Department of the Navy, Office of the Chief of Naval Operations, U.S. Naval History Division, Washington, D.C., 1963.

Friedan, Betty. *The Feminine Mystique.* New York: Dell Publishing, 1984.

Gann, Ernest. *Ernest K. Gann's Flying Circus*. New York: MacMillan Publishing, 1974.

Gardner, Donovan Dean. "Rags to Patches," *ca.* 1980.

Harris, Grace. *West to the Sunrise*. Ames, Iowa: The Iowa State University Press, 1980.

Hartney, Harold E. "The Civilian Pilot Training Program," *Aeronautics* 1:1 (September 4, 1940).

Hubbell, Charles H. *Famous Planes and Pilots*. Akron, Ohio and New York: Saalfield Publishing Company, 1939.

Hull, Robert. *A Season of Eagles*. Bay Village, Ohio: Bob Hull Books, 1984.

Hull, Robert. *September Champions*. Bay Village, Ohio: Bob Hull Books, 1979.

Jane's Encyclopedia of Aviation. New York: Portland House, 1989.

Kinert, Reed. *Racing Planes and Air Races, A Complete History*, Volumes I–XII. Fallbrook, Calif.: Aero Publishers, 1967–1976.

Kuralt, Charles. *On the Road with Charles Kuralt*. New York: G. P. Putnam's Sons, 1985.

Lomax, Judy. *Women of the Air*. New York: Dodd Mead, 1987.

Moolman, Valerie, and the editors of Time-Life Books. *Women Aloft*. Alexandria, Va.: Time-Life Books, 1981.

Morison, Samuel. *History of U.S. Naval Operations*, Vol. XIV: *Victory in the Pacific, 1945*. Boston, Mass.: Little, Brown & Company, 1960.

Planck, Charles. *Women with Wings*. New York: Harper & Bros., 1942.

Powder Puff Derby, The Record, 1947 to 1977, All-Woman Transcontinental Air Race, Inc., Sanctioned by N.A.A. and conducted under rules of the F.A.I., Endorsed by the Ninety-nines, Inc., 1985.

Rankin, Tex. "There Are All Kinds of Students." *Popular Aviation* (August 1939): 74.

Rogers, Mary Beth, Sherry A. Smith, and Janelle D. Scott. *We Can Fly, Stories of Katherine Stinson and Other Gutsy Texas Women*. Austin, Tex.: Ellen Temple Publisher, 1983.

Schmid, S. H. 'Wes,' and Major Truman C. 'Pappy' Weaver (USAF Ret.). *The Golden Age of Air Racing*, Volumes 1 and 2. Oshkosh, Wis.: EAA Aviation Foundation, 1983.

Tallman, Frank. *Flying the Old Planes*. Garden City, N.Y.: Doubleday & Co., 1973.

Tegler, John. *Gentlemen, You Have a Race: A History of the Reno National Championship Air Races 1964–1983*. Severna Park, Md.: Wings Publishing Company, 1984.

Thaden, Louise. *High, Wide and Frightened*. New York: Air Facts Press, 1973.

Veca, Donna, and Skip Mazzio. *Just Plane Crazy: Biography of Bobbi Trout*. Santa Clara, Calif.: Osborne Publisher, 1987.

Worthylake, Mary M. *Up In The Air*. Woodburn, Oreg.: self-published, 1979.

Index